the **60**ˢ in canada

the **60**^s in canada

Denise Leclerc and Pierre Dessureault

National Gallery of Canada
Canadian Museum of Contemporary Photography

2005

Published for the exhibition *The Sixties in Canada*, organized by the National Gallery of Canada and presented at Ottawa from 4 February to 24 April 2005, and the exhibition *The Sixties: Photography in Question*, organized by the Canadian Museum of Contemporary Photography and presented at Ottawa from 22 January to 24 April, 2005.

Produced by the Publications Division of the National Gallery of Canada, Ottawa
Chief: Serge Thériault
Editor: Lauren Walker
Picture Editor: Colleen Evans
Main texts and notes translated by Judith Terry
Foreword and Introduction translated by Arlette Francière

Designed by Fugazi, Montreal. Typeset in Helvetica and Clarendon
Printing: Tri-Graphic Printing (Ottawa) Limited

Front cover: Claude Tousignant, *Chromatic Accelerator 96–10–68* (detail), 1968, cat. 68 (NGC) © Claude Tousignant

Inside front and back covers: Marcel Barbeau, *Retina 999* (detail), 1966, cat. 4 (NGC) © SODRAC (Montreal), 2005

Back cover: AA Bronson, *Mirror Sequences* (detail), 1969–70, cat. 8 (CMCP)

On sale at your local bookstore or at The Bookstore, National Gallery of Canada, 380 Sussex Drive, P.O. Box 427, Station A, Ottawa, Ontario K1N 9N4

Cataloguing in Publication Data
Library and Archives Canada

Leclerc, Denise.
The Sixties in Canada

Catalogue of exhibitions held at the National Gallery of Canada and the Canadian Museum of Contemporary Photography.
Published also in French under the title: Les années soixante au Canada

Includes bibliographical references
ISBN 0-88884-796-3

1. Canadian Art – 20th Century – Exhibitions.
2. Photography – Canada – History – 20th Century – Exhibitions. 3. Nineteen Sixties – Exhibitions.
I. Dessureault, Pierre. II. National Gallery of Canada.
III. Canadian Museum of Contemporary Photography.
IV. Title.

N6545 L43 2005   709'.71'09046   C2004-986006-2

Contents

Foreword

In recent years we have witnessed a readiness to examine the sixties' outstanding contribution to our way of life – specifically to the world of art. A few major international exhibitions have already taken place, notably *Les années Pop 1956–1968* at the Centre Pompidou in Paris in 2001 and *Art and The Sixties: This Was Tomorrow* at the Tate Britain in London in 2004.

On the Canadian scene, the exhibitions *Making It New!: (The Big Sixties Show)* at the Art Gallery of Windsor and at the Glenbow Museum of Calgary and *Déclics, art et société. Le Québec des années 1960 et 1970* at the Musée d'art contemporain de Montréal and at the Musée de la civilisation de Québec, both held in 1999, have explored several striking features of that decade. A year earlier, a meeting between the National Gallery of Canada and the Canadian Centre for Architecture in Montreal set the foundation for an important collaborative project among seven museums.

Since then, some of these institutions have generously deployed their efforts towards an examination of many facets of this pivotal period. Noteworthy are the exhibitions *Global Village: The 60s* at the Montreal Museum of Fine Arts in 2003 and *The 60s: Montreal Thinks Big* now on view at the Canadian Centre for Architecture. By the winter of 2006, the McCord Museum of History and the Vancouver Art Gallery will have presented other exhibitions and public programs focused on the sixties. An exhibition devoted to design and the decorative arts will soon open at the Canadian Museum of Civilization.

The National Gallery of Canada and the Canadian Museum of Contemporary Photography in Ottawa now have the opportunity to offer an overview of the Canadian scene in the visual arts with two exhibitions: *The Sixties in Canada* and *The Sixties: Photography in Question*. Selecting and presenting nearly 180 works by Canadian artists that pinpoint the diversity of artistic expression throughout this remarkably prolific period has been a daring undertaking. Curators Denise Leclerc and Pierre Dessureault have met this challenge with care, enthusiasm, and determination. *The Sixties in Canada* at the National Gallery follows the numerous trends in Canadian artistic production during that decade which, fostered by popular iconography, new materials, and technological innovations, tested the conventional boundaries of artistic disciplines. The works selected from the impressive collection of the Canadian Museum of Contemporary Photography for the exhibition *The Sixties: Photography in Question* also testify to the experimentation and eclecticism that characterize Canadian photography. Professional photographers and the artists who adopt the camera as a tool explore the links between art and photography and in so doing, they transcend any division between the two in favour of a dialogue involving both disciplines. They borrow from the specific vocabulary of photography while challenging both formal boundaries and generally accepted ideas in an attempt to reconcile art and communication.

The success of these two exhibitions would not have been possible without the participation and the ingenuity of the artists themselves and the lenders who proved to be essential collaborators. We are deeply indebted to them. We also wish to thank our staff, particularly our curators Denise Leclerc and Pierre Dessureault, as well as the teams from Technical Services, Multimedia Services, Design, Exhibitions Management, Publications, Library and Archives, Collections Management, Communications, Conservation and Restoration, and Education, all of whom have devoted considerable time and effort.

May these two exhibitions pay tribute to the creative energies of our artists who have shaped the Canadian expression of this extraordinary period and provided a truer portrait of a society committed to renewal.

Pierre Théberge, O.C., C.Q.
Director
National Gallery of Canada

Martha Hanna
Director
Canadian Museum of Contemporary Photography

Acknowlegments

The authors of the catalogue would like to acknowledge:

Raven Amiro
Monique Baker-Wishart
David Bosschaart
Josée Drouin-Brisebois
Marnie Butvin
Jean-François Castonguay and the
Technical Services team
Clive Cretney
Colleen Evans
Louise Filiatrault
Richard Gagnier
John Gorman
Denis Gravel
Linda Grussani
Martha Hanna
Anouk Hoedeman
Julie Hodgson
Charles Hupé
Sue Lagasi

Clement Leahy
Marie-France Lemay
Nathalie Mantha
Danielle Martel
Ceridwen Maycock
Marc-Antoine Morel
Anne Newlands
Mark Paradis
Marie-Chantale Poisson
Megan Richardson
Carmen Robichaud
Geneviève Saulnier
Anne Tessier
Pierre Théberge
Yves Théoret
Serge Thériault
Alan Todd
Emily Tolot
Lisa Turcotte
Canadian Museum of Contemporary
        Photography and
        National Gallery of Canada, Ottawa

Christine Braun
Art Gallery of Hamilton

Cassandra Getty
Sandra Gill
Art Gallery of Windsor

Suzanne Wolfe
Canada Council Art Bank, Ottawa

François Martin
Réjean Myette
Fugazi, Montréal

Jan Vuori
Janet Wagner
Canadian Conservation Institute, Ottawa

Jim F. McDonnell
Library and Archives Canada, Ottawa

Barry Fair
London Museum, London (Ontario)

Janine Butler
McMichael Canadian Art Collection,
    Kleinburg (Ontario)

Krisztina Laszlo
Mary Williams
Morris and Belkin Art Gallery, Vancouver

Anne-Marie Zeppetelli
Musée d'art contemporain de Montréal

Stéphane Aquin
Montreal Museum of Fine Arts

Amy Marshall
Donald Rance
Barry Simpson
Art Gallery of Ontario, Toronto

Susan Sirovyak
Vancouver Art Gallery

James Patten
Formerly with the Winnipeg Art Gallery

Michel Martin
Musée national des beaux-arts du Québec,
    Quebec City

Stephen Bulger
Stephen Bulger Gallery, Toronto

Julie Desgagné
Arlette Francière
Yves Gagné
David Mirvish
Judith Terry
Lauren Walker
Brian Worobey

as well as numerous other people who
kindly assisted in the organization of these
exhibitions.

Denise Leclerc
Associate Curator
Modern Canadian Art
National Gallery of Canada

Pierre Dessureault
Associate Curator
Canadian Museum of Contemporary Photography

List of Lenders

AA Bronson, New York
Art Gallery of Hamilton, Ontario
Art Gallery of Ontario, Toronto
Art Gallery of Windsor, Ontario
Canada Council Art Bank, Ottawa
François Dallegret, Montreal
Department of Foreign Affairs and
    International Trade Canada, Ottawa
Estate of Pierre Elliott Trudeau, Montreal
Faculty of Law, University of Manitoba,
    Winnipeg
Anne Lazare-Mirvish, Toronto
McMichael Canadian Art Collection,
    Kleinburg, Ontario
Montreal Museum of Fine Arts
Morris and Helen Belkin Art Gallery, Vancouver
Michael Morris, Vancouver
Katerine Mousseau, Montreal
Musée d'art contemporain de Montréal
Musée national des beaux-arts du Québec,
    Quebec City

Museum London, Ontario
Power Corporation of Canada, Montreal
David Rabinowitch, New York
Geraldine Sherman and Robert Fulford,
    Toronto
Stephen Bulger Gallery, Toronto
The Robert McLaughlin Gallery, Oshawa,
    Ontario
Claude Tousignant, Montreal
Serge Tousignant, Montreal
University of Lethbridge Art Collection, Alberta
Vancouver Art Gallery
Bill Vazan, Montreal
Winnipeg Art Gallery

We would also like to extend our sincere
thanks to all the lenders who prefer to remain
anonymous.

intro

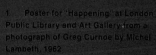

Even forty years later, the sixties are invariably associated with the collective awakening of Canadian society to advanced modernity on all fronts – political, economic, social, and cultural. Nonetheless, all the soul-searching, experimentation and reforms that occurred in this decade did not happen at once. Change in Canada did not take place at the same pace as in the United States or the rest of the western world. Canadian society was subjected to a plethora of forces, some of which were reactions to ideas that had been generally accepted since the Second World War. It is therefore not possible to give a proper account of the dynamics of the Canadian artistic output without first establishing the evolution in the consciousness of a society adapting to new circumstances on both the national and international scenes.

The International Socio-political and Cultural Context

The year 1960 heralded great hope for renewal. As a sign of the times, a young John F. Kennedy was elected president of the United States. The American pharmaceutical industry introduced the birth control pill on a large scale, ultimately providing a chemical boost for the burgeoning feminist movement. An emerging intercontinental satellite communications system ushered in a progressive change in collective thought (the first transatlantic Telstar communication occurred on July 10, 1962) as it brought international events into living rooms throughout the western world.

The immediacy and occasionally blunt clarity of media coverage of political events on the international scene stunned viewing audiences, causing polarization in attitudes and increased debate. A stark reminder of the ongoing cold war, the Berlin Wall was erected in 1961. That same year anti-segregationist demonstrations in Birmingham, Alabama brought the issue of the civil rights of Black Americans to centre stage. In 1962, the Cuban Missile Crisis tested the competence of the new American president who would be assassinated the following year (his brother, Senator Robert Kennedy, met the same fate in 1968.) The Civil Rights Movement reached its pinnacle in 1963 with the March on Washington when Martin Luther King delivered his memorable speech *I Have a Dream*. The Vietnam War, a conflict linked to the break-up of the European colonial empires, intensified in 1964 when the American government increased war efforts. Students on university campuses gathered en masse to organize demonstrations in Washington against the United States' intervention in Vietnam. Riots broke out in Harlem (New York, 1964) and Watts (Los Angeles, 1965). Violent flare-ups were marked by the assassinations of the radical Afro-American leader Malcolm X in 1965 and Martin Luther King in 1968. Americans were shaken to the core by this wave of upheaval.

This new climate of revolt spilled beyond the narrow political arena to foment dissent elsewhere. The creation of new departments of sociology at many universities on both sides of the Atlantic fostered further thought about a social system now seen as oppressive.[1] The works of political philosophers such as Herbert Marcuse – *Eros and Civilization* (1955) and *One-Dimensional Man* (1966) – served to debunk the post-war technocratic culture rampant in large organizations. In China, the Cultural Revolution under Mao Zedong aimed at recasting all "bourgeois" behaviour and thought patterns. The events of May 1968 in France provided a catalyst for young people looking for solidarity and means to overthrow all forms of authority. The sense of exhilaration born of a runaway prosperity[2] fed the need to rebuild everything from scratch.[3] The concepts of underground and counterculture took form and an emerging awareness of the environment, which coincided[4] with the hippie movement, challenged both consumer society (the "throw-away economy") and the use of nuclear power. *The Sexual Revolution* (1936) by Freudo-Marxist theoretician Wilhelm Reich had a posthumous impact on sexual relationships and behaviours. In 1969 the Woodstock Music Festival, a metaphor for the ideology of a new generation, brought the decade to a close on a note of love and peace.

The Major Intellectual Issues Relevant to Artistic Endeavours

To understand fully the issues that captivate Canadian artists, one must consider the under-lying major intellectual forces behind the artistic discourse. Furthermore, recent theoretical ideas bring about a better and more enlightened understanding of the activities of the sixties. Many thinkers believe that it was during this period that the Western world made the shift from modernity to post-modernity.[5] While modernity[6] is characterized by an unprecedented growth in knowledge, by specialization, and by autonomy within the various specialized fields, during the sixties the West embraced a new logic that allowed for a cross-fertilization of disciplines. American cultural critic Fredric Jameson states that the triumph of capitalist logic and a long process of commodification of all aspects of traditional life marked the end of the decade. The disappearance of borders between specialized fields signifies the emer-gence of a post-modern society and underlines the new contemporary will to value subject-ivity, interaction and fusion – notions at the antipodes of the pure ideals of modernity. It is then that, according to Jameson, economy and politics become cultural manifestations.[7] For the philosopher Jürgen Habermas the modern process is, however, ongoing.[8]

Aesthetically, the sixties see the emergence of a trend in architecture that would be deemed post-modern in the early seventies. An architectural project at Yale University led Robert Venturi[9] and his students to denounce the Bauhaus type of purist functionalism in favour of a vernacular urban architecture whose new approaches hark back to classical architectural models. That is how the term "post-modern" found its way into other artistic disciplines.

Scientific objectivity was also called into question in respect of the subjective rapport between "the observer and the observed."[10] The artistic prose during that decade reflected the thinking of the American philosopher and psychologist John Dewey as exemplified in his seminal work of 1934, *Art and Experience*, which had a lasting impact on artistic pedagogy. In his writings, Dewey discusses the way an individual adapts to his immediate environment. He insists on the therapeutic dynamics of experience (the direct confrontation of fears is encour-aged) and shies away from childhood memories favoured by psychoanalysis. In his view, one must embrace the present; as a corollary, the aesthetic dimension is rooted in everyday life accessible to all. Dewey rejects the legitimacy of the assertion that the aesthetic experi-ence is reserved for some privileged classes. Likewise, he also maintains that artists do not have the monopoly on creativity. That potential is latent in every intelligent person. The sixties' slogans that all aspects of art must be democratized are linked directly to Dewey's influence.

The scientific theories dealing with information and communication also take centre stage thanks to the technological breakthrough in cybernetics and mass communications. With the publication of *The Gutenberg Galaxy* (1962) and *Understanding Media* (1964), Marshall McLuhan adopted a humanist approach and popularized highly complex notions. Finally, a system of linguistic analysis – structuralism – instituted by the Swiss grammarian Ferdinand de Saussure, and its brilliant adaptation in 1958 by Claude Lévi-Strauss in his *Anthropologie structurale* (published in English as *Structural Anthropology* in 1963) had a resounding impact on the field of literary and artistic criticism. By doing away with historical perspective and by promoting the study of any phenomenon from the sole point of view of the place it occupies in a given system, structuralism provides grist to the mill of a decade unabashedly focused on the present.

The International Artistic Scene

The period of the sixties thus witnessed the breakup of modernism on the international scene. Additionally, the idealistic premises of modern society did not deliver all the intended results – namely, the unfolding of reason, the accumulation of wealth, the emancipation of workers, the advance of technology, the liberation of women, and the free expression of various forms of sexuality – as they ran counter to the strong traditions of non-Western countries.

Two major twentieth-century artistic tendencies that emerged at the start of the century clashed: the Russian formalism that contributed to the birth of Abstract Art and Dadaism. Tensions arose between art with a formalist slant, which was always in pursuit of its own purist refinement, and the more "popular" arts that took advantage of the new media. Artistic thought broadened the scope of its investigation.

Apart from borrowing from two conflicting trends, artistic expression changed course. Art that evolved by stepping back from other fields and following its own rules, opened up to a popular culture that urged artists to free themselves from artistic conventions. Instead of making each discipline the focus of an introspective approach, the artists favoured the fusion of all genres. During this period, which was dominated by a measure of eclecticism, another trend emerged: the rejection of the notion of craftsmanship in the production of art (the role of the hand) in favour of the conceptual in art – a transposition of the debate regarding the respective roles of the craftsman and the artist, which has recurred ever since the Renaissance. With the integration of technology in the practice of art, innovative equipments and industrial processes came to the fore. The smooth finish of Minimal Art and composites from industry were now considered "artistic." On that issue, the American art critic Hal Foster[11] went so far as to proclaim the demise of the humanist subject in art.

Soon there was a rapid shift from aesthetic criteria based on the Western artistic canon to a visual culture that included both the disparate and the heterogeneous. Veritable cultural organizers, several artists undertook to make culture more accessible to everybody. The artistic press played a vital role in informing the artistic community and fostering solidarity while increasing its readership. Celebrated authors such as Aldous Huxley promoted the artist as visionary: "What the rest of us see only under the influence of mescaline, the artist is congenitally equipped to see all the time."[12] "Bless the artist's vision of the present visible to him because of the freedom from the constant or stabilized environment,"[13] asserted Marshall McLuhan.

Finally, the decade saw an intense period of artistic activity during which the major artistic centres – London, Paris, New York, and Los Angeles – each took a turn on centre stage. As early as 1960, the art critic Pierre Restany and the painter Yves Klein founded *Nouveau Réalisme*, a movement in the wake of British Pop Art, where objects from the real world were paramount. In the United States, beginning in the mid-fifties, Robert Rauschenberg gave a major push to the techniques of collage and assemblage. In New York, gallery owners Sidney

Janis and Martha Jackson recognized the importance of the emerging pop tendencies. With the 1962 launch of the magazine *Artforum* rose the best debates on the new artistic stakes: Minimal Art, Conceptual Art, Land Art, etc.

The Canadian Socio-political and Cultural Background

The American version of the continuous process of modernization began to shatter some of the convictions relevant to the Canadian community, called into question the existing inter-pretation of historical facts, and fostered the emergence of new groupings. The important identity question that fed the political discourse in the decades to follow began to reflect a collective approach. By way of example, consider Canada's attraction to the very American values it partly tried to fend off, the shift from the term "French-Canadian" to "Quebecker," and the political and cultural activism of the First Nations. Let us not forget that the right to vote in federal elections without first renouncing their status was only allocated to people of the First Nations in 1960.

Moved by the desire to "catch-up"[14] with the rest of the continent, Quebec society changed in every way. In June 1960, the election of Jean Lesage's Liberals ushered in the Quiet Revolution. Launched by Lesage, the slogan *Maîtres chez nous* – literally, masters in our own homes – had repercussions that were hardly anticipated even ten years later. The process of modernization continued, bringing about the broadening of fields of expertise within the elite, and the secularization and the professionalization of many aspects of human activity. Like the railway that previously contributed to the unification of the land from East to West, the Trans-Canada Highway, completed in 1962, played a similar role. At the same time, however, as a harbinger of a split within Canadian unity, the first bombs of the *Front de Libé-ration du Québec* exploded in "federal" mailboxes in 1965. During a period marked by the demise of colonial empires, the majority of leftist groups – especially the intellectuals returning from prolonged study trips in Europe – began to feel the influence of Third World liberation movements. The world-famous anti-colonialist book by Frantz Fanon, *The Wretched of the Earth* (1963, first published in French in 1961), had major repercussions on local sympathizers. It also contributed to the publication in 1968 of its Quebec parallel, Pierre Vallières' *Nègres blancs d'Amérique* (published in English in 1971 under the title *White Niggers of America*).

Elected in 1963, Lester B. Pearson remained head of a minority liberal government until 1968 on the strength of his being an honest broker after playing the priceless diplomatic card of peace during the Suez Canal Crisis and arranging for the withdrawal of NATO troops from Gaza in 1956–57. Very much in the spirit of the sixties, the promotion of peace became the rallying cry for Canadian diplomats. The decision to opt for a new Canadian flag in 1965 (famous artists were asked to submit their designs) indicates that the country was distancing itself from its European heritage. The Canadian identity issue gained momentum as a result of policies introduced in 1968 by the Pearson government following the Royal Commission on Bilingualism and Biculturalism (Laurendeau-Dunton Commission, 1963–68).

1967 was a remarkable year in every respect. The many activities generated by the commemoration of the centenary of the Confederation (leading to numerous commissions for artists and architects) and the organization of the 1967 Universal Exhibition in Montreal projected a Canada that had reached a stage in its development that would allow its full potential to unfold. On the theme of Man and his World, after the famous book *Terre des*

Hommes by Antoine de Saint-Exupéry, Expo 67 remains an unequalled visual and sensory experience that would strongly influence generations to come. The event would attract more than fifty million visitors.

Pierre Elliott Trudeau succeeded Lester B. Pearson in 1968. The Trudeaumania phenomenon created by the media was a direct result of its new influence in political image making. To counter the nationalist and separatist political unrest on the Quebec scene, two other personalities, union leader Jean Marchand and journalist Gérard Pelletier ran for office and were elected to Parliament. The national unity issue now became crucial.

While the Quiet Revolution tried to give a new direction to Quebec society, Canadian society in general submitted to critical soul-searching. The incisive and influential book by Canadian sociologist John Porter, *The Vertical Mosaic* (1965), tackled inequalities of wealth, power, and learning opportunities. His ideas disturbed the conscience of a privileged generation who were still remembering their own parents' memories of hard times during the Great Depression. In *Lament for a Nation: The Defeat of Canadian Nationalism* (1965), George P. Grant raised the issue of Canadian sovereignty and the difficulty in maintaining independence in a continental context. According to Grant, the non-Americanization of the Anglophone Canadian citizen and the continuous efforts on the part of French-Canadian people to remain French are collective values difficult to pursue. Perhaps only the implementation and the staunch advocacy of social programs on a grand scale can establish a distinction between Canadian and American societies.

The telecommunications revolution accelerated during that period, thus helping to connect cities and regions spread over the vast Canadian territory. At the same time, Canadians grappled with the proliferation of popular American culture through the media, the drift from the land, and, as a result of opened immigration, an increasingly pluralist society.

The Scope of the Visual Art Scene in Canada

The exile and the death in Paris in 1960 of Paul-Émile Borduas, one of the best-known Canadian artists, had an impact on a people still largely unappreciative of the radicalization taking place in the art world. During the sixties, artists combatting indifference towards their ways of practising art no longer had to leave their birth country. Rather, trips outside Canada would be to gain access to larger markets or for other professional reasons.

Since 1957, travel grants from the Canada Council for the Arts have made it easier for artists to get further training abroad.[15] The Canada Council also helps to finance travel within Canada for artistic personalities so they can meet their peers. This enlightened form of artistic management stimulated such interest abroad that Henry Geldhazer, head of visual arts at the Washington National Council on the Arts, gave it high praise: "All our administrators look to it with respect, awe and envy."[16]

With no principal artistic hub during that decade, Canada experienced an incredible burgeoning of the arts in both large urban centres and regional communities. Artistic activities occurred both in public institutions and in alternative spaces. A vast number of Canadian artists exhibited their work in international exhibitions abroad or in events of international calibre at home. In 1960, the National Gallery of Canada moved to a renovated office building on Elgin Street in Ottawa. Beyond its regular program of exhibitions that gave a higher profile to contemporary Canadian art,[17] the institution orchestrated Canadian participation in the

Venice and São Paulo biennales. It also set up biennales for contemporary Canadian art on tour throughout Canada.

The Winnipeg Shows, ambitious juried exhibitions (with art for sale), were held annually at the Winnipeg Art Gallery. The amazing Emma Lake Artists' Workshops in Northern Saskatchewan were organized from Regina[18] and attracted such renowned artists and critics as Barnett Newman, Clement Greenberg and Jules Olitzki. For its part, the Art Gallery of Toronto (now the Art Gallery of Ontario) welcomed the most innovative artists from the Isaacs Gallery, while the artists associated with the Festival of the Contemporary Arts at the University of British Columbia proved themselves at the Vancouver Art Gallery.

An international sculpture symposium was held on Mount Royal in Montreal in 1964 and the Musée d'art contemporain de Montréal was founded the same year. At the end of the decade, the Nova Scotia College of Art and Design spearheaded the recognition of avant-garde art with its specialization in Conceptual Art.

Among the very dynamic galleries outside big cities, the London Regional Art Gallery established in 1962 by Greg Curnoe (fig. 1), Jack Chambers, and Tony Urquhart is noteworthy. The 20/20 Gallery, a co-op that opened its doors in London in 1966, testifies to the will of artists to grow roots in their own milieu. It was also in London that artists demanded, from public institutions and from the general public, recognition of their professional status and fair compensation for services rendered, at the same time initiating the debate about copyright. The Canadian Artists' Representation/Le Front des artistes canadiens (CARFAC) was founded there in 1968. Founder, president and principal spokesperson Jack Chambers quite rightly stated, "The artist is the only resource producer in our society who is not paid for his service or encouraged in the slightest to share in the profit and benefits from his work."[19]

Toward the end of the decade and at the beginning of the seventies, financial support from the Canadian government enabled the creation of artist-run centres, an initiative that afforded some respite to avant-garde artists who found it difficult to disseminate their works in commercial galleries and public institutions with a wider mandate. It may be that Marshall McLuhan's exhortation to "Blast those art galleries and museums which imprison and classify human spirit,"[20] was heeded.

The new ideals for the democratization of art were embodied in the creation of printmaking workshops, notably in Montreal, Winnipeg, and Halifax. In the same spirit, public participation was encouraged. Team projects were in evidence: the happenings at the Art Gallery of Toronto in 1965, the *Opération Déclic* in Montreal in 1968, and a variety of performances, experimental music recitals, and poetry readings at the Art Gallery of Vancouver and at the London Regional Art Gallery and other art institutions. People talked about environmental art and multi-disciplinary events. Some traces of these ephemeral activities can be found in photographs, film inserts and other paraphernalia that survive today, including Gathie Falk's theatrical objects that were exhibited at the Equinox Gallery in Vancouver in 2000.

To appreciate the contribution of the visual artists of that decade, one must keep in mind their commitment to reach the public (fig. 2). Many artists drew simultaneously on their new roles as communicators and presenters. Just as television solicits the viewer and enables him to live a present continually renewed, the artist avidly sought the active and playful participation of the spectator. Others followed a more arid modernist path, exploring the ramifications of a form that was increasingly more refined. Art magazines disseminated the new trends and the debates stemming from the practice of art. For example, in 1967 the magazine *Canadian Art* changes its name to *artscanada*, a sign of the multiplicity of artistic activities of great import on the Canadian scene. All things considered, the desire to test the limits of the possible and to decompartmentalize the arts marked the practice of art in that period. What better testimony than the oft-quoted assertion of multi-disciplinary artist Michael Snow: "My paintings are done by a filmmaker, sculpture by a musician, films by a painter, music by a filmmaker, paintings by a sculptor, sculpture by a filmmaker, films by a musician, music by a sculptor."[21]

1

The Return of Dada

I feel it is curious that in the last one hundred years the movement (Dada) has had two exposures. We were not satisfied with the first exposure of it. We needed another, and now we have it.[22]

Marcel Duchamp

3   Neo-Dada Exhibition, The Isaacs Gallery, 1962. Photo: Michel Lambeth
4   Chess Game "Performance," by Marcel Duchamp and John Cage, Ryerson Theatre, Toronto, March 5, 1968. Courtesy of the Centre for Contemporary Canadian Art, Toronto/ The Isaacs Gallery Project
5   Aftermath of the *Happening*, Art Gallery of Toronto, 1965. Photo: Michel Lambeth
6   Artists' Jazz Band, left to right: Nobuo Kubota, Graham Coughtry, Robert Markle, and Gordon Rayner. Photo: Kryn Taconis

7   Graham Coughtry, Gordon Rayner, and Robert Markle in Rayner's Toronto studio, spoofing the well-known Artists' Jazz Band, c. 1965. Photo: John Reeves
8   Nihilist Spasm Band behind the York Hotel, London, Ontario 1968. Left to right: Hugh McIntyre, Art Pratten, Archie Leitch, Murray Favro, John Clement, Bill Exley, John Boyle, Greg Curnoe. Photo: Ian MacEachern
9   The *groupe de l'Horloge* performing at Parc Lafontaine, Montreal, 6 June 1965. Musée d'art contemporain de Montréal, Médiathèque. Photo: Marc-André Gagné

A number of factors contributed to the international resurgence of interest in Dada that occurred in the early nineteen sixties. Born in Zurich in 1916, this subversive literary and art movement, which advocated irreverence towards the established social, political and artistic order, spread through Europe like wildfire. Around the same time, Dada underwent an important development with the permanent move to New York of the French-born painter Marcel Duchamp. Duchamp devoted part of his career to the production of ready-mades – randomly chosen everyday objects that he elevated to the rank of artworks by extracting them from their usual context. Fruit of a brilliant flash of artistic intuition, the ready-made acted as a catalyst, stimulating the emergence of several twentieth-century art movements, including conceptual art, which dominated the artistic landscape from the end of the sixties.

Rooted, like conceptual art, in the primacy of the idea and of the artist's freedom of choice (both essential tenets of Duchamp's art), "neo-Dada" made its appearance around 1958. The term was coined to describe a practice that formed a bridge between Abstract Expressionism and Pop Art. But several events earlier in the 1950s played a role in the US revival of Dada. In 1951, for example, the Abstract Expressionist painter Robert Motherwell published *The Dada Painters and Poets: An Anthology*, a comprehensive anthology of the Dada movement that had a major influence on American artists – notably Robert Rauschenberg, who in 1955 produced a tribute to the Dada heritage in the form of his "combine paintings." The 1950 donation to the Philadelphia Museum of Art of the Arensberg collection, which included Duchamp's major works, also helped broaden the circle of cognoscenti.

A few manifestations in the Dada spirit took place on the international stage in 1960. Europe's New Realists, creators of assemblages and accumulations of disparate objects, held a group exhibition at Milan's Galleria Apollinaire. And Kurt Schwitters (1887–1948), the grand master of collage and an assemblage technique he called *Merzbau* – a kind of sculpture-collage-assemblage-environment that became the definitive expression of his art – was honoured at the Venice Biennale. The following year, 1961, William C. Seitz mounted *The Art of Assemblage* at New York's Museum of Modern Art (MoMA), a major exhibition that had widespread impact.

The Toronto Scene

At the start of the decade, the neo-Dada movement was raising an opposition to the type of art dominated by formalism. A fever gripped art circles in Toronto and London: artists began turning to new techniques – collage, assemblage, environment – in preference to the traditional disciplines of painting and sculpture.

In Canada, neo-Dada found its most eloquent expression in the work of artists represented by Toronto's Isaacs Gallery, the charismatic Greg Curnoe and other anarchistic artists from London, Ontario. The Toronto presence of Michel Sanouillet, a leading expert on Dada who was at that time teaching at the University of Toronto, cannot be overlooked. In 1958 Sanouillet had published *Marchand du sel*, a collection of the writings of Marcel Duchamp, and it was at the Librairie française de Toronto, which he ran, that Curnoe first met the author who would later become his close friend.[23] It is also worth noting that in 1961 Michel Sanouillet gave a talk entitled *Dada's Eye* at the London Public Library and Art Museum, which coincided with Greg Curnoe's first solo show, *An Exhibition of Things*, held at the Richard E. Crouch

Branch Library in London. In November of the same year, the artist Tony Urquhart apparently gave Curnoe a lift to Detroit to hear a lecture being given by Marcel Duchamp at the Institute of Arts.[24]

The Isaacs Gallery's first Dada exhibition ran from 20 December 1961 to 9 January 1962 (fig. 3). Reviewing the show, Michel Sanouillet emphasized the unique character of Canada's Dada renaissance: "The Dadaist revival is by no means confined to Toronto … But, in a typically Dada fashion, the 'things' exhibited in the Toronto show give no evidence of being imitations. The artists claim to be unaware of similar agitation taking place elsewhere. Dada, they say, is just being re-born here, because our world has come to need its ultimate form of revolt again. There is but one way to hit one's head against the wall."[25] It was also around this time that artists became aware of the possibilities offered by the recycling of industrial material.

One of the most important events of the decade was certainly the famous chess game between Marcel Duchamp and the American composer John Cage, which took place in the auditorium of the Ryerson Polytechnical Institute, in Toronto, on 5 March 1968. The event, organized by the Isaacs Gallery, was promoted as a performance (fig. 4).

As the techniques of collage were evolving towards assemblage and environment, the work of a small group of artists was edging closer to the realm of scenography. By the early sixties, this shift was being manifested in such ephemeral artistic events as happenings and performances, "collages" of often improvised activities that likely had their roots in the absurd theatre of Samuel Beckett and Eugène Ionesco and its terminally disconnected dialogues. The theatrical theories of Antonin Artaud, outlined in his 1938 book *Le Théâtre et son double* (which appeared in English in 1958), lent support to the trend and largely inspired the theatrical experiments and improvisations undertaken in New York by Julian Beck and his Living Theatre troupe. During the sixties the terms "performance" and "happening" were often used interchangeably, but generally speaking a performance was more scripted. In contrast to drama productions, a happening was a one-off event that involved a high degree of audience participation.

Aside from its theatrical sources, there were two other events that stimulated the development of the happening.[26] In the summer of 1952, John Cage, then teaching at Black Mountain College in North Carolina – a veritable laboratory of new forms and ideas – created *Untitled Event*, which involved the presentation (in the company of Merce Cunningham and Robert Rauschenberg, among others) of a range of non-coordinated multidisciplinary activities.[27] His conception of chance and his emphasis on undefined elements allowed personal subjectivity to be completely eliminated from the creative act, leaving spectators to make their own sense of it. In fact, Cage's experiment was entirely in line with one aspect of Josef Albers' innovative teaching at Black Mountain College: "Art is concerned with the HOW and not the WHAT; not with literal content, but with the performance of the factual content. The performance – how it is done – that is the content of art."[28]

Yet it was thanks to Allan Kaprow, one of John Cage's students at the New York's New School for Social Research that the happening spread throughout the art world.[29] In October 1959, Kaprow organized an event at New York's Reuben Gallery called *18 Happenings in Six Parts*. Kaprow encouraged spectators to move around (although according to strict rules) within the environment formed by the three spaces in which the happenings occurred. The large splashes of paint that adorned various elements of the "set" were all applied by Kaprow. Through their shared attitude of nonchalance towards the art object, a new generation of artists began denouncing the inertia of institutions that focused solely on the preservation of artefacts. It was an attitude that, at the end of decade, would also characterize conceptual art.

The idea that art should be somehow fused with life was voiced widely at the time and used to validate the introduction of everyday objects into art. The notion became such common currency, in fact, that Andy Warhol, some of whose works were involved in the controversy,[30] felt compelled to publicly oppose it and to define the role of the object:

> But the statement about bridging the gap between art and life is, I think, a very nice metaphor or image, if that's what you'd call it, but I don't believe it. Everybody's using it now. I think it misleads. It's like a magic step, like – 'Oh, that's beautiful, it bridges art and life' – Well that's not so. If you can make it in life – and I don't say that's easy to do – then you can make it with art, but even that's just like saying if you make it with life then you can make it as a race-car driver. That's assuming art and life can be the same thing, those two poles. I make art. Other people make other things. There's art and there's life. I think life comes to art but if the object is used, then people say the object is used to bridge that gap. It's crazy. The object is used to make art, just like paint is used to make art.[31]

Toronto's first happening is said to have taken place in 1959 in the studio of Dennis Burton, whose fellow participants were Gordon Rayner, Graham Coughtry and CBC writer Murray Jessell.[32] In February 1965, the exhibition space of the Art Gallery of Ontario became the site of a spontaneous public happening, orchestrated by the original creative team of Burton and Rayner, accompanied this time by Richard Gorman, Harold Town and Walter Yarwood. The event, attended by a record two thousand people, testified to the AGO's new desire – under the stimulus of the Junior Women's Committee – to become more involved in avant-garde activities (fig. 5).

The Isaacs Gallery exhibitions were accompanied by all sorts of concurrent events. The gallery, which in 1961 had moved to a new location at 832 Yonge Street, offered its patrons concerts of free jazz featuring musicians linked to the visual arts scene (fig. 6), such as the Artists' Jazz Band (December 1964),[33] and John Cage-style composite concerts organized by the composer Udo Kasamets, together with experimental film and dance programs and a series of Mixed Media Concerts (November 1965 to May 1966). The gallery also served for a while as a publishing house, specializing in illustrated collections of poetry: "Poets have come to read their works in evening hours, and painters and poets have joined to produce a series of illustrated books bearing the Gallery's imprint."[34]

Gordon Rayner was among the artists who relished this flurry of activity. His piece entitled *Homage to the French Revolution* (1963, rep. 1) consists basically of an adjustable oval tabletop, presented vertically in the open position. The rails of the table's closing mechanism resemble the uprights of a guillotine, the decapitation machine developed during the French Revolution to ensure trouble-free executions. The artist has modified this found object by adding elements of wood and painted cardboard and reproducing the shadows created by

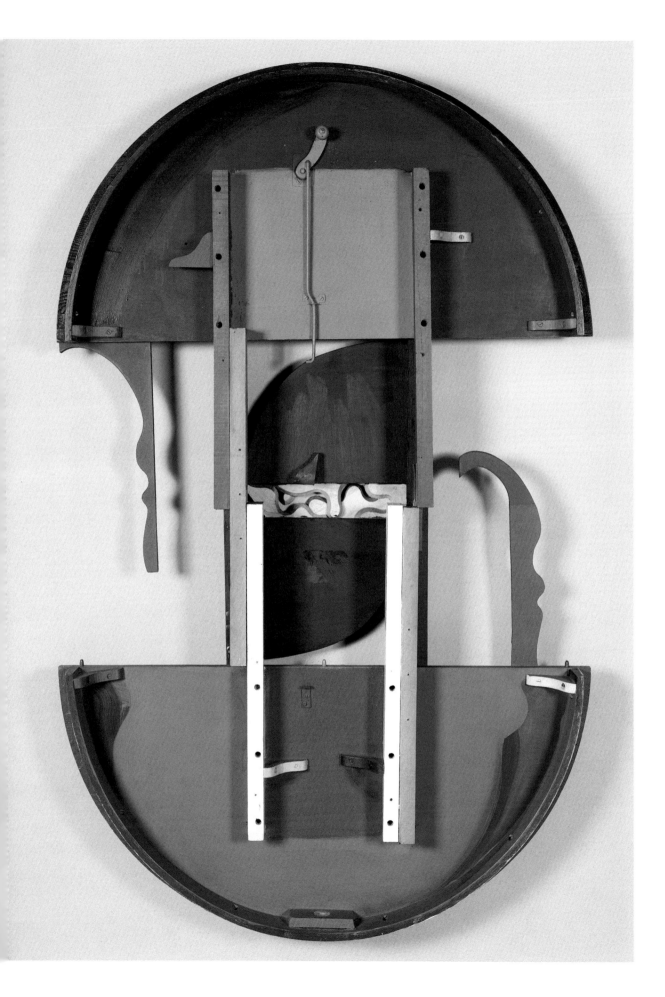

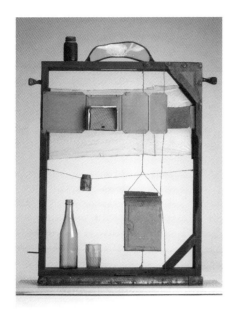

1   Gordon Rayner
Homage to the French Revolution 1963
cat. 59

2   Michael Snow
Window 1960
cat. 63

3   Joyce Wieland
Young Woman's Blues 1964
cat. 78

the lighting conditions (natural and artificial) in his studio. Graham Coughtry was apparently the source of the jokey title. In 1963 and 1964 Rayner produced a large number of constructions and reliefs that often show signs of the high-speed improvisation characteristic of the jazz of which he and his circle were so fond (fig. 7).

The multidisciplinary artist Michael Snow is also a jazz musician. His work *Window* (1960, rep. 2), which was included in the 1961–62 Dada exhibition at the Isaacs Gallery, is a kind of still-life of objects one might find on a desk – a bottle, a glass, glass jars, pieces of metal, an eye-shade, a rubber stamp – all in the same plane, some suspended with wire. This investigation into perceptual phenomena echoes the artist's earlier "topological" paintings of flattened tables and chairs. Here, however, emphasis is on the window frame that places natural boundaries on the gaze. As we shall see later (see "Perception, Perception, Perception," pp. 61–62), Snow became deeply interested in the image-capturing techniques of the still, film and video camera.

Joyce Wieland was another virtuoso of mixed media. Her painted assemblage entitled *Young Woman's Blues* (1964, rep. 3), basically a wooden box/drawer, plays on the semantics of the word "blues," which simultaneously denotes the colour, the popular musical form and a mood of melancholy. Although the subjects of disaster and death appear frequently in Wieland's works from this period, this piece is full of humour: love (the heart) can certainly give us wings (the plane), but it can also be painful, and the phallically positioned aircraft could well pierce the heart of the young woman, which we glimpse through a "veil" of translucent colour.

At the time she executed this work, Joyce Wieland was already well known as an experimental filmmaker, particularly in New York. Reminiscent of a film strip, *Home Movie* (1966, rep. 4) consists of a vertical row of coloured pockets, made of soft, transparent plastic, that contain two reels of film, cut-out pictures of an eye and a mouth, dried leaves and flowers, contact prints of shipwrecks and urban landscapes, and other memento-objects. Claes Oldenburg's huge soft sculptures served as a model, but Wieland has adapted them to suit a more intimate, mundane approach.

Les Levine – a native of Dublin who lived in Toronto from 1957 to 1964 and finally settled in New York – was closely involved in the Canadian art scene for several years. In his view, happenings allowed art to reveal its transitory nature, to move closer towards an aesthetic of the ephemeral. And since the art object no longer had to last, Levine, with considerable ingenuity, began exploring the properties of new synthetic materials and recent technologies. Using an assemblage approach that drew inspiration from American artist Joseph Cornell's famous boxes, Levine electrified the acrylic-fronted wooden structure of *Untitled* (1965, rep. 5), transforming it into a primitive light box. He added a significant human element to this potentially fruitful new technique by reproducing a chest X-ray on a sheet of acetate, reviving an image he had already employed as the basis of one of the prints in the *Toronto 20* portfolio.

In *Slipcover* (1966, rep. 6), Levine's goal is again to materialize a ghostlike presence – a recurring theme of his work. Originally created for the Art Gallery of Ontario in the fall of 1966,[35] the environment was reconstructed in April–May 1967 at the Architectural League in New York. It consists of reflecting surfaces – sheets of silver Mylar that inflate and deflate at varying speeds, like huge lungs – onto which coloured lights and slides of artworks are projected. Spectators' images and voices are captured on tape and relayed a few seconds later on the surrounding walls, which thus act as a kind of retroactive device. In fact, this interactive piece allows visitors to penetrate deeply into an enclosed world where muffled and distorted fragments of their recent actions combine with shimmering images showing an earlier occupation of the site.

The London Scene

Greg Curnoe played a leading role in the organization of London's first happening, *The Celebration*, held at the London Public Library and Art Museum in February 1962.[36] Fascinated by the most ordinary aspects of local life, Curnoe chose to highlight an obscure episode from 1922, when a Chinese restaurant owner was given a two-dollar fine for sprinkling salt on the sidewalk – a contravention of municipal regulations. Curnoe's choice was not arbitrary, however, for just a few years earlier his close friend Michel Sanouillet had published *Marchand du sel* (literally, "Salt Seller") whose title is a phonetic anagram of Marcel Duchamp's name. Sanouillet actually attended the happening along with Michael Snow and Joyce Wieland.[37]

Despite his belief that culture is entirely defined by its regional component and that art is necessarily rooted in everyday experience, Curnoe was influenced by Dadaism, especially in his approach to assemblage. This explains the dedications to the Dada artists who had inspired him – including Hugo Ball, Arthur Cravan, Isidore Ducasse (Lautréamont), Francis Picabia and Kurt Schwitters – that can be seen on the front of *Hurdle for Art Lovers* (1962,

4   Joyce Wieland
Home Movie 1966
cat. 79

5   Les Levine
Untitled 1965
cat. 36

6   Les Levine
Slipcover 1966
Installation at the Art Gallery of
Ontario in 1966
cat. 37

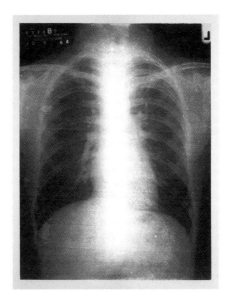

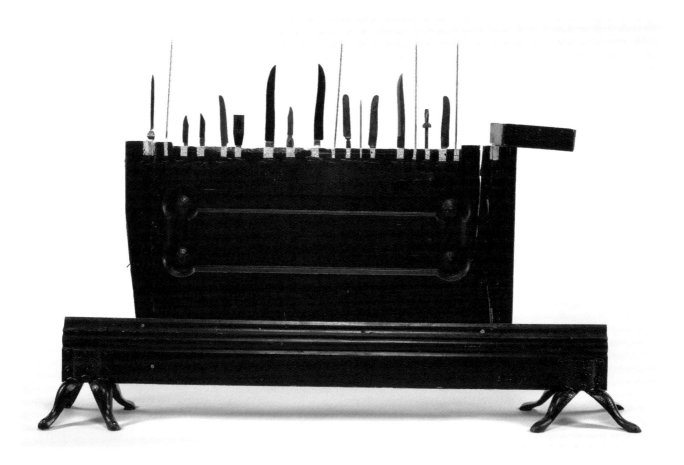

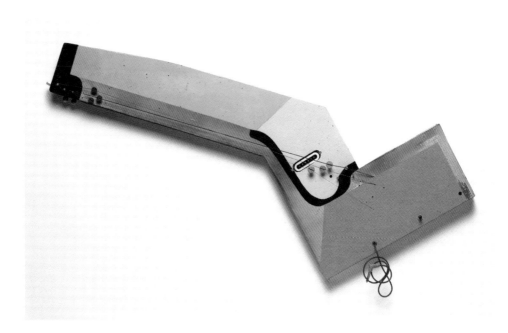

rep. 7). The inscription, where the names of athletes, right-wing politicians and dictators rank alongside those of poets, artists and composers, offers an interesting glimpse into the artist's personal and intellectual preoccupations.

Hurdle for Art Lovers is also a critique of the conservatism of Curnoe's native city. Such domestic objects as knives, knitting needles and tools are transformed into dangerous objects that could easily injure the genitals of anyone tempted to leap over the hurdle.[38] The diverse elements of the piece are united by the blue, white and red of the French flag, and there is in the title a tone of provocation, a desire to *épater le bourgeois* – shock the middle-classes – reminiscent of the artistic anarchism that abounded in early twentieth-century Paris.

The small city of London, Ontario, a positive hotbed of artistic creativity, was home to numerous other groundbreakers, including Murray Favro. Guitarist with the Nihilist Spasm Band (fig. 8), a group of "noise" musicians without any musical training,[39] Murray Favro made his own makeshift musical instruments, just like members of the blues "spasm" bands of early twentieth-century New Orleans. The group, which still exists, has with time earned an international reputation, particularly among Japanese fans of noise music. Favro's *Guitar #1* (1966, rep. 8) was the first in a long series of guitars that would evolve from homemade curiosities to instruments of immense visual sophistication. In a process that was the very antithesis of mass-production, Favro gave each of the guitars its own unique sonority and he would play the instrument until a collector or dealer chose to hang it on a wall, thus subjugating its musical function to its status as a material object. Just as the Cubists' deconstructed guitars coincided with the emergence of popular music, Favro's reconstruction of the electric version of the instrument mirrored its reign over the rock music of the period.

Finally, Tony Urquhart's papier mâché sculpture *Pillar Landscape* (1969, rep. 9) offers a glimpse into the mysterious world beneath the ground. Like the core samples used in mining, the sculpture reveals the sedimentary structure of its constitutents. Born into a family of undertakers, Urquhart realized very young that the earth is not a flat surface but a natural formation whose immeasurable depths are worth probing.

The Montreal Scene

In Montreal, the effects of neo-Dadaism were felt more strongly in the realms of poetry and the performing arts than in the visual arts. The exhibition *Art and the Found Object*, held at the Montreal Museum of Fine Arts in 1959, brought together works by Joseph Cornell, Marcel Duchamp, Louise Nevelson, Man Ray, Kurt Schwitters and Richard Stankiewicz. But the artistic avant-garde was obliged to contend with the pure geometric abstraction that then dominated the Montreal art scene. A group show held at the École des beaux-arts de Montréal in 1961 nevertheless introduced a new generation of artists, including Henry Saxe, Yves Gaucher, Jacques Hurtubise, Richard Lacroix and Peter Daglish, who called themselves "La Relève" and saw themselves as successors to the Automatistes and the Plasticiens.

In the painting-collage-assemblages he produced in 1961, such as *Collage No. 2* (1961, rep. 10), Henry Saxe introduced diverse found materials into an abstract composition – here, a piece of fencing from Papineau Street in Montreal where he had his studio. The monochromatic purity of the velvety black recalls the long, black sculptural walls of Louise Nevelson. In his subsequent works, Saxe would attach foreign objects to a panel or perforate it with nails, staples and other found objects. This piece belonging to the Montreal Museum of Fine Arts can be related to the National Gallery of Canada's *Other Fence* (1961), which also incorporates the tip of a fence post. Henry Saxe would later align himself with the founding members of Fusion des arts, a group that promoted the dissolution of artistic boundaries, genre crossovers, multidisciplinary experiments and group creations.

Charles Gagnon returned to Montreal in April 1960 after five years of study and creation in New York. In 1961 he made a series of boxes containing collages comprising fragments of different objects in either two or three dimensions, which, like Henry Saxe, he unified using an Abstract Expressionist painting technique. These works resemble windows (although they have also been described as "medicine cabinets"),[40] through which spectators may examine the diverse contents while ignoring the glass barrier. In *No Vacancy* (1962, rep. 11), the broken mirror at the lower right reflects what is happening outside the box, encouraging the spectator to become part of the work. Among the various objects that make up the collage-assemblage is a torn advertisement that reads, bilingually, "Chambre à louer/Room to Let." Yet the room, as the title humorously points out, is taken.

In Montreal, as in other major art centres, a few individuals began pushing towards a new democratization of the arts. Very early in the sixties Serge Lemoyne emerged as one of the foremost defenders of this vision, organizing more than a hundred improvisations and shows that merged art and everyday life. In November 1964, for example, at the Grand National Theatre, he showed "objects not reassembled but recycled by painting. Transforming ordinary objects by painting in this way, turning an ironing board into an object ready to leap into space [see rep. 12], de-realizing reality, as it were, by putting paint everywhere and on anything, meant running the risk of seeing reality permanently at one remove."[41]

9   Tony Urquhart
Pillar Landscape 1969
cat. **70**

10   Henry Saxe
Collage No. 2 1961
cat. **61**

11   Charles Gagnon
No Vacancy 1962
cat. **22**

Throughout his career, Serge Lemoyne was motivated by the motto "After global refusal, total art."[42] In 1960, when he was "thrown out of the École des Beaux-Arts for 'lack of talent,'"[43] Lemoyne adopted an art form that focused on everyday objects. Poem-posters and improvisations of poetry and jazz – involving, among others, Gilles Boisvert, Serge Tousignant, Armand Vaillancourt and Robert Charlebois – were among the politico-cultural activities he organized at the Bar des Arts in 1963. During La Semaine "A" held at the Centre social de l'Université de Montréal in April 1964, an event whose goal was to show artists at work, Lemoyne splattered paint everywhere, including on the tables, chairs and window blinds. "In my work, I use everything to hand," he wrote at the time. "I like to integrate into the surrounding atmosphere the objects it encompasses. I paint canvases – objects composed of horse bones, brooms, car license plates … And in spite of myself, these processes have become a kind of critique of everything I see around me."[44]

In the mockingly ironic spirit typical of Dada, *Ironing Board (Cap Canaveral)* (1963, rep. 12) employs the overlapping of genres (object, painting, sculpture), an effect many artists sought to capture at the time. In what may or may not be a coincidence, a 1963 article in *Art in America* (no. 51) reported that a group of artists had recently been invited by NASA to witness and sketch a launch at Cape Canaveral. In 1969, when asked by Greg Curnoe to present a performance at London's 20/20 Gallery, Lemoyne painted a number of large surfaces using hockey sticks. This event marked the first step in a ten-year exploration, during which he restricted his palette mostly to red, white and blue – the colours of the Montreal Canadiens hockey team (see *Quebec Prisoner of Confederation*, 1969, rep. 13).

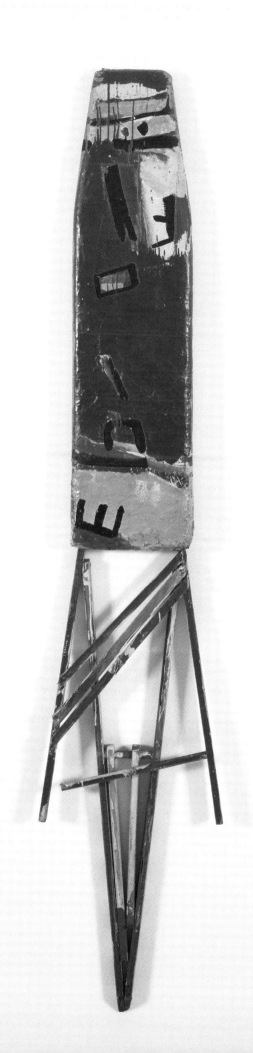

During the sixties, Lemoyne founded and participated in a number of multidisciplinary groups, including Nouvel Âge, which held several improvisation shows in 1964, and L'Horloge (also known as the Horlogers du Nouvel Âge),[45] which, after a "hallucinatory" spectacle presented in Lafontaine Park in June 1965 (fig. 9), was reborn the following fall as Zirmate. Pursuing their quest to synthesize individual practices into a total art, the members of Zirmate drew inspiration from the world of science fiction for the "infragalactic event" they presented at the Youth Pavilion of Expo 67.

These activities were not happenings in the strict sense of the term, but on 15 October 1966 Serge Lemoyne organized a genuine happening at Montreal's Musée d'art contemporain. He saw the happening as a necessity, "a need to make use of as many dimensions as possible, to involve time, the environment … A happening is closer to life, is more vital than a painting because human beings are constantly performing in it … The happening … is a total art."[46]

Also notable and extremely active among the circle of Montreal intellectuals and artists who sought to create a bridge between art and everyday life was the poet and journalist Patrick Straram, also known as "Le Bison ravi" (The Delighted Bison), renowned for his earlier contact with the European Situationists. The Situationists, worthy successors to the Dadaists and Surrealists, were deeply interested in everyday life, considering it the main theatre of action in the struggle against the middle-classes and Judeo-Christian ideology.[47]

Before moving on, mention must be made of the collages of Bill Vazan, a Toronto artist who settled in Montreal in the early sixties and still resides there. Vazan later embarked on a conceptual and Land Art practice in which photography would play a central role (see "A New Role for Photography," pp. 109–110 and "Photography in Question," pp. 152–153), but at the start of his career he was absorbed by the dissection of maps. For *Land Filling (Water Depletion – Silting – Land Reclamation [Political])* (1966–69, rep. 14) he deconstructed Esso road maps and, in anticipation of a major ecological disaster that would redefine the geography of the region, rearranged the pieces so that certain previously distant US states border on Ontario. In *North Reclaim (Lakes Dry Up – Sediment Pile Up – Rebound Up – French Reclaim)* (1966–69), he has linked the cities and populations of northern Ontario to a "French reclaim" of the land. As the two subtitles imply, however, it is the imperceptible yet irreversible movement of the earth itself that preoccupies the artist and that will prevail over the territorial and political claims he describes.

Through their assemblages, happenings and environments, a number of Canadian artists challenged artistic convention by employing an unprecedented fusion of genres and focusing their attention largely on the everyday object. As we shall see in the next chapter, one of the effects of this creative outburst was to encourage a revival of representation – a shift that would be eagerly seized upon by the proponents of Pop Art.

13   Serge Lemoyne
Quebec Prisoner of Confederation
1969
cat. 34

14   Bill Vazan
Land Filling (Water Depletion – Silting – Land Reclamation [Political]) 1966–69
cat. 71

15   Bill Vazan
North Reclaim (Lakes Dry Up – Sediment Pile Up – Rebound Up – French Reclaim) 1966–69
cat. 72

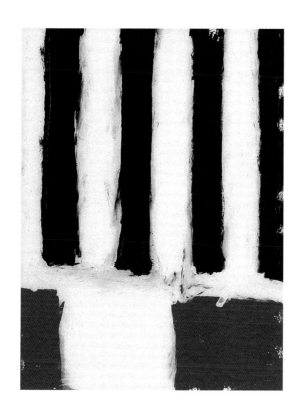

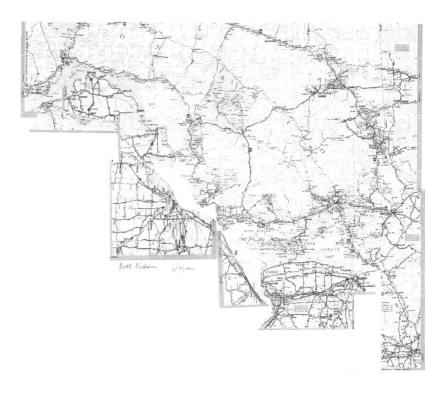

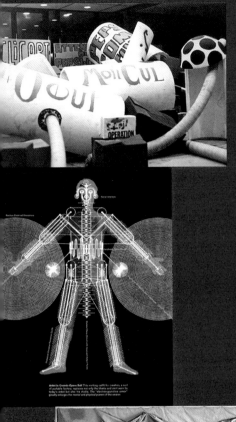

2
The Pop Aesthetic

10   Collective sculpture by Y. Trudeau,
P. Gnass, P. Chamberland, R. Duguay,
I. Fortier, C. Paradis, and M. and L.
Boisvert during the *Opération Déclic*
in front of the Musée d'art contem-
porain de Montréal 1968. Photo: Marc-
André Gagné. Fonds Yves Robillard,
Université du Québec à Montréal
11   François Dallegret. *Artist in
Cosmic-Opera Suit* (1966). Collection
of the artist. Photo courtesy of the
artist
12   Joyce Wieland *Heart-on* (1962),
NGC, Ottawa

13   *Prisma*, an environment by
Michael Morris and Gary Lee-Nova,
Vancouver Art Gallery, 1968

The British artist Richard Hamilton once offered this marvellous definition of Pop Art: "Popular, transient, expendable, low cost, mass produced, witty, sexy, gimmicky, glamorous, big business. This is just a beginning."[48] In England, around the middle of the nineteen fifties, the artists of the Independent Group, which included Hamilton and Eduardo Paolozzi, began introducing fragments of popular culture into their works. It was the critic Lawrence Alloway, a fellow member of the group, who coined the term "Pop Art." The exhibition *This Is Tomorrow*, which he organized in 1956 at London's Whitechapel Art Gallery, brought immediate fame to Richard Hamilton's collage *Just What Is It that Makes Today's Homes So Different, So Appealing?* (Kunsthalle Tübingen, 1956) and launched the movement. But it was a handful of American artists, including Claes Oldenburg, Jim Dine, Roy Lichtenstein, James Rosenquist, George Segal and most notably Andy Warhol, who turned it into a major art phenomenon.

During the sixties, then, popular culture took on a new respectability, ennobled by the interest of avant-garde artists. In the wake of the neo-Dada movement, which saw the integration of ordinary objects into works of art as an alternative to the purist constraints of abstraction, Pop Art ironically brought elitist art and mass taste closer together. A number of objects and subjects of popular culture – Andy Warhol's silkscreen portraits of Marilyn Monroe, for example – would become veritable icons.

Pop Art was characterized by either a direct borrowing of elements from mass culture or a use of images manipulated and disseminated by the media. The artistic appropriation of media-processed images substantially altered conventional modes of representation: "Pop signalled a major revival of figurative art after half a century of abstraction … The term Pop Art defines neither a manner nor a particular style but an iconography, a reference to the urban and commercial environment and to the media … Pop images are extraordinarily readable and often like a transparent overlay of the reality they depict."[49]

Manifestations of the Pop movement were rarely unequivocal in Canada, but its effects could be felt here and there. Representation once again dominated the work of a number of avant-garde artists, and political and sexual themes were freely and seriously explored. In Quebec theatre and literature of the mid-sixties, the contemporary folklore of the *ti-pop* movement liberated language by deliberately employing an irreverent, slangy vocabulary and openly mocking the remnants of religiosity that lingered among a recently urbanized population.

The Montreal Scene
Quebec society – and more especially that of its metropolis – was at the time in a state of upheaval. Eager to play a role, armed with a caustic pen and considerable fervour, a group of young intellectuals founded the influential review *Parti Pris* (1963–68), whose proclaimed goal was nothing less than the radical transformation of society. Its editors saw 1963, year of the publication's founding, as Year One of the Quebec independence movement:

> By opting for "objectivity," the intellectuals of the generation preceding us played the role of impartial spectator … their universalism was a way of avoiding our particular situation … our only goal in describing our society is to transform it … The conditions for change are now all present … Quebec society has entered a revolutionary period.[50]

Although *Parti Pris* was committed to the arts in general, it gave pride of place to poetry and, to a lesser degree, jazz.

The province's art schools were a particular focus of disruption. A succession of strikes organized by the students of the École des beaux-arts de Montréal – the one of 18 November 1965, to demand the holding of a Royal Commission into art education in the province (which resulted in the Rioux report), and those of March 1966 and October 1968 (the latter took the form of an occupation) – radically transformed traditional fine arts education. The École des beaux-arts eventually became part of the Université du Québec à Montréal, and in 1969 obtained the right to award university degrees.

This protest movement, having manifested itself first in the realm of higher art education, soon spread. From 7 to 11 November 1968, for example, a number of demonstrations and debates took place at the Bibliothèque nationale du Québec. Entitled *Opération déclic* and aimed at a re-examination of the relations between art and society, this milestone event attracted a large number of artists of all kinds, including members of such professional associations as the Association des sculpteurs du Québec and the Société des artistes professionnels du Québec (fig. 10). Many pamphlets were distributed during the week, but one of the most succinct contained the following slogans: "'OPÉRATION DÉCLIC' proclaims the continued relevance of Borduas's Refus Global. 'OPÉRATION DÉCLIC' aims essentially to QUESTION, question the Art-Society tandem. 'OPÉRATION DÉCLIC' aims to be an EXPERIENCE CENTRE OF CONFRONTATION site of a DEVELOPING AWARENESS. 'OPÉRATION DÉCLIC' is ACTION, ACTIVATED MANIFESTO".[51] The role of the arts and strategies for self-management were the main issues under discussion.[52]

Mirroring the gradual democratization of the arts and a new sharing of the artistic means of production, printmaking workshops blossomed during the sixties. Following in the footsteps of Albert Dumouchel, long-time teacher at Montreal's École des beaux-arts, a younger generation began opening art print centres. In 1963 Richard Lacroix founded the Atelier libre de Recherches graphiques, which was succeeded by the Guilde Graphique in 1966. Pierre Ayot, another leading figure on Montreal's art scene, ran the print studio at the École des beaux-arts de Montréal from 1964 to1972. In 1966 Ayot founded the Atelier libre 848, which was renamed Graff, centre de conception graphique Inc. in 1972 and is still in operation today. Boasting a wide range of sophisticated equipment used in linocut, etching, lithography, serigraphy, photomechanical serigraphy, photography with view camera and arc lamps, and Plexiglas processing, this cooperative workshop – way ahead of the outdated facilities offered by École des beaux-arts – was the embodiment of the new desire to make art both accessible and inexpensive.

In *Untitled* (1966, rep. 16), where a number of styles converge, Ayot has placed a figurative motif in an abstract context. Using flat, unmodulated colour, he gives a painted portrait the look of a silkscreen print, a medium that had known huge commercial success since the Second World War.[53] Executed using a stencil, the woman's head is similar in style to the popular posters featuring the revolutionary leader Che Guevara.[54] The collage-like elements that structure the composition seem to have been derived from hard-edge abstract painting or from Abstract Expressionism, while the comic-strip "bubble" recalls the work of Roy Lichtenstein – although the message it contains ("From 420/to 86/12 ski-days") remains obscure. By multiplying his references, Ayot has here successfully fused the abstract and the representational.

16 **Pierre Ayot**
Untitled 1966
cat. 2

In 1967, Ayot gave up painting and lithography in favour of serigraphy. *You Let My Toast Burn Again* (1969, rep. 17), whose evocative title is drawn straight from everyday life, consists of a black and white photo-serigraph of a toaster, accompanied by two real slices of overdone toast that have apparently just popped out of the appliance. Ayot's preoccupation here is clearly the object and its image – or its illusion.

François Dallegret can be located at the intersection of several disciplines, including design, graphic design, sculpture and architecture, as well as the interface between all these and technology. In 1962, after graduating in architecture from the École nationale supérieure des beaux-arts in Paris, he exhibited a series of technical drawings of automobiles at the Galerie Iris Clert, in the French capital. He moved to Montreal in 1964. In *Artist in Cosmic-Opera Suit* (1966, fig. 11), Dallegret echoes the mysteries of British Pop-fiction, presenting the artist in a humorously make-believe world of integrated circuits. Wearing "electropuncture armour," the skeletal form looks like a pseudo-functional diagram that is apparently receiving electric emanations via cosmic rays.

Among Dallegret's highly popular manipulable creations are *Atomix* (1966), which resembles a square plastic magnifying glass containing thousands of tiny stainless steel balls that conjure the endless fluidity of atomic particles, and *Kiik* (1969), a shiny metal bar with bulging ends. *US Paper Dollar* (1968, rep. 18) and *US Silver Dollar* (1968, rep. 19) herald the brilliance and shape of the later *Kiik*. Here, optical effects and graphic manipulations expand the surface of the all-powerful American currency, soon to become a Pop icon. Dallegret employed a similar design in his 1968 project for a poster for the International Design Conference held in Aspen, Colorado.

In the work of Guy Montpetit, a serial approach that combines the grid and the hard-edge geometric form provides the context for variations on a motif that recalls the jointed cardboard figures and the construction games of childhood. In *Series E – Sex Machine No. 8* (1969, rep. 20), as in the rest of his Series E, Montpetit uses areas of flat colour to present schematic close-up views of different sexual positions – an amusing tribute to the "mechanics" of a satisfying sex life.

The sixties were, moreover, a time of new sexual attitudes and a new openness towards the whole subject of sex. The pioneering research of Masters and Johnson, published in the US in 1966 in their book *Human Sexual Response*, toppled many prejudices. The Montreal magazine *Sexus*, whose name was borrowed from the title of a novel by the American writer Henry Miller that was banned for many years for its sexual frankness, began publication in August 1967.

The Toronto and London Scenes

It was largely thanks to exhibitions held by gallery owners Jerrold Morris and David Mirvish that the Toronto public was introduced to American Pop Art, which was far more clearly defined than its Canadian counterpart. A number of local artists, however, shared its preoccupations.

In the early sixties, Dennis Burton, initially an abstract painter, adopted a comic strip-inspired graphic style to energetically explore the theme of sexual pleasure – as in *The Game of Life* (1960, Ottawa, NGC, no. 15444). Borrowing freely from erotic magazines and women's underwear ads, his production became even more sexually charged towards the middle of the decade. *Mother, Earth, Love* (1965, rep. 21), with its echoes of geometric abstraction,[55]

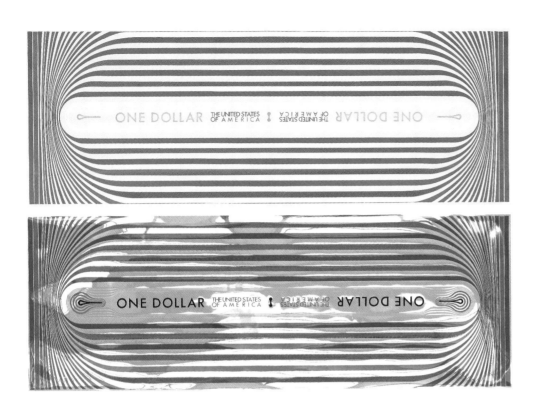

17   Pierre Ayot
You Let My Toast Burn Again 1969
cat. 3

18   François Dallegret
US Paper Dollar 1968
cat. 17

19   François Dallegret
US Silver Dollar 1968
cat. 18

20   Guy Montpetit
Series E – Sex Machine No. 8 1969
cat. 44

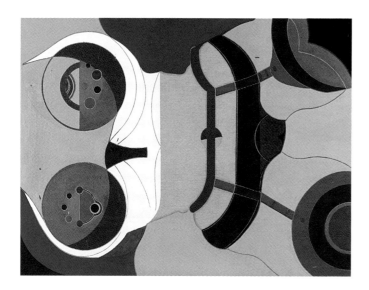

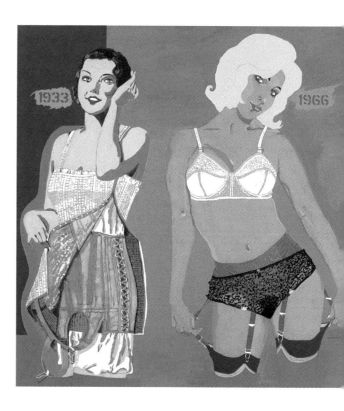

promotes the mythical image of the sexualized goddess-mother – in this case a cosmic image drawn from the world of science fiction:

> In it, I approached the figure from a landscape point of view, seen from above. I focused on the breasts, accentuating their size and shape by adapting the design of a French nursing brassiere. Then I suggested the panty-briefs and the garterbelt straps. At the same time, since I've always been deeply interested in astronomy, I made the breast areas suggestive of circular planetary orbits. This, then, was not only a landscape of earth viewed aerially, but a landscape of 'Mother Universe.'[56]

An old Simpson's catalogue from 1933 was the source of the corset worn by the model Diane Pungen, a friend of Burton's, for the painting *Mothers and Daughters* (1966, rep. 22). During the thirties, women's underwear was designed to conceal and support; this dual image is an amusing reminder of the evolution in female lingerie and its new function of revealing the body and attracting attention.

In May 1965 the dynamic Toronto gallery owner Dorothy Cameron organized an exhibition of erotica by a talented group of artists. Entitled *Eros 65*, the exhibition would become a *cause célèbre* of Canadian censorship for it was raided by police and Cameron was obliged to close her gallery on grounds of "obscenity."

Joyce Wieland had earlier ventured boldly into the expression of female sexuality with her work *Balling* (1961, rep. 23). The splashes of paint that cover the canvas, inevitably conjuring the culmination of a sexual encounter, can be interpreted almost like the blots

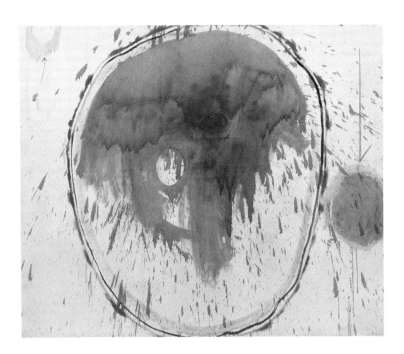

of a Rorschach test. But the full meaning of this Abstract Expressionist work is undoubtedly revealed by its title. Throughout the decade, Wieland conducted a light-hearted exploration of sexuality in which the genitals often look like something out of a comic book. But what set Wieland apart from her peers was the frankness with which she treated the more intimate aspects of femininity, such as menstruation, and her endless technical experimentation. In the marvellous *Heart-on* (1961, fig. 12), for example, Wieland has impregnated a piece of raw linen canvas with red ink.

In the latter part of the sixties, inspired by an interest in traditionally "feminine" techniques, Wieland produced *Reason over Passion* (1968, rep. 24) and *La raison avant la passion* (1968–69, rep. 25), two works that occupy the borderland between art and politics. The impact of the two brightly coloured quilts – one in each official language – is nothing if not ambivalent, for the appeal of the charmingly twirling hearts seems to run counter to the sobriety of the message.

The circumstances that triggered Wieland's execution of these works are worth recalling. Already well established as an experimental filmmaker, the artist attended the 1968 Liberal leadership convention in Ottawa with her friend Mary Mitchell, where she filmed part of the proceedings. On the plane home, the two friends read a report that included a reference to Pierre Elliott Trudeau's famous "reason over passion" remark:

> As Liberals, we rely on that most unlikely bulwark, the individual citizen, you and
> me, the young and the old, the famous and the unknown, the Arctic nomad and
> the suburbanite. It was this confidence in the individual which set me on the road

24   Joyce Wieland
Reason over Passion 1968
cat. 81

25   Joyce Wieland
La raison avant la passion 1968–69
cat. 82

which has led me to my present quest. For many years, I have been fighting for the triumph of reason over passion in politics, for the protection of the individual freedoms against the tyranny of the group, and for a just distribution of our national wealth. It was my concern with these values which led me to the Liberal party.[57]

Wieland immediately decided she was going to make a quilt based on the phrase. Back in New York, she and a group of artists and friends began sending letters to Ottawa in support of Trudeau's candidature: "Eventually it got into the papers that there was this huge movement in New York and Trudeau was asked about it and he answered, 'Reason over passion; that's the theme of all my writings.'"[58] A woman of considerable insight, Wieland was fascinated by this public figure and the contradictory political reactions he inspired. Since that time there have been many plays on the famous motto, including the title of the autobiography published by the politician's ex-wife: *Margaret Trudeau: Beyond Reason*.[59]

When she became one of the leading artists invited in the late sixties to make lithographs at the print workshops of the Nova Scotia College of Art and Design, in Halifax (see "A New Role for Photography," p. 108), Joyce Wieland used her own lipstick as the grease medium and "kissed" the lithographic stone to create the sublimely patriotic work *O Canada* (1969, rep. 26).

As several of Wieland's works illustrate, words took on greater aesthetic significance during the sixties with the rise of conceptual art – an approach that focused largely on the ideas behind artworks and on the verbal language suited to describing these abstract mental images. In the case of Greg Curnoe, an enthusiastic writer and keeper of a daily journal, the

shift from paper to canvas as the support for writing was, technically speaking, a bold one. He had large rubber stamps specially made for this lettering technique, but the results of stamping ink directly onto canvas were not always uniform. In *The True North Strong and Free (No. 1 – Canada Feeds the Brain! G.C.), The True North Strong and Free (No. 2 – Close the 49th Parallel, Etc.), The True North Strong and Free (No. 3 – Can. Costs Less than Drugs), The True North Strong and Free (No. 4 – Canada Always Loses!), The True North Strong and Free (No. 5 – Did Chartier Die in Vain??)* (1968, rep. 27), Curnoe is quoting from the English version of Canada's national anthem and adding his own slogans or paraphrasing other sources. He said later that the works in "THE TRUE NORTH STRONG AND FREE series were consciously made as slogans, CANADA COST LESS THAN DRUGS was a paraphrase of a subheading in a catalogue for The Sanden Electric Hurculex Belt as was CANADA FEEDS THE BRAIN."[60]

All his life Greg Curnoe was vehemently anti-American, and in the late sixties he continued to oppose US culture and politics by promoting a regionalist approach that centred on the artist's own immediate surroundings. After a first series devoted to a lettered work, he replaced words by images in *View of Victoria Hospital, Second Series (February 10, 1969– March 10, 1971)* (rep. 28), one of the works he presented at the 1976 Venice Biennale. Deeply attached to his milieu, Curnoe always enjoyed looking out of his wide studio windows at London's Victoria Hospital where he was born in 1936 and where, in a tragic turn of fate, his body was taken after he was killed in a cycling accident on 14 November 1992. The simple coloured forms represent the elements of a landscape seen from afar. The circled numbers (an amusing reference to painting-by-numbers) are linked to an explanatory notebook where rubber-stamped letters record 120 phenomena – weather conditions, visits from friends, light effects, sudden puffs of smoke, insects and birds, traffic, the passage of the seasons – observed by the artist as he was executing the painting between February 1969 and March 1971. The language of the notebook is simple, and the descriptions precise. The work is also accompanied by an audiotape of ambient noises recorded by the artist during the same period. The painting's central division corresponds exactly to the transom of the window that opens onto a panoramic view of the hospital and its environs. The hospital, a place of birth, life and death, has here become a kind of sacred territory.

The painter and filmmaker Jack Chambers was born – like Curnoe – at London's Victoria Hospital, and it was also there that he died of leukaemia in 1978. The two artists began making paintings of the hospital around the same time, using more or less the same viewpoint: Chambers from the roof of Curnoe's studio on Weston Street, and Curnoe from the studio window. Chambers began by photographing the hospital from the studio roof, using a wide-angle lens. Nineteen sixty-nine was a fruitful year for Chambers: it saw the production of such major works as *401 Towards London No. 1* (Toronto, Art Gallery of Ontario), *Sunday Morning No. 2* (private collection) and *Chrysanthemums* (Museum London). It was towards the end of the year that he embarked on *Victoria Hospital* (1969–70, rep. 29). In this extremely subtle winter scene, a blanket of snow softly unites all the elements of the composition. During his studies at the school of fine arts in Madrid the artist had been much drawn to the Spanish realist tradition and he frequently employed photography as an intermediary step to define depth in his images. Chambers' enthralling pictures, painted slowly and with meticulous care, seem to crystallize privileged moments of perception. In the fall of the same year, in a theor-

29   Jack Chambers
Victoria Hospital 1969–70
cat. 13

30   John Boyle
Rebel Series: Totem; Big Bear and
Brendan; Louis and Gregory 1967
cat. 7

etical "manifesto" summarizing the foundations of his art, he wrote: "… man's art, I call *experience* and the intention to imitate experience by art-craft, I call *perceptual realism* … The perception of the natural world and its objects, creatures and people is the source of truth about oneself because not only what we project but also what we receive is ourselves."[61] In other words, it is in the act of perception that we learn to perceive ourselves.

In a quite different spirit is John Boyle's *Rebel Series* (1967, rep. 30), a painting/sculpture composed of cut-outs. The rebel heroes it depicts include Louis Riel, the Métis chief who led the Manitoba Rebellion of 1885 and was later seen as the founding father of the province; Woodie Guthrie (died 1967), singer-songwriter of politico-social folk songs (*Dust Bowl Ballads*) and father of Arlo Guthrie, the popular sixties folksinger; and a member of the Dukhobor community, a pacifist Russian peasant sect that settled in Western Canada. On the other side of the mobile can be seen the architectural visionary Buckminster Fuller, along with a self-portrait of the artist as a young man. The second part of the work portrays Big Bear, a Cree chief who refused to sign a treaty with the Canadian government because he considered it detrimental to his people; and on the verso is Brendan Behan, the Irish playwright who was imprisoned for his activities on behalf of the Irish Republican Army. Finally, in the third section, Louis Riel reappears on the opposite side of Gregory Corso, an American beat poet who took up writing while in jail.

John Boyle's work deals with the nature of the Canadian identity, the vestiges of the colonial mentality, and powerful feelings of political and artistic marginality. In his efforts to determine the essence of "being Canadian," Boyle has attempted to explore the *genius loci* – the associations, local history and traditions (now threatened by mass culture) – of southwestern Ontario, before it disappears forever.

In 1970, at the Agnes Etherington Art Centre in Kingston, Boyle (supported by Greg Curnoe) presented his manifesto *Continental Refusal*, whose title no doubt alludes to Borduas' 1948 *Refus global*. It includes the following statement: "Indeed, a Canadian patriotism might very well be based on anti-Americanism. As well as an increased awareness of the real Canadian culture, a culture developed by people living in the country drawing upon their environment, as opposed to professionals working along lines developed in international cities."[62]

The anarchist ideology of London's visual artists is well known, and can also be felt in the work of the artist-musicians of the Nihilist Spasm Band. The emergence of such a trend in an essentially conservative city such as London is intriguing. Interestingly, during his extensive research into local history, Greg Curnoe discovered that London had a substantial Jewish anarchist community, located around Grey and Waterloo streets, and that it invited Emma Goldman to lecture there in the 1930s.[63] Emma Goldman, a legendary Lithuanian-born anarchist who had emigrated to the United States, died in exile in Toronto in 1940. She features, moreover, in a painted assemblage by John Boyle entitled *Making Bombs* (1965, Ottawa, NGC, no. 40426).

The Vancouver Scene

Vancouver became Canada's California. The relatively mild climate of the city and of the whole province attracted a large hippie population composed in part of American draft dodgers – who were opposed to the Vietnam war and US draft laws, but often also to the homogenization of consumer society and to traditional social values. A heady mix of drugs, Oriental philosophy and new communications technologies helped create a vibrant, exciting milieu.

Although New York exerted a strong pull for artists on Canada's east coast, those in Vancouver were more interested in the cultural dynamism of England's capital, which was revolutionizing fashion, design and music. A sign of this fascination was the 1965 presentation at the Vancouver Art Gallery of the exhibition *London, The New Scene*, mounted by Martin Friedman of the Walker Art Centre in Minneapolis. This major exhibition offered an American perspective on the London scene – the first on this scale to be held in North America.

Vancouver's Pop-formalist artists worked initially in the hard-edge mode of geometric abstraction before experimenting with the iconography of popular culture. Gary Lee-Nova's *Menthol Filter Kings* (1967, rep. 31) contains vague references to menthol cigarettes, whose popularity among women at the time can be attributed to the increasingly persuasive power of advertising. Lee-Nova is a master of the optical illusion, especially the kind that seems to imbue his forms with a volume that takes them outside the two-dimensional frame. In 1968 he collaborated with Michael Morris on the creation of an environment entitled *Prisma* at the Vancouver Art Gallery (fig. 13), continuing as the decade ended to explore other expressive approaches, including experimental film.

There was no better interpreter of the darker side of the sixties than Claude Breeze. Inspired by an anti-segregationist poster that was put out by the Student Nonviolent Coordinating Committee of Atlanta and published in the University of British Columbia's student newspaper, his painting *Sunday Afternoon: From an Old American Photograph* (c. 1964–65, rep. 32) portrays a dreadful scene. Breeze's semi-expressionist adaptation of the photograph of a lynching in the southern United States reveals the full horror of the crime. The nudity of one of the figures – a modification introduced by the artist – is a brutal reminder of the victim's vulnerability, while the expression on the witness's face seems to draw the spectator into a conspiracy of silence. Breeze would execute other scenes of violence, often based on images

31 Gary Lee-Nova
Menthol Filter Kings 1967
cat. 32

32 Claude Breeze
Sunday Afternoon: From an Old
American Photograph c. 1964–65
cat. 8

33 Iain Baxter
Red Still Life 1965
cat. 5

of Vietnam – the first televised war – or of passionate battles between lovers. His work from this period can be related to that of the English painter Francis Bacon, another artist who exploited a semi-expressionist manner in a highly distinct way.

Through the nature of both his work and his contacts, Iain Baxter contributed significantly to the internationalization of the Vancouver art scene. Before founding the N.E. Thing Co. in 1966 with Ingrid Baxter (see "A New Role for Photography," pp. 104–105), Baxter pursued his fascination for the work of the Italian painter Giorgio Morandi. He became particularly interested in ordinary objects, especially ones made of plastic. In *Red Still Life* (1965, rep. 33), he used an industrial vacuum moulding technique to transform coloured plastic into a bas-relief. The perfectly aligned bottles (modern versions of early pottery forms) evoke the assembly line that is the key to mass production. In Baxter's skilful hands, industrial techniques and materials become art.

So, in Montreal, Toronto and Vancouver alike – and in the form of instantly readable, often playful images that reflected the general mood of social protest and ferment – a Pop aesthetic edged its way into the consciousness of those eager to tighten the links between art and daily life.

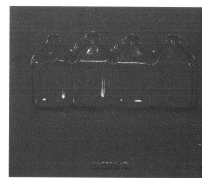

3

Perception, Perception, Perception

14   Claude Tousignant removing tape
from his gong, 1966
15   Charles Gagnon in his studio
16   Av Isaacs with Michael Snow's
Walking Woman banner, Centre for
Contemporary Canadian Art, Toronto/
The Isaacs Gallery Project

We touched briefly in the last chapter on the notion of perceptual realism introduced by Jack Chambers and the phenomenological approach underlying Greg Curnoe's picture of Victoria Hospital – both methods that describe everyday events in perceptual terms. The lingering impact of existentialism, and more particularly of Merleau-Ponty's phenomenology of perception, which places enormous emphasis on the role of the body in the human experience of the world, shaped artistic visions and opened new avenues. People became deeply interested in the sensory aspects of perception. Theories of communications and technology – notably those of the celebrated Marshall McLuhan – stimulated research into perception.

> Seen as extensions of man, all technologies inevitably affect our senses, and call for new models of perception in whatever culture they appear. To study the dominant models of perception in any culture whatever, can best be done through the arts of that culture. To be able to spot such models as they appear … becomes necessary today as we live more and more in all the cultures of the world simultaneously.[64]

Different theories of perception – philosophical, scientific and even literary – thus had an indirect influence on a number of artistic practices. The popularity of Aldous Huxley's book *The Doors of Perception*,[65] which opens with a quote from William Blake ("If the doors of perception were cleansed, everything would appear to man as it is, infinite")[66] and explores the effects of so-called psychedelic drugs,[67] gave impetus to these preoccupations. In his book, Huxley observes that "mescaline raises all colours to a higher power and makes the percipient aware of innumerable fine shades of difference, to which, at ordinary times, he is completely blind."[68]

LSD occupies a special place in the history of hallucinogenic drug research. It was discovered in 1938 by the Swiss chemist Albert Hofmann and introduced into the US by Dr. Max Rinkel eleven years later. Intrigued by the drug's psychotropic properties, which produce powerful phantasmagorical images in kaleidoscopic colours, scientists attempted to develop it for therapeutic use in various types of addiction, including alcoholism, and in cases of mental illness such as schizophrenia. The most famous research project, immortalized by Tom Wolfe in his novel *The Electric Kool-Aid Acid Test* (1968), was conducted in 1960 at Harvard by behavioural psychologist and professor Timothy Leary (although not within strict scientific parameters). This drug "guru" was dismissed from the university in 1963 for promoting the general use of LSD. Throughout the fifties, researchers and doctors had been trying to understand the hallucinatory effects experienced by users, which range from the blurring of the boundaries between objects to major emotional changes that can culminate in a profound mystical experience. The similarities observed between the manifestations of certain psychoses and the psychotropic effects of LSD eventually led to the theory that chemical imbalances in the organism could be at the root of certain mental illnesses.

A number of institutional research programs focusing on LSD were undertaken in Canada during this period. One part of the study conducted by Dr. Humphry Osmond during the fifties at the Weyburn Mental Hospital in Saskatchewan explored the links between artistic creativity and hallucinogenic effects, and Art McKay and Ted Godwin were among the artists who took part.[69] On the West Coast, similar therapeutic studies were run between 1958 and 1965 by

Drs. J. R. MacLean, D. C. MacDonald, F. Ogden and F. Wilby at Hollywood Hospital in New Westminster, British Columbia. For his part, Dr. A. M. Hubbard of Vancouver was particularly interested in the spiritual experiences that can be triggered by the drug. During the sixties, other types of research that were officially approved at the time – but later severely criticized – were conducted at the Kingston and Millhaven penitentiaries in Ontario, under the direction of psychiatrist Dr. George Scott of Canadian Federal Corrections, in partnership with Dr. Ewen Cameron of the Allen Memorial Psychiatric Institute of Montreal's McGill University. Funding for their work was provided by Canada's Department of National Defence and the US Central Intelligence Agency. These government bodies were interested in the revelatory effects of hallucinogenic drugs and their possible use in interrogation.

Although by no means a sudden phenomenon, the exploration of the optical possibilities of artistic expression gained momentum in the mid-sixties, coinciding with the first appearance of the term "Op Art" in *Time* magazine in 1964. The form had attracted public interest a few years earlier thanks to the work of the Hungarian artist Victor Vasarely, who would play a leading role in the founding of the Groupe de Recherches d'Art Visuel (GRAV) in Paris. Between 1960 and 1968 this group made use of the parameters of geometric abstraction to expand the boundaries of Op Art. Meanwhile, in the very early sixties, the British artist Bridget Riley produced a series of landmark optical works that would have international impact.

One of the characteristic features of Op is the generation of lines, shapes and movements that are not real, but caused by the natural physical reaction of the eye. The advertising and fashion worlds began energetically exploiting these perceptual anomalies, and an exhibition held at New York's MoMA in 1965, entitled *The Responsive Eye*, placed the seal of respectability on the movement. Although paintings by two Canadians – Guido Molinari and Claude Tousignant – were included in this exhibition, both artists rejected the "Op" label. Moreover, the fame of the movement, considered essentially decorative and lightweight by the powerful US art milieu, was short-lived.

Notable among the small group of Canadian artists who experimented with this style is Marcel Barbeau, a versatile painter whose roots were in Automatisme. In the early sixties, having become aware of the reversibility potential of black and white (a realization that had earlier marked the practice of Paul-Émile Borduas), Barbeau restricted his palette to these two colours. In 1963, after seeing an exhibition of Victor Vasarely's works in Paris, he moved closer to geometric abstraction and began employing certain optical effects. In August 1964 he began living in New York, where, along with the member of GRAV, he took part in an international conference on Op Art organized by Fairleigh Dickinson University.[70] In 1965 New York's East Hampton Gallery, which was focusing on this type of art at the time, held exhibitions of both Barbeau's and Claude Tousignant's works.

The canvases of Barbeau's aptly titled series *Retina*, which spanned a couple of years, remind us forcefully how this sensitive membrane of the eye captures the light effects of optical art and transmits them to the brain. *Retina 999* (1966, rep. 34) is a particularly good example: the optico-psychological result of the tension between undulating parallel lines and Bridget Riley-style chevrons is the generation of a virtual line at the point where the two motifs meet.

Hard-edge painting lends itself almost naturally to optical illusion, as witness the vibrations that can often be observed at the dividing line between two colours. The Vancouver

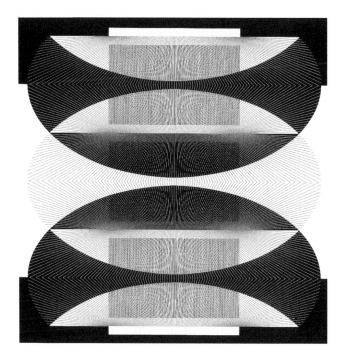

artist Brian Fisher ventured deep into the realm of Op. The arcs that cover the entire surface of his painting *Indirections No. 1* (1968, rep. 35) generate multiple virtual images. In computer science, "indirection" refers to the manipulation of data via its address, using a pointer. In more ordinary language, the word can denote a deceitful or misleading action. Fisher's delicate, subtle work is a tapestry of illusion. Carried away by the virtuosity of his imagination, he continued until the early seventies to create optical works whose complexity and extremely close tones (white and cream, for example) leave us confounded.

If there is one practice that is concerned with expression through sense data, through pure sensation, it is that of Claude Tousignant. In *Chromatic Accelerator 96–10–68* (1968, rep. 36), the correspondence between the inner rings and the painting's round format render palpable the artist's ongoing reflection on the ontological nature of pictorial space. His canvases of narrow concentric bands of colour – the *Chromatic Transformer*, *Gong* and *Chromatic Accelerator* series – met with considerable acclaim, both in Canada and abroad. In the sixties, rigorously and boldly exploring the expressive power of pure chroma, Tousignant presented colour as a vibrating discharge of energy. The introduction of new acrylic paints and a skilful use of masking tape (enabling him to create perfectly circular edges) resulted in paintings that sharpen and challenge the spectator's visual acuity. In 1965, in the *Chromatic Transformer* series, he began exploiting the attraction-repulsion of centripetal and centrifugal forces. In the *Gongs*, created the following year, he conceived new synesthetic[71] correspondences based on the acoustic reverberations of the gong (fig. 14). Finally, in the 1967–68 *Chromatic Accelerators* he achieved a chromatic interaction that was even more dynamic by ordering

36   Claude Tousignant
Chromatic Accelerator 96–10–68
October 1968
cat. 68

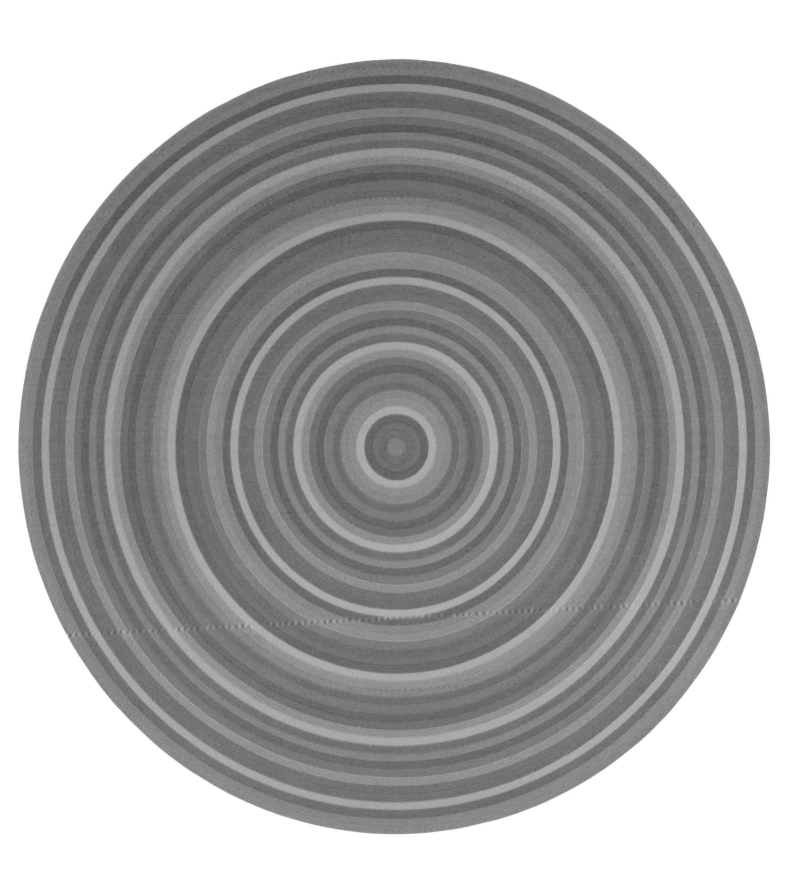

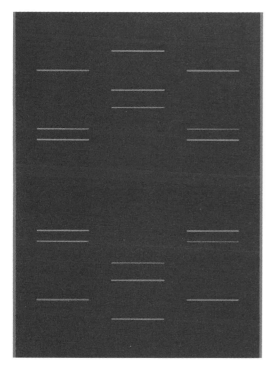  

the narrow bands in systematized sequences of alternating colour. According to the artist, the serial structure "creates an aleatory system of vision"[72] that can be compared to the random component of contemporary music, like that of one of the pioneers of aleatory music, Iannis Xenakis.

Through the vibrating energy of the colour, the viewer is caught up in a dizzying optical whirlwind. But the artist's objective is much broader: "My goal is that the painting become a vast field of chromatic vibration, that it be the very rhythm of the colour that speaks. I use optical effects, but for purposes of expression: to express the different qualities of chromatic vibration so that each painting has its own particular respiration."[73]

In contrast to the vibrational impact of Claude Tousignant's circular works, the subtle nuances explored by Yves Gaucher encourage a mood of silent contemplation. Gaucher's subsequent paintings feature variations of grey on grey, so *Triptych: Signals, Another Summer; Signals, Very Softly; Silences/Silence* (1966, rep. 37) is somewhat atypical in its use of the three primary colours. In 1966 Gaucher embarked on a series of works whose coloured surfaces are punctuated here and there by lines of equal length, like bars of light.[74] In this triptych, whose elements were executed separately and then assembled, there is constant interplay between the horizontality of the three conjoined canvases, the verticality of the columns formed by the "signals," and the horizontality of the bar/signals themselves. Explains curator Michel Martin: "Formally the same but of varying intensities, these contrasting signals produce a kinetic effect, a dichotomic push-and-pull movement that draws the spectator into spaces that owe their instability largely to the relations between the colours and the eye's capacity to perceive and experience these relations."[75]

37 Yves Gaucher
Triptych: Signals, Another Summer; Signals, Very Softly; Silences/Silence
1966
cat. 24

38 Charles Gagnon
November Steps 1967–68
cat. 23

Yves Gaucher, too, was deeply interested in contemporary music, particularly the atonal compositions of Anton Webern and the principle of repetition and sequential variation that is the basis of serial music. Signals incised with exquisite delicacy and surgical precision on a coloured ground offer the viewer a synesthetic experience of fields full of silence. "I prefer the murmur to the shout, for in silence, there is real presence," said the artist in 1969.[76]

Charles Gagnon was also drawing inspiration from music when he executed *November Steps* (1967–68, rep. 38), a work that encourages a relationship of communion with the spectator. Executed in Montreal on Gagnon's return from Japan, the painting takes it name from a musical work composed in 1967 by his friend Toru Takemitsu, who had been commissioned by the New York Philharmonic to write a piece celebrating the musical encounter of East and West. The influence of both photography and film – modes in which Gagnon also expressed himself – can be sensed in the broad, gesturally handled white areas and the smooth black bands that frame the pictorial space. The almost photographic/filmic framing of the work would remain a dominant feature of Gagnon's painting until the end of the decade and beyond (fig.15). This painting actually appears (along with Gagnon himself) in a silent black and white film he made around the same time, entitled *Le Son d'un espace*. By thus imprisoning the painting inside the camera's frame, Gagnon placed it in a kind of *mise en abyme*. The series of eight serigraphs he produced in 1967 called *The Colour of Time, The Sound of Space* is another manifestation of the desire to highlight interaction between the senses.

As Gagnon's practice hints, our way of seeing is conditioned by the visual devices we invent. Michael Snow has probed deeply into the mechanisms of visual perception, both natural and artificial. In *Atlantic* (1967, rep. 39), Snow placed photographs of slightly varying

waves at the back of a series of metal compartments. The metal's reflective surface creates a sense of depth, transforming the two-dimensional photos into moving ocean images. By standing at a precise distance from the piece, the viewer can also perceive its point of convergence – the spot where all thirty photographs fuse into a single image. Often described as a cinematic work, *Atlantic* is at the intersection of film, photography and sculpture.

Between 1961 and 1967, Snow explored issues of perception and media influence using multiple variants of his "Walking Woman" silhouette (fig. 16). Whatever the material, the figure is always the same – although it may be flattened, three-dimensional, dressed, naked, cut out, rolled up, folded, painted, sculpted or filmed. Exhibited for the most part in New York and Toronto, the Walking Woman also made an appearance at Montreal's Expo 67 and sometimes became part of the urban scene in the form of posters or silkscreened T-shirts. In *Five Girl-Panels* (1964, rep. 40) the artist uses the same Pop image, but here as if seen in the distorting mirrors often found at the time in fairs and science and technology museums.

Hinting at Michael Snow's *Authorization* (see "Photography in Question," p. 146), the images captured by the camera in *Topesthesia 1968* (1968, rep. 41), by Les Levine, raise a number of questions concerning the perception of the body by the media. Symbols of three of the artist's senses – eye, ear and mouth – are shown in close-up on a series of television screens. This work, whose title denotes the power of localizing a tactile sensation, was included in Levine's exhibition *Body Control Systems*, held at the Isaacs Gallery in 1970. According to Levine: "Man has entered a state of post-consciousness; we are all extensions of a main circuit. Real systems, body technology and ecological conditions control our cultural thrust rather

than any previous idea of consciousness we may have had."[77] Speaking of his photographic practice, Levine describes himself as a "post-production artist." Placing everything within a conceptual framework, he maintains that "good camera artworks are those that abdicate any aesthetic authority."[78]

During the sixties, in all types of artistic discipline, the perceptual experience of the natural and artificial environments in which artists found themselves became an object of artistic reflection. Let us now look at how sculpture was in its turn transformed by the act of perception.

40   Michael Snow
Five Girl-Panels 1964
cat. 65

41   Les Levine
Topesthesia 1968 1968
cat. 38

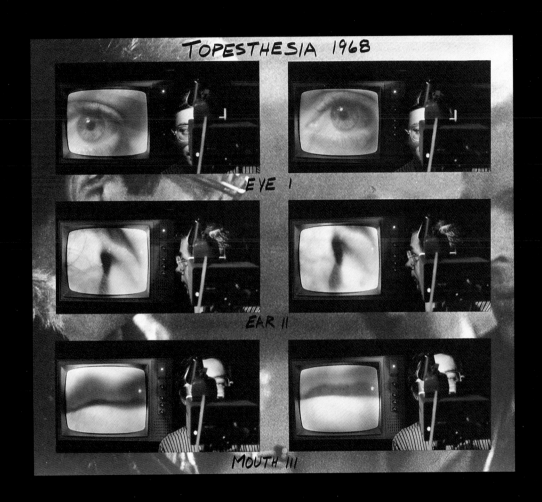

4 Sculpture at Ground Level

17   Royden Rabinowitch *Barrel-Constructions 1964, Toronto/Edinburgh* (1983), National Gallery of Canada, Ottawa.

18   Royden Rabinowitch, David Rabinowitch and Pierre Théberge in a studio, 1968

19   Artist Walter Redinger

During the sixties, abstract sculpture followed a path parallel to that of modernist painting, voluntarily reducing its means of expression and embarking on an in-depth examination of its own foundations. Several sculptors of this period who had been trained as painters began fusing the two disciplines. The abandonment of the human figure as the defining model allowed sculptors to explore new aesthetic qualities – notably horizontality, a concept that freed them from the tyranny of gravity. The angle of the spectator's gaze gradually shifted: hitherto horizontal or slightly raised, it was now directed downwards.

As minimalism and reductionism began to dominate sculpture internationally, the pioneer American sculptor Carl Andre brought it down to ground level. The decade, which saw many commissions for abstract, often monumental sculpture projects, can be considered something of a high point in the history of the discipline. North America's first ever international sculpture symposium took place in Montreal in 1964, a year before the one held in Long Beach, California.

In the Toronto region, meanwhile, sculptor Royden Rabinowitch was adopting an almost conceptual approach in his choice of assemblage techniques. His *Barrel Construction* series consists of about fifty assemblages composed of the staves and bottoms of oak barrels[79] – materials that no doubt reminded him of his youth, when he would play with the barrel staves and hoops in the yard behind Toronto's Gooderham & Worts distillery, near his home. The inside of whiskey barrels are generally charred so as to give a particular flavour to the liquor during the aging process, which explains the burnt inside surfaces of the staves employed by Rabinowitch. Throughout this series the artist plays with both the dimensionality and the surface treatment of components that started out as ready-mades.

The works entitled *Barrel Construction: Double Curvature at Right Angles* (1966 ?, reps. 42, 43 and 44) are an exercise in deconstruction/reconstruction: depending on their relative positions, the staves placed parallel or at right angles to one another on the ground create a number of convex and concave forms, achieving a fragile equilibrium that is both subtle and complex. The bulging cylinder of the barrel shape is, for Rabinowitch, an ideal metaphor for the earth itself and its lines of longitude and latitude. The artist's lithograph entitled *Barrel Construction 1964, Toronto/Edinburgh* (fig. 17) evokes another of his favourite images – the elongated air balloon. Perhaps significantly, the original Charliere gas balloons were filled with hydrogen contained in a wooden barrel.

Fascinated by diverse mathematical and philosophical theories, Rabinowitch has drawn inspiration from a number of studies, including Johannes Kepler's treatise on the volumes of wine barrels, *Stereometria Doliorum Vinariorum* (The Stereometry of Wine Barrels). In addition, the distinctions drawn by the French mathematician Henri Poincaré between abstract space and the space of experience have led him to strive in his own sculpture for an "ordinary space of experience." His work certainly makes us aware of different types of space: rational mathematical space, visual space (with its multiple viewpoints), and space as the source of the subjective experience of body and time.

The sculpture of David Rabinowitch (fig. 18), Royden's brother, offers an opportunity to study the properties that condition the viewer's experience. An elegant work, *The Phantom: Conic (Elliptical) Plane with 2 Double Breaks I (Convergent)* (1967, rep. 45) consists of a metal ellipse (originally painted), whose converging pleats give the piece volume and draw the gaze into a narrowing channel. Rabinowitch has a fondness for the marks that typically appear on

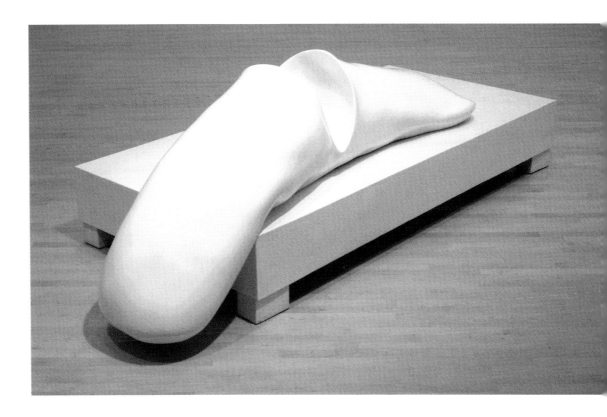

the surface of steel sheets treated with a hydraulic press – an industrial process that alters the metal in unpredictable ways. Vehemently dissociating himself from art that depends on illusion, David Rabinowitch practices reductionism but rejects the "minimalist" label. Like a number of his contemporaries, however, he takes a holistic rather than a fragmented approach to the work. Geometry is the abstract method of representing space, and Rabinowitch's reasoning proceeds differently; for him, on the contrary, the object is a concretization of mental processes. Deeply concerned with perception, the artist compels the viewer to approach his work from multiple angles: "From the side, the *Phantom* lives up to its name. It becomes aerodynamically sleek, almost like something glimpsed in flight, nearly on the point of breaking some uncalibrated visibility barrier. The transitions between these views are all the more startling for their smoothness and unforeseeability."[98] For David Rabinowitch, the purpose of sculpture is the exploration of the relational interplay between the work's inherent properties and the external perceptions it produces.

Sculptor Walter Redinger (fig. 19) could be singled out during the sixties for his penchant for organic forms and his early use of fibreglass, a new material that lent itself perfectly to curved lines, folds and surface distortions. His work *Spermatogenesis # 1* (1968, rep. 46) possesses something of the Pop spirit: on a scale much larger than life, it powerfully suggests the soft, boneless flesh of the male genital organ. The surface of the form that spills over the edge of its platform is at once hard and soft to the touch, qualities that are contradictory enough to evoke alternative images. Some years after it was executed, the artist explained: "I was developing a technique of multi-associations, of minimal shape with an encasement of the human body. It was combined and simultaneous use of the human body form in, and with, minimal sculptural shape. This was a breakthrough for me … After 1965, the human body became a reference point, a bridge to the largest concept I know – life and life forms."[81] The Art Gallery of Ontario owns a second, larger version of this work.

The paradoxical also plays a fundamental role in the sculptural oeuvre of Serge Tousignant, of Montreal, as his painted sculpture *Exit* (1966, rep. 47) clearly demonstrates. "Sculpture is not a sculpture," said the artist in 1968, "it is the formulation of an idea that does not initially have a sculptural perspective and that is only clearly defined in the execution."[82] In fact, the open structure of these coloured cubes gradually eliminates the notion of volume, deforming the cube in a linear sequence and ultimately giving the metal the lightness of a sheet of paper. As has recently been noted, "*Exit* … illustrates this passage from three-dimensional form to surface: in four coloured steps, an enamelled steel cube collapses until it is almost completely flat."[83] In other sculptures from the same period, Tousignant would employ mirrors to create illusions that are simultaneously optical and conceptual.

In the mid-sixties, before taking a more conceptual direction at the start of the following decade, Jean-Marie Delavalle – a versatile artist who studied in Montreal and later moved to Boucherville – executed a number of painted steel sculptures in the minimalist mode. In *Roller* (1968, rep. 48), a roller that appears to be flattening a three-dimensional square focuses attention on the triangle of one of its corners. With its two monochrome components – red and white – the piece embodies a subtle use of high density metal and an interesting exploration of the inclined surface. The artist had previously made another compression roller part of *Eloise* (1967), a work that belongs to the Canada Council Art Bank.

5 The Expanding Field of Painting

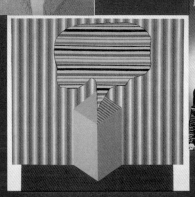

20   Guido Molinari in his studio
21   Artist Rita Letendre
22   Michael Morris *The Problem of Nothing* (1966), Vancouver Art Gallery
23   The collective General Idea, from left to right, AA Bronson, Jorge Zontal, Felix Partz, 1982

49 Jean McEwen
Jubilant Red 1963
cat. 40

A number of young painters who had attracted attention in Canada during the mid-fifties took up the challenge of large-scale painting in their subsequent careers. Both the promotion of monumental works by their American counterparts and an escalation in public commissions encouraged painters to increase the dimensions of their canvases and adapt the all-over technique to large-scale composition. Towards the end of the sixties, then, late modernist painting expanded. Labelled variously "hard-edge," "colour field" or "minimal," the trend was too complex to be encapsulated by any single term. Some practices placed emphasis on process, while others were nourished by a new and incisive criticality. It was a fruitful period for the country's leading painters working in this mode.

One of these artists was Jean McEwen, who had moved away from Automatisme in 1955 to align himself more closely with Montreal's Plasticiens, sharing their deep interest in the dynamic properties of colour. Unwilling to accept the physical and material constraints of the very large canvas, McEwen sometimes joined smaller ones together. We see this technique in the five panel *Jubilant Red* (1963, rep. 49), which was commissioned by the architect John Parkin for Toronto's airport.[84] Like an all-consuming fire, the red offers glimpses of a charred black underlayer. The many stratae beneath the pictorial surface multiply the expressive possibilities of the warm/cool, light/dark dichotomies. Subtle divisions and bands of varying widths create an impression of verticality reminiscent of the work of Barnett Newman. Generally eschewing the paintbrush and working directly with his fingers, the artist would make the surface of the canvas vibrate like a drum, "rubbing the colour into the varnish"[85] in order to obtain effects of transparency and opalescence. The year this painting was executed,

1963, was a good one for McEwen: he showed at Martha Jackson's gallery in New York and sent six paintings to the biennale in São Paulo, Brazil, receiving an honourable mention for the works as a group.

Orange and Green Bi-serial (1967, rep. 50), by Guido Molinari, is one of the most accomplished large-format paintings from this period. Using the principles of seriality and bi-seriality, which allowed him to repeat ad infinitum a strict arrangement of coloured bands (fig. 20), Molinari escaped the thrall of Mondrian's grid – the starting point of all his aesthetic reflections and research. Like Gaucher and several other artists during this decade (see "Perception, Perception, Perception," p. 60), Molinari invoked the notion of musical seriality in explaining his application onto canvas of sequences of coloured bands:

> In 1964, I began my real research into seriality, arranging the elements in series where the chromatic units are repeated two, three or four times but the order of each series is different. In some paintings there is a simple repetition of the initial series, demonstrating that the relational position – for example, the fact that the second band of the first series occupies the sixth position in the next series – creates a qualitative tension that is perceived by the spectator and permits him or her to create an experience of spatiality through selection of this structural possibility inherent to the composition.[86]

Molinari borrowed this notion of "structural possibility" from the field of linguistics, which was developing at an extraordinary rate during these years.

This concept [of structure] is very close to the approach used in linguistics ... it's the equivalent of phonetics ... the plane, like the phoneme, is a "building block" ... introduced in the idea of constant transformation. So the plane ... can be seen as a syntactic notion ... what became central to my work on the series was ... how similar or identical structures could appear entirely different depending on juxtaposition or position. In this sense, it's an almost semiotic approach.[87]

The interaction of colour within a repetitive structure creates a kind of "fictional" space (sometimes called an optical space) that can be perceived by the spectator. As a result of the interaction between bands of energy, colour plays a varying role depending on its position within the structure. Necessitating a high degree of spectator participation, the painting only becomes fully operational if the perceptual act lasts long enough for the rhythm of the vertical bands to be apprehended.

In 1967 the Toronto painter Jack Bush also began working with bands, or stripes, in preference to the sash, tie, column and chevron forms that had previously been his trademark. By emphasizing composition in his continuing explorations into colour the artist was moving closer to a more geometric type of formalism – possibly evidence of an affinity for the works of Frank Stella and Kenneth Noland being exhibited in Toronto around this time by David Mirvish. The upward thrust characteristic of Bush's works from the early sixties was no longer evident and the whole pictorial field was now in a state of dynamic interaction. In *English Visit* (1967, rep. 51), for example, the viewer is drawn into a chromatic struggle of epic dimensions between groups of vertical, horizontal and diagonal bands that are caught up in a constantly vacillating push-and-pull movement. A dedicated colourist, Bush has made full use of the new acrylic paints and wide range of colours available, applying uneasy combinations of colour directly onto raw canvas with a masterly skill that bespeaks his years of experience. The edges of the different areas of colour are not "hard," however, for they were painted freehand (like those of Rita Letendre before she discovered masking tape). The title of the work is probably a lighthearted reference to the form of the Union Jack flag, which combines the classical red cross of St. George (patron saint of England), the diagonal white cross of St. Andrew (patron saint of Scotland) and the diagonal red cross of St. Patrick (patron saint of Ireland). During the seventies, both Guido Molinari and Yves Gaucher would re-examine the notion of the oblique, which absorbed Bush for a time.

Montrealer Rita Letendre took part in all the chief Automatiste exhibitions of the fifties (*Les Rebelles* in 1950, *La matière chante* in 1954, *Espace 55* in 1955), as well as a number of major Canadian exhibitions held around the turn of the decade (fig. 21). During this ebullient period she integrated and adapted the lessons of Automatisme and Abstract Expressionism to develop a highly personal approach. In 1965 she moved to a more hard-edge style in executing the commission for a mural for the campus of California State College in Long Beach, where an international sculpture symposium was held that year. For the huge *Sunforce* (7.3 by 6 metres) – one of North America's first exterior murals – Letendre was obliged to abandon her expressionist impastos and use a flatter paint layer that adhered better to the support. The oblique flashes created by the collision of two black masses would soon evolve into the multicoloured diagonal beam forms that earned her many commissions during the seventies, especially in Toronto, where she later lived.

The energy of the oblique infuses Letendre's work with an unusual power. She likes to compare the diagonal arrow-form[88] traversing the pictorial space to a comet lighting up the sky for a few fractions of a second. Obsessed with light, she continued to narrow her forms and combine contrasting colours despite the technical difficulty of obtaining perfectly sharp edges. "All through my life as a painter … I've had a need for an image that has strength and power," says Letendre[89] – a statement dramatically confirmed by the evocative cosmic rays and light beams of *Lodestar* (1970, rep. 52).

A hard-edge technique and a stripe motif were also for a time part of the artistic vision of Bodo Pfeifer. Born in Düsseldorf and educated in Hamburg, he moved to Canada in 1956. After a period studying at the Vancouver School of Art under Roy Kiyooka, his work took an unexpected turn. Pfeifer began producing large, striking paintings in which novel arrangements of stripes and zigzag forms share the picture plane with areas of unmodulated monochrome. Echoing a technique employed by Matisse, Pfeifer and several Vancouver colleagues invented a form of hard-edge cut-out. His brilliantly coloured *Untitled* (1967, rep. 53) was reproduced on the cover of the catalogue of *Joy and Celebration*, an exhibition celebrating the centenary of Confederation held at the University of British Columbia's Fine Arts Gallery during the summer of 1967. This specialist of the large scale saw close collaboration with architects as a way of exploring the architectural possibilities of painting. "We could solve spatial problems with colour. The painting would become part of the function of the building, part of its space and environment – a total relationship with architecture," he concluded later that year.[90]

The stripes of Michael Morris's *Peking Letter* (1968, rep. 54) – another large painting – are more delicate, created by subtle gradations of tone. With its embedded V-shaped mirrors, the work offers an experience with narcissistic overtones. It was executed in Vancouver on the artist's return from a two-year stay in the English capital funded by a Canada Council grant.

52 Rita Letendre
Lodestar 1970
cat. 35

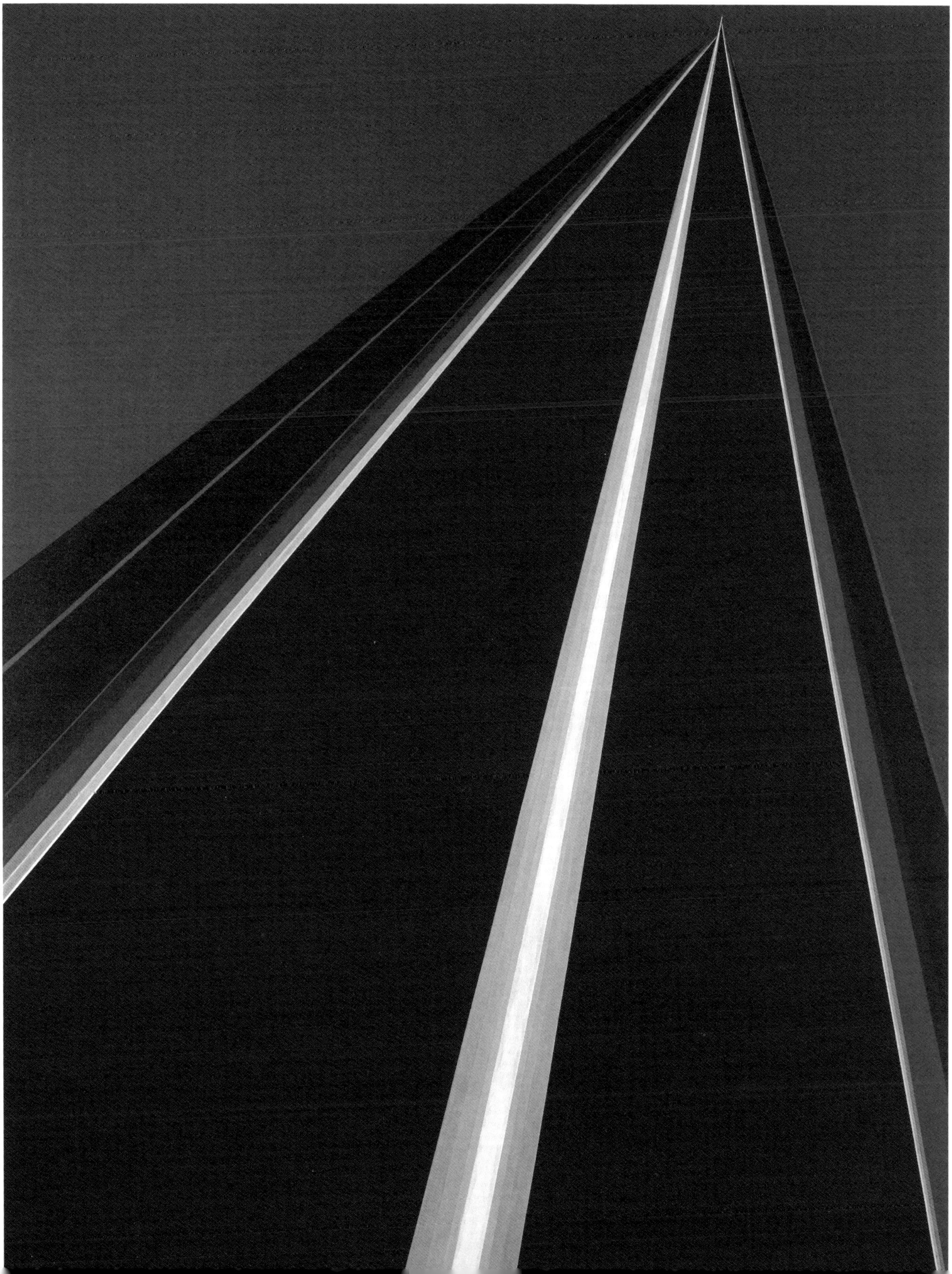

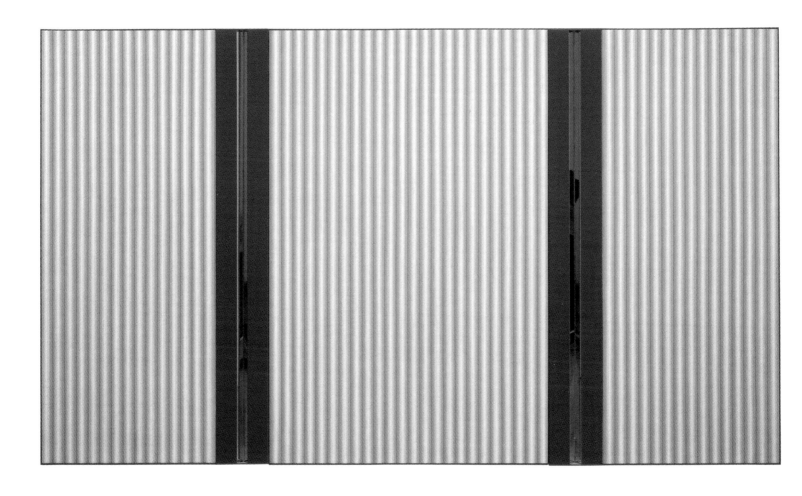

Inviting the spectator to observe the effect of light reflecting off the two strips of bevelled mirror, the painting is an example of Morris's variant of Pop abstraction, whose palette at this period conjured the world of advertising and commercial packaging.

The use of the word "letter" in the title is significant: during the sixties, art magazines often published letters (under a variety of column headings) from the world's major cities, in which critics offered regular reviews of local exhibitions. Detesting the "parochialism" that often paralyzes regional areas,[91] Morris saw these imaginary correspondences as a perfect way of developing links with the outside world, of "dragging [a] place out of itself."[92] In 1968 Morris received a letter from Ray Johnson, the father of mail art,[93] written after Johnson had seen a reproduction of Morris's painting *The Problem of Nothing* (fig. 22) in *Artforum*. As he indicated in his letter, Johnson had called his earlier performances "Nothings." That same year, keen to encourage exchange between artists, Morris joined with Vincent Trasov in founding the Image Bank and maintained an artistic correspondence with Ray Johnson that lasted many years.

Eric Cameron's square painting *Reds and Yellows on Green (type 111q, ½" tape)* (1968, rep. 55) appears to have its roots in the experimentations of Op Art, but in fact the work's true source was the process of its execution. Using a mask of Scotch tape laid vertically and then horizontally, Cameron has created a grid of neat straight lines. Since the artist's hand cannot achieve the perfection of a machine, however, the grid shows certain irregularities.

> The interaction is between the paint, considered as a fluid that behaves in a particular way, and the taped mask. In theory, it should be have been possible to achieve a perfectly regular grid, but in practice various unpredictable internal rhythms were set up amongst the squares as a result of the slight irregularities created by the impossibility of laying out the tape perfectly straight.[94]

The unpredictability of the optical rhythms resulting from the harmonious chromatic interaction between the red, yellow and green seems to indicate that this is abstraction of a more intellectual type. It was the transformational dynamic inherent to the artistic act that had led Cameron to create his Process Paintings (of which this is an example) and that also prompted him in 1978 to begin his Thick Paintings. The multiple paint layers used in this later series are a concrete manifestation of the accumulative addition that is integral to his painting. Later, while serving as head of the Fine Arts Program at the lively Nova Scotia College of Art and Design (1976–87) and of the Department of Fine Arts at the University of Calgary (1987–97), Cameron would write a number of theoretical texts on the creative process.

Apparently an example of abstract painting, General Idea's *Pascal* (1968–69, rep. 56) has another significance entirely. In 1969, steeped in sixties counter-culture and drawing inspiration from the artistically collaborative model of Intermedia, in Vancouver (see "A New Role for Photography," p. 104), this three-artist collective (whose corporate-sounding name was borrowed directly from William Burroughs) embarked on its mission of mounting a frontal attack on the new consumer society and the advertising on which it depended (fig. 23).[95] By appropriating and parodying the forms, symbols and icons of popular art, General Idea adopted the strategy of invading and transforming the media and art worlds and turning themselves into celebrities – notably through the publication of *FILE*, a humorous take-off of the famous *LIFE* magazine, and their Miss General Idea Pavilion construction project planned for 1984, a metaphor for the artificiality of the art world.

Pascal, executed in fact by Felix Partz (born Ronald Gabe), one of General Idea's three founding members, consists of a chromatically imaginative image in which the paint has been applied directly onto unprimed canvas. This was a technique taught by Kenneth Lochhead, a member of the Regina Five and Partz's professor at the University of Manitoba. According to another General Idea member, AA Bronson (born Michael Tims), the ziggurat motif introduced by Partz was triggered by a trip to North Africa.

> The idea of the ziggurat paintings was woven into the fabric of much that we did together and so we decided at a later date to claim the series as General Idea paintings, although they were executed immediately before we actually began together. At that point we named each painting after one of the "female" characters in our ongoing semi-fictional narrative … "Pascal" was the transgendered performer (drag queen, I guess) who lived with us in the early seventies and performed as "the entertainment" at the 1971 Miss General Idea Pageant at the AGO.[96]

The ziggurat motif would become the cornerstone of the Miss General Idea Pavilion (never built) and provide the basis for the plan showing the position of the 1,984 audience seats in the hall where the 1984 Miss General Idea Pageant would be held.

Stimulated by the shift towards abstraction that had marked the previous decade, a number of Canadian artists came to the forefront during the sixties with a painting practice that was ambitious in both scale and intent. At the same time, other artists were beginning to explore new materials and technologies and this is the trend we shall examine closely in the next chapter.

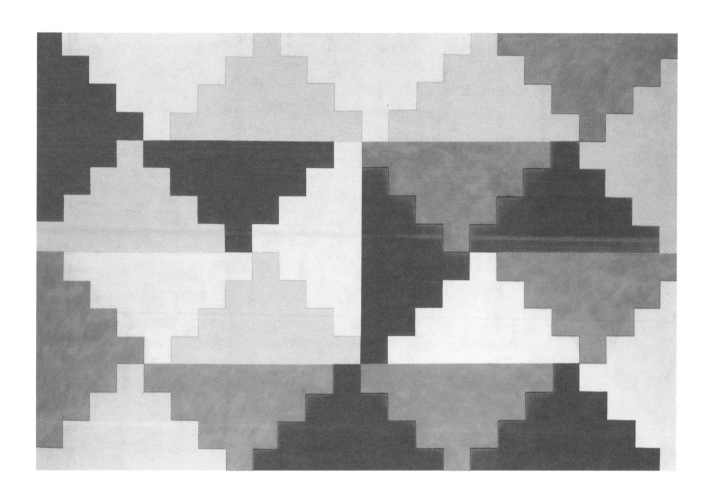

56   General Idea
Pascal 1968–69
cat. 25

6

The Lure of New Materials

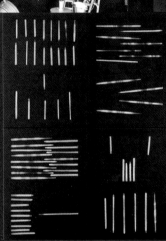

24   Billy Klüver lectures in a Toronto
television studio in 1967. The artists'
first suggestions for *9 Evenings:
Theatre and Engineering* (1966) are
projected on a screen in the background. Experiments in Art and
Technology

25   *Synthèse des arts*. Sculpture
created by Richard Lacroix and
other members of Fusion des arts for
the Canadian Pavilion Expo 1967

26   Les Levine, *Quartette* (1964).
NGC, Ottawa

The many new materials invading the market, often available in sheet form, caught the interest of Canadian artists, who had since the fifties been increasingly open to experimentation. Plastic materials such as polystyrene, phenolic resin, polyethylene and fibreglass, for example, together with the technologies used to transform them, including vacuum thermoforming, were more and more accessible. On another front, the new communications technologies that were reshaping everyday existence attracted a handful of artists eager to involve the general public in their global efforts to merge art and life.

The impact of technological development on the human consciousness was a subject of hot public debate continually stimulated by the ideas of Marshall McLuhan: "There is a great deal developing here in our Centre for Technology and Culture [in Toronto] for the study of the psychic and social consequences of the extensions of man."[97] In McLuhan's view, the media serve as "artificial extensions of sensory experience."[98] Already familiar with various industrial processes, artists began studying the creative potential of the machine. Spectacular light and sound effects were being seriously explored – as in Zbigniew Blazeje's *Audio-Kinetic Environment*, presented at the Art Gallery of Toronto during the winter of 1966.

Among the groups whose aim was to fuse art and technology were E.A.T. (Experiments in Art and Technology), an internationally known American group, and the Montreal group Fusion des arts (Fusion of the Arts), which took advantage of Expo 67 to execute some of its projects.

Among the members of E.A.T., which was founded in 1966, were the artist Robert Rauschenberg and Billy Klüver, an engineer working for Bell Telephone Laboratories. Eager to have the artistic, scientific and industrial milieus channel their energies in collaborative projects, E.A.T. encouraged the development of new expressive forms that used the latest technologies, including computer-generated images and sounds, video, synthetic materials and robotics. The most famous series of events organized by the group was *9 Evenings: Theatre and Engineering*, held in New York in October 1966 and attended by more than 10,000 spectators. The following year, Billy Klüver was invited to give a talk in a Toronto television studio (fig. 24).

The Fusion des arts collective was created in 1964 by printmaker Richard Lacroix, painter and sculptor Henry Saxe, sculptor François Soucy, architect François Rousseau, and art historian, designer and critic Yves Robillard. In their 1965 manifesto they defined their concept/title as "the total union of all the arts and a new concept of aesthetics" and the "sense of a radiating point of energy." "Fusion," they concluded, "is resolutely modernist."[99] By establishing themselves as a company the group became eligible to submit their installation project *Synthesis of the Arts* (fig. 25) to the organizers of Expo 67, and it eventually occupied a space in the Canadian pavilion. The work was composed of large pivoting disks made of coloured plastic, accompanied by sound elements. The group also gave thirty presentations of a piece entitled *The Mechanics* in the theatre of Expo 67's Youth Pavilion. During the fifteen-minute show, spectators were invited to handle a selection of novel musical instruments made out of a variety of objects.

In Winnipeg, meanwhile, Tony Tascona was determinedly exploring the artistic potential of industrial materials. He attributes his facility with new materials to his experience in the aeronautical industry: "I began to work with the kind of materials being implemented in the aircraft industry: aluminum, high-grade paints, lacquers, enamels ...The sophisticated tools

that they use, the incredible shapes of jet engines … in fact, that's where the sculptural qual-ity came into my work."**100** The smooth flawlessness of the thickly lacquered surface of *Yellow Transmission* (1969, rep. 57) would later prompt the artist to spray lacquer onto aluminium in his effort to achieve an absolutely perfect finish. In this geometric work, a superimposed drawing seems to break away from the coloured lines and shapes. The electrifying yellows and (to a lesser extent) the oranges create a marked contrast with the vaguely conifer-like triangular green forms. After having been exposed to several theories of colour during his stud-ies at the Winnipeg School of Art and the University of Manitoba School of Fine Arts, Tascona opted for a geometric painting approach following contact with the Montreal art milieu. This artist has also made use of plastic resins in his sculptural practice.

Fibreglass and coloured resin were among Jean-Paul Mousseau's favourite materials. After figuring as a young man among the signatories of *Refus Global*, this versatile artist would later collaborate with architects on the design and realization of a number of murals. In 1959 he was already exhibiting decorative panels made of fibreglass and he also employed this material for a series of hanging lamps. In a similar spirit, his sculpture *Untitled (Dolmen Series)* (1961, rep. 58) – equipped with an electrical mechanism, neon tubes and a rheostat – triggers reactions among viewers to variations in the intensity of light it emits. The title of the series evokes the architectural majesty of these ancient megalithic structures. In creating *Light and Movement in Colour* in 1962, his mural for Hydro-Québec's head office in Montreal, Mousseau chose to work on a monumental scale. Restored in 2002, the piece now includes 1,280 metres of neon tubing in eight different colours, which, thanks to today's technology, can be recomposed in a virtually infinite number of light and colour variations.

Jacques Hurtubise has also used electrical devices to artistic ends. Back in Montreal in 1961 after a year in New York that had brought him into contact with Abstract Expressionism and its drippings, he became friendly with Plasticiens Claude Tousignant and Guido Molinari. For a number of years subsequently, Hurtubise would seek to elucidate the opposition between expressionism and geometric formalism. In 1966–67 his approach became increasingly "Op" as he began experimenting with fluorescence in both paint and light form. In other works of this period the spectator is literally dazzled by certain works from this period, which combine ordinary electric light bulbs and neon tubes in dramatic zigzag shapes that slice the space like lightning. With considerable mastery, the artist transforms and disposes light effects in a way that mirrors the chaotic rhythm of the artificial light inundating the great cities of the world. In *Héloïse* (1969, rep. 59), Hurtubise has combined neon indicator tubes, electric light bulbs and aluminum in a palette of playful, pleasing colour.

More interested in conception than execution, Les Levine developed a fascination for industrial manufacturing processes. He actually became so knowledgeable and expert in them that he was able to simply phone his instructions from New York to a factory in Toronto. In *Plug Assist II* (1966, rep. 60), a sheet of Uvex plastic, vacuum moulded and spray-painted on the back with metallic paint, presents a soft, sensual image. Shaped by the outline of two chairs, the surface conjures a strange human presence similar to the one that inhabits *Slipcover* (see "The Return of Dada," p. 26). This use of the chair as an art object was not new: Levine had already exhibited "embalmed" chairs in environmental situations,[101] and for *Quartette* (fig. 26) he had used the rungs of a chair to produce the white markings that appear on the black canvas. The thermoforming technique employed for *Plug Assist II* also enabled

59   Jacques Hurtubise
Eloise 1969
cat. 27

60   Les Levine
Plug Assist II 1966
cat. 39

Levine to produce a series of small inexpensive works that were designed to be disposable. Ironically, and contrary to the artist's intent, the value of these objects has increased and they have become collector's items.

Sculptor Michael Hayden was a member of the Toronto-based multidisciplinary group Intersystems (incorporated in 1967), which also initially included electronic music composer John Mills-Cockell, poet Blake Parker, and architect Dick Zander. Hayden's interactive sculpture *Head Machine* (1967, rep. 61) consists of an anodized aluminum cube perforated at varying heights with round openings into which spectators of all sizes can insert their heads. When they do, they are exposed to a combination of kinetic elements, stroboscopic and ultraviolet light, and electronic sounds that induce a near-psychedelic state. The work was circulated throughout Canada with considerable ceremony in 1968.

This group's activities were not limited to the visual arts. They recorded and produced a number of albums, including the 1967 *Peachy*, which was strongly influenced by John Cage's piece *Indeterminancy*. The soundtrack of their psychedelic installation *Mind Excursion Center*, presented in Montreal in 1968, was also made into a record, entitled *Free Psychedelic Poster Inside/À l'intérieur un poster psychédélique gratuit*. During the numerous multi-media performances organized by Intersystems in a thoroughly McLuhanesque spirit, spectators were assailed with a mind-bending mix of artificial mist, strobe lights, fluorescent paint, synthesizers and closed circuit television.[102]

Experimental filmmaker Michael Snow also made use of cutting-edge technology in creating his cinematic and kinetic sculpture *De la* (1969–72, rep. 62), which is actually an automatic movie-making machine (which Snow tried to have patented) used in the making of his film *La Région Centrale* (180 min, October 1970). This "Camera Activating Machine,"[103] built by Montreal mechanic Pierre Abbeloos and originally equipped with a 16mm Arriflex, allows the camera to rotate and pivot through 360 degrees and thus capture comprehensively panoramic views; it can also be operated by remote control. Snow has described the film he made with the device as "a gigantic landscape film equal in terms of film to the great landscape paintings of Cézanne, Poussin, Corot, Monet, Matisse and in Canada the Group of Seven."[104] In the fall of 1970, in order to shoot the movie, he had the machine transported by helicopter to the top of a slope situated in a barren, frigid region about 160 kilometres north of Sept-Îles, in Quebec.

Critics were impressed by the device's physical characteristics: "*La Région Centrale* defies the imagination. A special camera, capable of pivoting through 360 degrees, horizontally, vertically, diagonally, with a complex movement that multiplies displacement."[105] In an interview, Michael Snow explained how the camera's movements were ingeniously controlled by audiotapes: "There were two ways of controlling the movements of the camera. One was through composing sound tapes which contained the information, the orders to the machine telling it which way to move. Another way was by means of dials which were divided in 'horizontal,' 'vertical,' 'rotation,' and 'zoom,' each being able to run at different speeds (between fast and slow) and in various combinations; like you could have the 'horizontal' at the medium speed, or the 'vertical' at, say fast speed."[106] Now fitted with a surveillance camera, the machine-sculpture records and reproduces the space it occupies. Visitors who find themselves by chance in front of the moving lens see themselves projected onto the monitors surrounding the device.

61   Michael Hayden
Head Machine 1967
cat. 26

62   Michael Snow
De La 1969–72
Installation at the National Gallery of
Canada (on Elgin Street) in 1971
cat. 66

7

Traces of Age-Old Memories

27   Pole-raising ceremony in honour
of a Kwakwaka'wakw totem pole,
Indian Pavilion, Expo 67. Circular panel
in background is *Beaver Crossing
Indian Colours* by Alex Janvier.
Courtesy of Russ Moses/Indians of
Canada Pavilion
28   Norval Morrisseau with
Jack Pollock. Courtesy of Methuen
Publications
29   Ronald Bloore and his work *White
Sun – Green Rim* (1960)

The art world was not focused exclusively during the sixties on the here and now; the tabula rasa of modernism was, moreover, beginning to show signs of erosion. The growing body of knowledge resulting from anthropological, ethnological and archaeological research into non-Western cultures permitted a new appraisal of indigenous and folk art, and of the artistic legacies of foreign and ancient traditions. The very distant past became a revitalizing source for some artists, and oriental philosophies, First Nations legends, syncretic movements and esotericism began to form the substrata of novel modes of artistic expression.

Across Canada, Aboriginal art was being revived and modernized by a new visual language that drew nourishment from its own past. An increase in public commissions stimulated by Expo 67 and the centennial of Canadian confederation gave added impetus to already emerging modern trends. Those responsible for the construction of Expo 67's Indians of Canada pavilion commissioned a number of well-known Aboriginal artists to execute a totem pole, three murals, five circular panels, and a large sign. The artists involved were Alex Janvier, Norval Morrisseau, Henry Hunt, Tony Hunt, George Clutesi, Gerald Tailfeathers, Noel Wuttunee, Ross Woods, Francis Kagige, Tom Hill, and Jean-Marie Gros-Louis.

Although Canadian government authorities were proud to display Aboriginal culture to the world as a distinctive feature of Canada' identity, they were less eager to give Native communities the chance to present their version of history. The creation of the Indians of Canada pavilion actually marked a turning point: from this period on, Aboriginal people have played an increasingly dominant role in defining official discourse.[107]

> It was Delisle [Mohawk chief Andrew Delisle] who was the driving force in ensuring an Aboriginal presence at Expo 67. "There were problems getting the pavilion because it was considered too controversial at the time. The governments felt we were too aggressive in telling the history of Native people from our perspective," Delisle recalled. Delisle smilingly recounted how he parlayed a friendship with then-Mayor Jean Drapeau into hard political currency: "While everyone else was opposing us, Drapeau made it clear that if there was to be an Expo, it would have to have a Native Pavilion the way we wanted it."[108]

That same year the Vancouver Art Gallery presented a major exhibition entitled *Arts of the Raven: Masterworks by the Northwest Coast Indian*, the goal of which was to assign historical works by West Coast Native artists their rightful place in the world of international art. "This is an exhibition of art, high art, not ethnology,"[109] proclaimed Doris Shadbolt, one of the show's curators.

Alex Janvier, one of the most skilful Aboriginal explorers of modern artistic expression, executed a circular panel for Expo 67's Indian pavilion whose abstract character and provocative title appealed little to the organizers. Originally titled *Unpredictable East*, Janvier's work would eventually be called *Beaver Crossing Indian Colours*, and it was moved from the front to the rear of the pavilion (fig. 27).

The career of Norval Morrisseau – another leading exponent of contemporary Native art, and a major repository of traditional knowledge – took an unexpected turn when an exhibition of his work held at the Jack Pollock Gallery, in Toronto, proved an astonishing success (fig. 28). The brilliant colours of Morrisseau's paintings, and their forms, which seem to embody ancient ancestral beings, have a powerful effect on the viewer's imagination. *Merman Ruler of Water* (1969, rep. 63) recounts the Anishinabe legend of Nepii-Naba, half-man, half-fish.[110] Morrisseau draws inspiration from the rock paintings of Agawa Bay, the petroglyphs of Peterborough, the sacred scrolls of the Midewewin, and the literature on Native art of the American Southwest and Arizona, expressing himself in an inventive and highly influential style. A shaman-artist, deeply committed to the practice of art, Morrisseau uses visual language first and foremost as a way of transmitting rites, myths and legends.

While new printmaking workshops proliferated in the south of the country, the studio of the West Baffin Eskimo Co-operative expanded under the influence of Terrence Ryan and of local artists eager to diversify. James Houston's stay in Cape Dorset, which lasted from 1951 to 1962, also stimulated production of sculpture in the area and made printmaking a permanent activity in the region. To this day, prints from Cape Dorset are renowned throughout Canada and the world.

The introduction of graphic art techniques contributed to the emergence of women artists, less attracted by sculpture. Among these was Pitseolak Ashoona, who moved to Cape Dorset permanently after the death of her husband.[111] After she had worked for a while making clothes for James Houston, he began encouraging her to capture the places and events of her people's traditional life on paper. Longing to escape from a modern existence that seemed to her too sedentary, she began to draw: "I draw the things I have never seen," she said, "the monsters and spirits, and I draw the old ways, the things we did long ago before there were many white men."[112] She took her initial inspiration from Kiakshuk, an older artist who liked to picture shamans and spirits. Since Pitseolak's husband Ashoona was an excellent hunter, she had been supplied while he was alive with beautiful skins to make clothes. The image of *Woman Hiding from Spirit* (1968, rep. 64) is thus nourished by personal experience: a well-dressed woman holding an ulu bows down before a spirit that is part-seal, part-goose and part-fish. Conjuring each goose by the presence of a single feather, the work conveys the symbiotic relationship between human and animal with tenderness and humility. Eegyvudluk Pootoogook was responsible for reproducing the drawing as a stonecut print.

Sakiassie Ragee, also a skilled hunter, lived a traditional Inuit life for many years at Camp Tikirak, near Cape Dorset. He took up drawing in the late fifties, but only practiced his art during the short summer season. Although he enjoyed drawing and sculpting small animals, it was the picturing of surreal figures extracted from age-old strata of myth and fantasy that really sparked his imagination – as witness the fish-men portrayed in his work *The Old Way of Drawing* (1959, Kleinburg, Ontario, McMichael Canadian Art Collection). Explaining this title, the artist said: "The old way of drawing was very different. There was a lot of imagination then. Now actual creatures and other things are drawn …"[113] In *Sea Goddess Feeding Young* (1961, rep. 65), a fluidly composed image where the figures seem to float, a half-human, half-fish goddess breast feeds a pair of twins. Ragee ceased drawing in 1962, when he gave up the nomadic life to settle permanently in Cape Dorset. Here again, the stonecut print of the drawing was made by Eegyvudluk Pootoogook.

The practices of Ronald Bloore, Art McKay and John Meredith reflect the interest shared by some artists in the representation of a non-Western cultural heritage.

It would be a mistake to imagine that on his return in 1963 from a trip to Greece, Egypt and Turkey, Ronald Bloore succumbed to the reductionist pressures of minimalism. Bloore,

63   Norval Morrisseau (Copper
Thunderbird)
Merman Ruler of Water 1969
cat. 46

64   Pitseolak Ashoona
Woman Hiding from Spirit 1968
cat. 1

65   Sakiassie Ragee
Sea Goddess Feeding Young 1961
cat. 58

66   Ronald Bloore
Painting No. 11 1965
cat. 6

67   Art McKay
Blue Image 1966
cat. 41

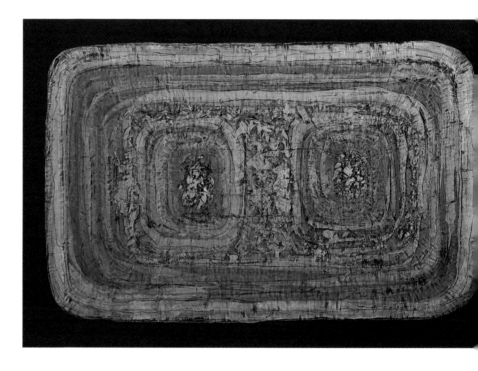

who had studied art history and archaeology, had actually been seduced by the brilliance of the whitewashed walls of the Mediterranean and by the richness of the region's iconographical legacy embodied in countless symbolic motifs.[114] Renouncing his earlier work and rejecting the post-Renaissance art so valued in the West, he embarked on a new and highly purified approach (fig.29). Limiting himself to white paint on Masonite panel, he began celebrating the redeeming power of artistic creation through reliefs featuring repeated motifs. As an inhabitant of a land of snow, Bloore is skilled at capturing the many shades of white on a diversity of surfaces. He is also much opposed to trends that focus exclusively on ephemerality: "I think it's necessary to try to get away from the here and now," he has said. "Art must sustain multiple experiences in perpetuity."[115]

Bloore made *Painting No. 11* (1965, rep. 66) especially for a solo exhibition held at the Dorothy Cameron Gallery, in Toronto. Famous for having been the first artist in Regina to employ a heavy-impasto technique similar to Borduas's,[116] Bloore often applies paint with the generosity of a mason layering cement. In *Painting No. 11*, light steals gently over a rigorously symmetrical, maze-like composition that is defined by the shadows cast by scraped up ridges of pigment.

Art McKay was another artist who from the start of his career showed a marked interest in oriental thought and esotericism – stimulated largely in his case by his father's extensive library. Through his reading, McKay became extremely knowledgeable about different belief systems and their impact on political regimes. In 1956 he attended a lecture in New York given by Dr. D.T. Suzuki, who would play a major role in the spread of Zen Buddhism throughout the West. During studies at the Barnes Foundation in Merion, Pennsylvania, McKay was introduced to an unorthodox method of aesthetic appreciation involving multiple observations of the same painting. He learned that the more one looks at a work, the more entrancing it is likely to become.

Accordingly, McKay executed the abstract monochrome mandala *Blue Image* (1966, rep. 67) and a number of other circular and rectangular mandalas with the aim of triggering an attitude of attentive observation among his viewers. The oriental mandala symbol was a popular image in the drug-taking psychedelic circles frequented by McKay at the time. Long before LSD became widely known, the artist served as a subject in a study into the effects of the drug on artistic creativity. He would later say that the study failed to produce conclusive results regarding LSD's capacity to enhance creativity (see note 69), but added that the meditative state it can induce is beneficial to artistic appreciation. Using a scraping technique on the initial paint layer, McKay would gradually lighten the tone of his mandala series. Each one, though, has an impact on the viewer's receptivity: "These paintings are attempts to re establish contact with and immersion in feeling and therefore are introverted, hypnotic and mostly a combination of concentric and eccentric movement … They are contemplative. The titles … are intended to indicate what the painting 'does' or what it is 'about' in terms of the feeling that is embodied in it."[117]

John Meredith was a member of the generation of Toronto artists that succeeded Painters Eleven.[118] His work from the sixties is dominated by the graphic sign, which he used to create abstract images that seem to have arisen for the most part from his subconscious. Through their suggestive titles – *Bengal*, *Karma*, *Ulysses*, *Atlantis* and *Eden*, for example – Meredith strove to imbue his works with a mood of Oriental exoticism. The striking palette of

Prophecy (1967, rep. 68) and the unexpected combination of highly saturated orange and turquoise tones gives the work an inadvertently psychedelic feel. The artist's mental landscape seems to open onto an esoteric past:

> *my paintings are the mystery iceberg*
> *of my past, but there is a way of knowing the mystery.*
> *it is the future…*
> *my paintings are themselves. they are oriental.*
> *they are me. I am not oriental.*[119]

The art of Jack Shadbolt entered a vital new phase in the late sixties, after a period of personal transformation that prompted him to fill his images with multiple and diverse references to the art of the past. The vertical or horizontal juxtaposition of large sheets of watercolour board provided him with a generous support on which to display his remarkable talents as a draftsman. With considerable skill, he applied acrylic and latex paints as if they were watercolour or gouache. For *The Bride* (1969–74, rep. 69), Shadbolt drew inspiration from the famous Isenheim altarpiece (1512–16), which he had seen twice in Colmar, France. The sense of suffering emanating from the painted panels of Matthias Grünewald's triptych of the *Crucifixion* made a profound impression on the artist.

Shadbolt has divided the central panel of *The Bride* horizontally into two. In the upper section, painted in 1969, we see the highly ornamental head of the "bride," wearing an Edwardian collar and cameo,[120] and flanked by two small side motifs that evoke the male and

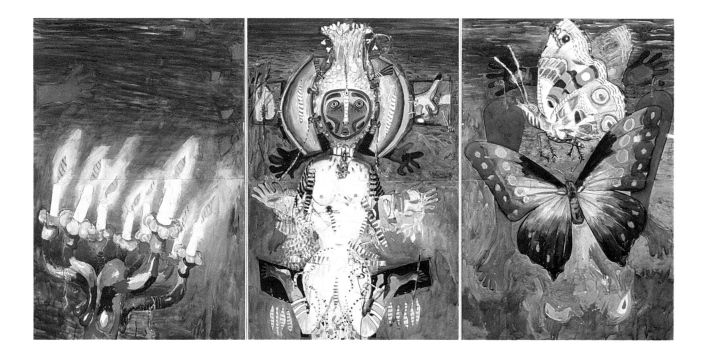

female genital organs. Menacing hand shapes seem to blend into the purple ground. In the lower panel, which dates from 1970, the bride's naked body, with its stigmatized hands and pierced feet, is presented as a sacrifice, hung here and there with decorative fetishes. Like the dismembered parts of a puppet, the hands with their stigmata and the cut-out legs reappear floating in the right-hand panel, where the bride's body is replaced by two butterflies. The candelabra that illuminates the left-hand panel, which looks vaguely like a menorah, reinforces the ceremonial character of the work. Born of a shamanic world, *The Bride* conjures a state of transformation, a seasonally cyclical metamorphosis charged with eroticism. In this syncretically inspired piece, the butterflies symbolize at once an ephemeral and fragile beauty violently debased by ritual sacrifice and the all-powerful will to survive.

69   Jack Shadbolt
The Bride 1969–74
cat. 62

Young
already old
splendored in ritual display
she is crucified on an evening shore

her hands bloom like flowers

silent phallic flutes
flame in the dusk

opened like a flower
and withered
lost
between desire and day
dark hands have claimed her

she is gone
like lost lovely things
her flowers have gone
like evening moths hovering
like fritillary dreams[121]

8 A New Role for Photography

30   Performance by Al Neil, Intermedia, Vancouver, 1968. Photo: Michael
de Courcy
31   *Bagged Place*, N.E. Thing Co.,
Vancouver, Fine Arts Gallery of the
University of British Columbia, 1966
32   Artist Roy Kiyooka

33   Lithography Workshop staff,
1969–70. Left to right: Murray Lively,
Robert Rogers, Richards Jarden,
Jerry Raidiger, Martha Rogers, Jack
Lemon (seated). Photo: Nova Scotia
College of Art and Design

Towards the end of the decade, conceptual art was developing steadily under the influence of artists who were gradually integrating photography as a material component of their work. Frequently not themselves products of the realm of photography – which boasts its own conventions, aesthetic movements and exhibition centres – these artists cared little about it as a craft. For them, photography served rather as a strategic support for new ideas focusing on the "dematerialization"[122] of the art object, the depersonalization of the practice of art and its immunity to judgements of an aesthetic nature. As we saw earlier, opposition to the capitalist system was accompanied by a rejection of the commodification of the work of art. The introduction of industrial production methods and the ascendancy of concept over execution helped divest art of any personal dimension. For these artists, photography with its low market value was a "mechanical" operation not necessarily linked to the aesthetic function. Photography became one of the many approaches that contributed towards the flourishing of conceptual art, a powerful movement that would open the way to the globalization of contemporary art.

The Vancouver Scene
In the summer of 1959, conscious of the predominant role being played by the virtually instantaneous circulation of information in modern society, the University of British Columbia invited Marshall McLuhan to give a lecture. Beginning in 1961 and for a decade to come, the university would host the ambitious Festival of the Contemporary Arts, organized by its fine arts department. Alvin Balkind, appointed curator of the faculty's art gallery in 1962, succeeded the event's founders, B.C. Binning and June Binkert, as the festival's organizer. In 1964, McLuhan (who had recently received a Canadian Governor General's Award for non-fiction) was invited back by Balkind to discuss the question of the electronic revolution. Balkind was quite frank in recording his impressions of McLuhan's two lectures – feelings that were no doubt shared by academia in general: "McLuhan's talks were complex exercises in medieval Catholic metaphysics as seen through the TV screen. His generalities were broad, his information often unscholarly and irritating, yet oddly enough, his general theories remain relatively valid."[123]

Balkind's critical reaction did not, however, prevent him from presenting the February 1965 festival under the banner of McLuhan's famous aphorism, "The medium is the message." A first multisensorial happening/performance was produced for the occasion by Iain Baxter, Arthur Erickson, Helen Goodwin and Takao Tanabe, with Abraham Rogatnik (supported by the school of architecture) in charge of staging and coordination. The Festival of the Contemporary Arts became the instigator of numerous activities in the spheres of poetry, experimental film, electronic music, underground theatre and dance, as well as organizing annual exhibitions of the very latest in visual arts productions. Balkind, a highly skilled communicator, had set himself the goal of making Vancouver a centre of artistic innovation on a par with such major American cities as Los Angeles, San Francisco and New York.

Meanwhile, the Douglas Gallery took over the former New Design Gallery, founded by Balkind, and continued to promote the Vancouver art scene abroad. The owner of the Douglas Gallery, Douglas Christmas, was also director of the Ace Gallery in Los Angeles. In his Vancouver gallery he showed works by Robert Rauschenberg, Frank Stella, Robert Morris, Robert Smithson and Carl Andre, and in 1968 he invited dancer Deborah Hay – who had participated in activities organized by the New York group E.A.T. – to give a performance.

He also collaborated with Toronto's Isaacs Gallery. In a 1967 letter to Christmas, Av Isaacs reiterated his promise to support the *Vancouver 5* exhibition: "It is to be [a] show that is to be as far out as possible of Canadians working in new materials and with new attitudes."[124]

The decade also saw the emergence of loose groups of independent artists working within local organizations. In 1965–66, the Sound Gallery held evening events in Gregg Simpson's painting studio, at which dancer Helen Goodwin, artist Gary Lee-Nova and the musicians of the Al Neil Trio were regulars. Sam Perry would project films during the various performances with the aim of creating a mind-altering atmosphere. During meetings held at Jack Shadbolt's house in the fall and winter of 1966, a number of artists expressed the need for increased access to the new techniques of creation. Shadbolt proposed the establishment of a multimedia studio and applied for a Canada Council grant on behalf of the group. With considerable discernment, the Council officer in charge of the visual arts, David Silcox, recognized the validity of the proposal and awarded the group the sum of $40,000 to found Intermedia. This project, which spanned a period of five years, would involve over two hundred artists in "interdisciplinary attempts to move outside the bounds of artistic tradition by way of drugs, non-Western thought and technological innovation."[125]

Photographer Michael de Courcy, who was a member of Intermedia (fig. 30), sums up the climate that reigned among the group: "We had no need to work [government programs also provided funding for specific projects]. New ideas in psychiatry and social awareness emphasized the importance of touching and feeling."[126]

From 1968 to 1970, Intermedia and the Vancouver Art Gallery worked closely together on a number of projects: the Intermedia evenings of 1968 were followed by two exhibitions – *Electrical Connection* in April 1969 and the *Dome Show* in May 1970. The public also flocked to a series of lunchtime activities presented by Intermedia at the Gallery. Under the urging of curator Doris Shadbolt and director Anthony Emery, the Vancouver Art Gallery simultaneously exposed the general public to the latest work of the city's artists and kept the latter informed about art events happening abroad, notably in Los Angeles.

In 1968 Michael Morris, Vincent Trasov and Gary Lee-Nova, all members of Intermedia, launched the Image Bank, a venture that made use of the mail system and other forms of communication to solicit and disseminate images throughout its member network. Another of the more memorable activities of the decade was the 1966 Trips Festival, the first sound-and-light show to go down in history as an unforgettable multisensorial, hallucinatory experience. The show starred the musicians of the Al Neil Trio and the Californian rock group the Grateful Dead.

Foremost among the artists who enlivened Vancouver's sixties art scene with humour and intelligence was the duo of Iain Baxter and Ingrid Baxter, founders in 1966 of the N.E. Thing Co. Formally incorporated in 1969, this firm constituted a witty parody of the corporate model and its bureaucratic procedures. Just like a major corporation, the company was subdivided into different departments: Thing, Research, Cop (an abbreviation referring to the "copying" – with modifications – of known works), Service, Photography, Film, Printing, Projects, Fashion, ACT (Aesthetically Claimed Things), ART (Aesthetically Rejected Things) and ANT (Aesthetically Neutral Things – a department that never actually existed). The N.E. Thing Co. was formed following the consolidation of two earlier organizations: IT (in collaboration with John Friel) and the N.E. Baxter Thing Co.

70　N.E. Thing Co.
ACT No. 19: Marcel Duchamp's Total
Art Production Except His Total Ready-
Made Production (1968)/ ART No. 19:
Marcel Duchamp's Total Ready-Made
Production Except His Total Art Pro-
duction (1968) 1969
cat. 48

71　N.E. Thing Co.
ART No. 16: Robert Smithson's "Non-
Sites" (1968) 1969
cat. 49

In a thoroughly McLuhanesque spirit, the Baxters saw themselves as "visual informers," moving – under their slogan "Art Is All Over" – into the hitherto neglected corporate realm. When invited to exhibit at the art gallery of the University of British Columbia in February 1966, they transformed the space into a four-room furnished apartment where the walls and all the contents were entirely covered in clear plastic sheeting. Called *Bagged Place*, it was an ambitious environmental work (fig. 31). The folds and ripples of the plastic both metamorphosed an apparently domestic interior and deprived the viewer of a total sensorial experience. In 1969 the N.E. Thing Co. "corporatized" the ground floor of the National Gallery of Canada in Ottawa during the retrospective of their work mounted by the institution.

ACT No. 19: Marcel Duchamp's Total Art Production Except His Total Ready-Made Production (1968)/ART No. 19: Marcel Duchamp's Total Ready-Made Production Except His Total Art Production (1968) (1969, rep. 70) apparently restores Marcel Duchamp's original intention, for in Iain Baxter's view Duchamp was unwilling at the outset to assign any aesthetic value to his ready-mades.[127] Another interestingly ironical feature of the work is the snow scattered across the portrait of Duchamp. Was the artists' aim to eliminate the aesthetic impact of the work in order to place it in the category of Aesthetically Neutral Things, or simply to give Duchamp's picture a northern feel? The image is ambiguous, but the seal of certification at the lower left is absolutely clear. By appropriating the Good Housekeeping seal of approval, Iain and Ingrid Baxter were denouncing corporate invasion of the domestic world. In *ART No. 16: Robert Smithson's "Non-Sites" (1968)* (1969, rep. 71), they have reinterpreted a work by Robert Smithson consisting of four pyramid-shaped containers filled with rough-hewn stones

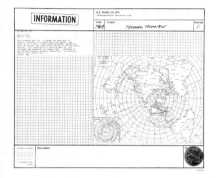 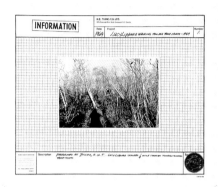 

from a single location. In extracting the material, Smithson both denatured the site and freed the rock fragments from any connection to it. After drawing inspiration from Land Art and earthworks, around 1968 the Baxters would also execute a number of "waterworks."

The instantaneity of communications by telex or fax, increasingly in use towards the end of the sixties, attracted the interest of the N.E. Thing Co. The Baxters were, in fact, among the first North American artists to employ the telex as a source of conceptual works and a means by which art could be cleverly introduced into the business world. This incursion of art into everyday life via technology would foreshadow a later, less positive phenomenon: the junk e-mails that now clog the Internet. For their 1969 work *Telexed Triangle* (rep. 72), the N.E. Thing Co. traced on a North Pole-centred world map the triangular route of a message sent by telex from Inuvik to Vancouver, from Vancouver to Halifax, and from Halifax to Inuvik.

The photograph on squared paper that constitutes *Lucy Lippard Walking Towards True North* (1969, rep. 73) provides a record of the N.E. Thing Co.'s activities and of a half-kilometre walk taken through the tundra by art critic Lucy Lippard. Lippard, who was interested in the Canadian artists' original approach to conceptual art, travelled to Inuvik in September 1969 with the Baxters, Harry Savage of Edmonton and Lawrence Wiener of New York to undertake the walk as part of an N.E. Thing Co. conceptual project. *Circular Walk Inside Arctic Circle Around Inuvik, N.W.T* (1969, rep. 74) records a walk of seven kilometres (or 10,314 steps) undertaken by Iain and Ingrid Baxter during the same trip.

When visiting the construction site of Expo '70 in Osaka prior to executing the sculpture he had been commissioned to make for the Canadian pavilion, Roy Kiyooka (fig. 32) was

fascinated by the number of worn and dirty gloves left discarded by construction workers. He got hold of a camera, and over the next four months took several thousand photographs. "I discovered that the camera … can be a perfect extension of the individual eye," he said. "I resist the temptation to organize the subject, but I do organize the camera in relation to it … What interested me most on the Expo site wasn't the architecture and design, but the gloves dropped by the workmen who wore them out at a terrific rate."[128] The three pictures entitled *StoneDGloves* (1970, reps. 75, 76 and 77) are part of a group of between three and four hundred photographs taken in December 1969 that the artist intended to present as an exhibition, accompanied by poems. The National Gallery of Canada circulated a selection of around forty of the prints between 1970 and 1972. "The thought of these black and white images of very ordinary gloves travelling halfway across the world delights my proletarian heart,"[129] said the artist when the exhibition concluded its tour at the Canadian Cultural Centre, in Paris.

A marvellous metaphor for the fleetingness of life, these cement-heavy gloves also testify to human enterprise and the durability of the commonplace. "Imagine, gloves talking about what WORLD FAIRS really are! The photos will stand without Expo, of course. Fact is, they're going to be standing straight up, long after the last bldg. has come down with a CRASH!!!!"[130] The exhibition's nearly two-year tour across Canada raised the profile of both oeuvre and artist, and the StoneDGloves project would prove to be his breakthrough into photo-conceptualism.[131] A photographic and poetic essay titled *StoneDGloves* was published in 1970 by Toronto's Coach House Press. Here is a short extract:

The way they fell
The way they lay there
the dust sifting down
hiding all the clues ...

...

glove

equals

leaf

equals

stone

equals

wood

equals

bone[132]

The Halifax Scene

In 1973 Les Levine wrote an article for the magazine *Art in America* about the Nova Scotia College of Art and Design, in Halifax (well known by its acronym of NSCAD), under a title implying that it might well be the best art school in North America.[133] Levine made particular mention in his article of the school's innovative artist-in-residence program, which had succeeded in attracting a number of leading figures of American and (to a lesser degree) Canadian minimal and conceptual art. One by one, a group that included Vito Acconci, Carl Andre, John Baldessari, Joseph Beuys (during a stay in North America), John Chamberlain, Joseph Kosuth, Robert Morris, Dennis Oppenheim, Richard Serra, Michael Snow and Joyce Wieland made the trip to Halifax to work with the college's students or to exhibit their art.

Following in the footsteps of the famous Tamarind Lithography Workshop, founded in Los Angeles in 1960 and affiliated since 1970 with the University of New Mexico, NSCAD set up its dynamic Lithography Workshop in the late sixties with the idea of enabling artists working mainly in other mediums to make lithographs. Joyce Wieland's *O Canada* (rep. 26), for example, was executed there, and the talents of the Lithography Workshop's master printer, Bob Rogers, helped enhance the reputations of a number of other artists (fig. 33). Between 1969 and 1976, at least 186 editions of prints were produced there.

In 1969, works by such artists as Joseph Kosuth, Vito Acconci, David Askevold, Dan Graham and John Baldessari adorned the walls of NSCAD's two exhibition spaces – the Mezzanine Gallery and the Anna Leonowens Gallery. One of Baldessari's pieces, entitled *I Will Not Make Any More Boring Art*, offers an amusing comment on the often rather tedious conceptual art of the period. Sol Lewitt, Lawrence Wiener, Mel Bochner and the N.E. Thing Co. all conceived class projects for the students. In October of 1969, for instance, the N.E. Thing Co. invited students to come up with an artistic response to instructions sent from Vancouver. The resulting works illustrate how the exchange of information can become a source of creation.

As in Montreal, there were acrimonious discussions about the curricula and teaching methods employed in art schools. It was not NSCAD's students, however, but its board of governors who shattered the status quo in 1967, by appointing the progressive Garry Neill

Kennedy as the college's first president. Kennedy had studied at the Ontario College of Art (a school that had come under harsh criticism from artists), earned a Master's degree in fine arts from Ohio State University and served as head of the art department at Northland College, in Wisconsin.

When the NSCAD's board of governors suggested that the college be merged with the fine art department of Dalhousie University to solve the problem of the validity of the degrees offered, Kennedy opposed the idea: "In my judgment," he later explained, "the best way to go was to take an individual course. We would have been like another art department in another university. History has shown that NSCAD is not in the same league. The excellence of what goes on here is so far beyond what goes on in any of the other universities."[134] Kennedy's approach, which was based on the importance of attracting known artists to smaller centres, was possibly influenced by the strategy adopted by the organizers of the summer workshops held at Emma Lake in northern Saskatchewan.

Several sources credit the Nova Scotia College of Art and Design with organizing the first international conference on minimal and conceptual art. Held in October 1970, with the backing of Seth Siegelaub of New York, the event was attended by Carl Andre, Iain Baxter, Ronald Bladen, Joseph Beuys, Daniel Buren, John Chamberlain, Jan Dibbetts, Al Held, Robert Irwin, Mario Merz, Robert Murray, Michael Snow, Robert Morris, Richard Serra, Robert Smithson, and Lawrence Wiener. Several participants left before the conference was over, however, when they learned that it was not open to the students, who were only permitted to watch the proceedings on closed-circuit monitors. Critic Lucy Lippard also protested the absence of women artists: Joan Jonas, Joyce Wieland and Ingrid Baxter had all been refused admission.[135] Nevertheless, under the leadership of Garry Neill Kennedy, assisted from early on by Gerald Ferguson, a key step was taken in the history of art education in Canada, and the Nova Scotia College of Art and Design in Halifax established itself at the cutting edge of contemporary art research.

As an artist Garry Neill Kennedy would become best known for his conceptual paintings, but his early approach was more diversified, sometimes encompassing photography. *Bisected* (1969, rep. 78) offers a panoramic view of the human body via forty-one snapshots displayed in a single row on the wall. The images dissect the body into rectangular fragments, simultaneously continuous and discontinuous, forcing the spectator to dwell on details that generally go unnoticed – the orientation of hairs on the skin, for example, or the network of veins just beneath its surface.

In the late sixties, also in the Maritimes, Bill Vazan executed several Land Art pieces at Paul's Bluff, on Prince Edward Island, employing the photographic medium to record the geometric shapes he had traced in the sand or the tide levels he had observed so closely. While serving initially to document his onsite creations, photography gradually became a form of expression in its own right. The works on view – *14 Time Lines Readied* (1969)/*Square of Ripples* (1967–69, rep. 79), *Two Angles Readied* (1969)/*Square with Tangents* (1967–69, rep. 80), *Low Tide Sand Forms – Level – Side to Side* (1967–69)/*Low Tide Sand Forms Pyramid After High Tide –* (1967–69, rep. 81), *Low Tide Sand Form – Impact Crater* (1969)/*2" High Tide Level* (1969, rep. 82) and *Low Tide Sand Form* (1969)/*After One High Tide* (1969, rep. 83) – were all printed for the first time or reprinted in 2004 by Bill Vazan especially for this exhibition.

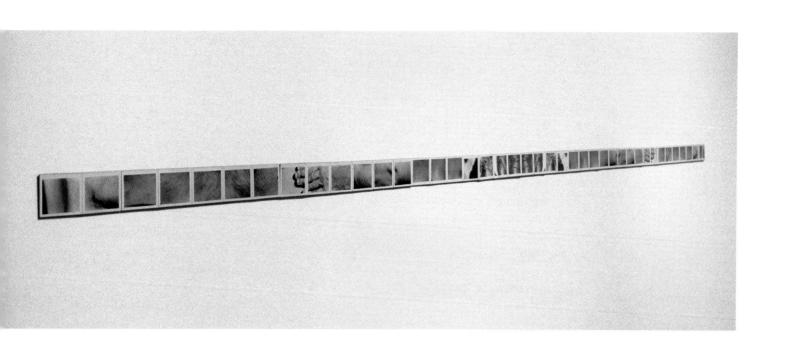

Since his paintings of the early sixties, Bill Vazan has been interested in the evanescent forms of nature, which he tries momentarily to "geometrize": "Whether the work lasts minutes or many years, it is all ephemeral. Time, by definition, is ephemeral."[136] He sees the marks made on the sands of Prince Edward Island as an attempt to draw on a large scale: "What is a drawing? It is a two-dimensional rendering. Where do I work? On the surface of the earth. It's a two-dimensional rendering. Usually I don't go high, and I don't go deep. I may go down a foot. I may go up a foot. In the end, it has the basic physical form of drawing but on a bigger scale."[137]

In short, then, towards the end of the sixties artists trained in the visual arts began turning to photography to document and provide evidence of (generally ephemeral) conceptual works. During the same period, professional photographers – whose work will be examined by Pierre Dessureault in the following chapter – undertook a rigorous reassessment of the medium's rules and conventions in an effort to shift it into the realm of personal expression and make it part of the emerging world of images.

78 Garry Neill Kennedy
Bisected 1969
cat. 28

79 Bill Vazan
14 Time Lines Readied 1969 (printed 2004)
Square of Ripples 1967–69 (printed 2004)
cat. 73

80 Bill Vazan
Two Angles Readied 1969 (printed 2004)
Square with Tangents 1967–69 **(printed 2004)**
cat. 74

81   Bill Vazan
Low Tide Sand Form – Level – Side to Side 1967–69 (reprinted 2004)
Low Tide Sand Form Pyramid After High Tide 1967–69 (reprinted 2004)
cat. 75

82   Bill Vazan
Low Tide Sand Form – Impact Crater 1969 (reprinted 2004)
2" High Tide Level 1969 (reprinted 2004)
cat. 76

83   Bill Vazan
Low Tide Sand Form 1969 (reprinted 2004)
After One High Tide 1969 (reprinted 2004)
cat. 77

9 Photography in Question

… the theme of the world since photography [is] a
Brothel-without-Walls.[138]

Marshall McLuhan

In this prescient phrase, McLuhan signalled the death of the typographical world that had held sway in the West since Gutenberg's invention of the printing press in 1438. Printing, at the very heart of the mechanical and alphabetical culture, resulted in a world of continuity and seriality. The proliferation of the photographic image and the advent of the technological media it has generated – cinema, television and video – created a rift in humanity's way of conceiving the world. The new universe is one of discontinuity and diversity: in its images, time and space are chopped up, broken into fragments and then reassembled into a whole that is presented as an object of communication. "The effects of technology do not occur at the level of opinions or concepts, but alter sense ratios or patterns of perception steadily and without any resistance. The serious artist is the only person able to encounter technology with impunity, just because he is an expert aware of the changes in sense perception."[139]

At the dawn of the sixties, two opposing conceptions of photography and its uses emerged that would shape the public's perceptions and receptions of the medium throughout the decade. The exhibition *The Family of Man*, produced by Edward Steichen in 1955 for New York's MoMA, was seen by over two million visitors during its lengthy international tour, organized by the United States Information Agency. It was shown at the National Gallery of Canada from February 1 to 22, 1957.

The exhibition's extraordinary popular success was due largely to its theme, which capitalized on post-war optimism. The show, which consisted of 503 photographs made by seventy-three photographers from sixty-eight countries, "was conceived as a mirror of the universal elements and emotions in the everydayness of life – as a mirror of the essential oneness of mankind throughout the world."[140] This idea that there is a human nature shared by all, regardless of such accidents as skin colour, social circumstance or nationality, underlies the message that the orchestrator of this huge, Hollywood-style production wished to convey. Alternating thematically defined groupings of photographic enlargements of varying formats, the exhibition forged links and juxtapositions between images of widely diverse sources. These enlargements, all cropped, created a polyphony of sizes and scenes in which the visions of the different photographers and the specificity of their works were obliterated by the "idealist" and "humanist" discourse of the demiurge Steichen, in whose hands the photograph became simply a raw material.

The other significant event was the publication (in Paris in 1958, and in New York in 1959) of Robert Frank's book *The Americans*, assembled from a series of photographs taken during a two-year trip across the United States. Frank's approach was unapologetically subjective, offering a personal and critical view that made no claim to descriptive accuracy. Like Kerouac's spontaneous prose and Coltrane's sinuous improvisations, both of which disarticulated the structure of their respective languages, Frank rejected the photographic canons of his time – linked to the production of beautiful, meaningful images – in favour of the spontaneity of the moment seized in its entirety. This translated into snapshots with blurred, grainy images in which perspectives are in a state of perpetual imbalance. These photographs, tinted with a kind of disillusioned lyricism, are replete with signs of the alienation of American life. Everything – jukeboxes, the ubiquitous American flag, automobiles, diners, deserted streets and parking lots – speaks of materialism and of emptiness.

The ambiguous nature of the medium and its ceaseless efforts to find a place for itself in the allied fields of mass communication and art were manifest in Canada at the start of the sixties. Still widely perceived as utilitarian, photography was employed principally in illustrated magazines and by government agencies such as the National Film Board's Still Photography Division, who saw their informational mission as a means of creating an image of national progress and disseminating a sense of national identity. In accordance with the ideas of John Grierson, for whom the camera was a mass communications and education tool, the medium was used as the vehicle of choice for informing the general public and consolidating their collective values.

The works of Lutz Dille, Roloff Beny, Walter Curtin, Kryn Taconis and Sam Tata are examples of this approach to photography, which aimed to present a particular idea of the human condition and its embodiment in different cultures

Lutz Dille was born in Leipzig, Germany. A conscript in the German army, he first became interested in photography in 1941, while serving on the Russian front. After the war he immigrated to Canada, settling in Toronto in 1952. Setting up as a freelance photographer, he worked frequently on commission for the CBC and for numerous publications of the period. As well as this "bread-and-butter" work, however, Dille would set off whenever he could (finances permitting) in search of more personal images, combing the streets of Europe, the United States and South America.

Dille belonged to the European humanist tradition expressed in the work of Robert Doisneau, Izis and André Kertesz. He was a *photographer-flâneur*, an observer of street life and minor everyday events. "During the Fifties and Sixties walking city streets was for me a fascinating experience. I am a photographer – and I wanted to catch It – the exciting chance encounter – at the right time – in the right location – under the right light … to capture on my film, happiness, humour, sorrow … To be able to record the human condition with a camera and film is I think one of the great steps forward in our time."[141]

Dille's often ironic eye dwelt on the drollery of his subjects and captured the instants most revealing of the personalities facing his camera (see rep. 84). There is invariably a tenderness, however, in his candid vision of humanity and its performance on the world's stage. Around 1965 Dille abandoned photography in favour of documentary cinema, in which he became interested when the CBC produced four animated films based on his photographs of London, Mexico and New York.

In contrast to Dille, who immersed himself in moments of consummate humanity and the cultures that were their backdrop, Roloff Beny travelled the world with a well-defined plan to photograph ancient cultures. He turned to photography in 1951, after having studied painting, printmaking, art history, architecture and archaeology. Already a painter of some repute, Beny used photography initially as an *aide-mémoire* in his painting process. But as he later wrote: "I … began to be aware of light as opposed to paint and to compose my photographs as I did my drawings."[142]

Beny presented his photographic work in a series of lavish books, the third of which, *Pleasure of Ruins*, was published in 1964. Built around the travel memoir of British novelist and essayist Rose Macaulay, it aims to "explore the various kinds of pleasure given to various people at various epochs by the spectacle of ruined buildings."[143] In the grand tradition of

84 Lutz Dille
New York, U.S.A. 1962
cat. 14

the nineteenth-century traveller, Beny offers a magnificent catalogue of the meccas of human history and heritage. In his year-long world tour, during which he visited 140 archaeological sites in some thirty countries, he sought to capture the timeless beauty of ruins. His images, with their spectacular viewpoints and rich tonalities, capture the spirit of each place in its most favourable light (see rep. 85). The eye of the aesthete passes over the particularities of each culture and the lives of the various countries' inhabitants to focus exclusively on the enduring significance of the myths inherited from humanity's glorious past.

Walter Curtin, Kryn Taconis and Sam Tata were among the leading photojournalists who left their stamp on humanist reporting and helped shape its development throughout the sixties. Henri Cartier-Bresson had been one of the first to define the photo essay:

> What actually *is* a photographic reportage, a picture-story? Sometimes there is one unique picture whose composition possesses such vigor and richness, and whose content so radiates outward from it, that this single picture is a whole story in itself. But this rarely happens. The elements which, together, can strike sparks out of a subject, are often scattered – either in terms of space or time – and bringing them together by force is a "stage management," and, I feel, cheating. But if it is possible to make pictures of the "core" as well as the struck-off sparks of the subject, this is a picture-story; and the page serves to reunite the complementary elements which are dispersed throughout several photographs. The picture-story involves a joint operation of the brain, the eye, and the heart.[144]

Born in Vienna, Walter Curtin left Austria in 1939 for England. In 1946, after studying photography and printmaking, he became apprenticed to a portrait photographer. He opened his own studio in 1948, and worked for several years as an illustrator in the publishing field. In 1952 he immigrated to Toronto, where he embarked on a long and fruitful career as a photojournalist. His works were commissioned and published by such major Canadian magazines of the period as *Maclean's*, *Weekend* and *Chatelaine*.

Stripper Ann Howe with Reporter Robert Thomas Allen (1960, rep. 86) is typical of Curtin's production. A single image summarizes the subject of the article – the encounter between a journalist and a stripper. Ann Howe, cigarette in hand and wearing the dress in which she regularly began her act, stands answering the questions of the journalist seated before her. The scene takes place outside the theatre where the stripper performed, as witness the posters. But despite its apparent naturalism, the image was arranged by the photographer, to ensure that every element contributed to the meaning of the whole. This practice, common among photojournalists, was here essential: the delicate subject was one that could hardly be approached directly in a family magazine. The tone of Allen's article vacillates, moreover, between caricature and moralism.

Sam Tata arrived in Montreal in 1956, having already worked for twenty years as a self-taught photographer. Among his subjects had been the 1949 fall of Shanghai to Mao's troops. Photography served him as a means by which to discover and understand Montreal and the diverse cultures that have moulded its identity. Wandering through the streets of its different neighbourhoods, he captured picture after picture of his adopted city and its many contrasts. Tata is present as observer and witness, never as judge. Often, he is moved by what he sees, sometimes amused. His report on the 1962 and 1963 Saint-Jean-Baptiste Day celebrations, commissioned by *Magazine Maclean,* the French-language monthly, swings back and forth between lighthearted humour and a surrealism that seems integral to the event (see rep. 87). Tata never adopts an attitude of accusatory cynicism or social criticism; rather, he remains at a studied distance from his subject to avoid an excess of local colour or the superficially picturesque. Each of his photographs is a convergence of multiple cultural features that he juxtaposes with absolute freedom.

Tata would always reject the role of illustrator assigned restrictively by so many publications to the photojournalist, defending instead a personal vision nourished by culture:

> Photojournalism is actually a composite profession. It relies far more on a cultured background than upon technical ability. Painting, music, poetry and art are wonderful training grounds. Their study breeds sensitivity. Reading too is wonderfully beneficial, since there is no better way that I know of, outside of travel, to broaden the horizon. All these things, when coupled with experience, sharpen the perception. A photographer, to be any good in this business, needs perception of the world and its people's problems more than he needs anything else on earth.[145]

Another major figure in this group of photojournalists, Kryn Taconis, was born in Rotterdam, Holland, in 1918. He made his first photographs while serving with the Dutch resistance. After the war, he worked for *Life* magazine as a freelance photographer based in the Benelux countries, and in 1950, on the invitation of Robert Capa, he joined the Magnum agency. He moved to Toronto in 1959, and left Magnum in 1960 to set up on his own. One of his preferred clients was the *Star Weekly*, for which he undertook numerous assignments, as well as self-initiated projects. His wife and close collaborator, Tess Taconis, describes her husband's approach:

> Kryn always went off into the blue in his *Star Weekly* essays. He would say "I would like to do this and this and that" and they would say: "Sure, go ahead." And he would just go and do it. He would be back two weeks later and he would have his two or three stories. He worked fast. He knew exactly how to establish himself right away in a situation. He was very easy to have around as a photographer because he always said: "I'm not there to tell them who I am. I'm there to explain who they are, and if I can be the paper on the wall, so much the better.[146]

Like the great classics of the genre, Taconis's photo essays reflect a profound interest in human beings and events, which focuses on their essence. A young blind boy called Barry Scheur and the people of the Hutterite community (see rep. 88) are the subjects of two of his best-known pieces.[147] The Hutterites, an Anabaptist sect, live in self-sufficient colonies and follow the principles of primitive Christianity. Their lifestyle, language and customs have placed them on the fringe of modern society. Taconis made himself almost invisible as he studied these subjects and explored their sense of identification with their culture. The accompanying text, written by Harry Bruce, does more than simply repeat in words the content of Taconis's images – it complements them by throwing light on the unique world of the Hutterite colonies.

With neither pity nor condescension, Taconis and Bruce celebrate the Hutterites' difference, describing the values that cement a communal life lived discreetly, out of the public eye. Ultimately, their images and words combine to make this community seem far less strange.

Michel Lambeth, Nina Raginsky and Michael Semak can be seen as part of a "new wave" of humanist photographers who turned away from current events to offer their personal view of a selected subject, more often than not without the commercial constraints of an assignment.

Born in Toronto in 1923, Michel Lambeth enlisted in the Canadian army during the Second World War. After demobilization, he spent some time in London and then Paris, where he studied art, notably sculpture in the studio of Ossip Zadkine. He returned to Toronto in 1948, taking up photography in 1955 and producing numerous stories for the *Star Weekly* between 1959 and 1968. An avid reader of philosophy, history and politics, Lambeth was one of the first people to reflect on photography and its role in the expressive realm. His approach was essentially humanist in its preoccupation with his "human brothers," but also in the way he saw himself in them. In his oeuvre, observation and personal identification are continually combined. "Feeling as expressed in emotional freedom with photography becomes at once a diary of and a monument to the particular, unique existence of one man or woman. I believe that what our Greek-derived, science-bound word 'photography' fails to say is said succinctly in a two-ideogram character by the Japanese: the reflection of existence."[148]

Many of Lambeth's photographs reveal their subjects' inner nature through facial expression and body language. A good example is *St. Joseph's Convent School* (1960, rep. 89), captured in the yard of a Toronto orphanage, where the aged body and deeply lined face of the man in the foreground creates a powerful sense of vulnerability that contrasts with the jolly faces of the two young nuns at the rear. Utterly different universes are aligned through judicious framing. By exploiting visual dissonance and juxtaposing several discordant elements in a single space, Lambeth uses the language of photography to express a personal vision of reality – exactly like a painter.

Born in Montreal, Nina Raginsky studied painting and sculpture at Rutgers University in New Jersey. She began photographing on her return to Montreal in 1962. In 1966 she moved to London, and her photographs began appearing in *Queen Magazine*, the *Daily London Telegraph Magazine* and the French magazine *L'Express*.

Raginsky is not concerned with celebrities or people in the news. The appeal of her subjects, all ordinary people, resides in the lives they have created for themselves. She pictures these everyday heroes in their natural surroundings, often accompanied by objects that reveal their personalities or their achievements. *Colonel Langley with his Dog Toga* (1967, rep. 90) pose next to a flag. The frank, relaxed relationship that clearly exists between this pair and the photographer conjures the mood of a family photo album, and the picture actually respects several of the conventions of the snapshot: an alliance between the photographer and the subjects, who are shown face-on and full-length (thus maintaining a respectful distance between subject and camera). Worlds away from both the definitive portrait, designed to convey an individual's essential nature, and the photo reportage, which would aim to describe their social circumstances, Raginsky's practice is defined by the ritual associated with the actual taking of the photograph: "I am interested in the timelessness that surrounds the moment of interaction between the people that I photograph and myself."[149]

122

Michael Semak's work is notable for its involvement in social reality and its unwavering faith in the power of images. During the sixties, Semak produced a number of self-assigned projects on subjects that were hard to approach or in some way marginalized, including biker gangs, minority cultural communities, children with behavioural problems, slaughterhouses and mental institutions.

> Photography is principally a way of recording reality. If a photographer is capable
> of realizing that reality itself is always astonishing if looked at through a unique and
> original point of view, there is no limit to the possibilities of creative endeavour …
> The photographer, I feel, has to have one foot inside the world of the subject and
> one foot in his own world, so as to give his impression, a very personal expression
> of what he sees.[150]

While Semak asserts that reality serves as the cornerstone of his photography, his work is never detached or neutral, for it never lacks the stamp of the photographer's own personality and his own view of his subjects. The snapshot entitled *Italian Community, Toronto* (1963, rep. 91) is particularly eloquent: a composition of staggered planes presents a large and diverse group of people – male and female, young and old. The photo's frame becomes a window that imposes a structure on a multiplicity of activities and worlds. And through the quality of his prints, Semak intensifies the mood of these quickly snapped scenes: the deep blacks and brilliant whites focus attention on the main subject, which stands out from the ground like a cut-out. Nothing distracts the viewer's eye.

Documentary Photography

Several major documentary projects were undertaken in the late sixties. The genre had been developed during the 1930s by such figures as the German August Sander and the American Walker Evans, whose belief in a photography that "sees things as they are" was a reaction to decades of "artistic" photography shaped by studio wizardry, the artifices of Pictorialism and the formalism of the avant-garde. In creating their images they chose to focus on the subject, which was recorded in the simplest possible way. Many photographers of this category adopted a systematic approach towards their theme and a serial presentation of their images. Unlike photojournalists, documentary photographers explored their subjects over an extended period, striving to offer an exhaustive account.

Pierre Gaudard's series *Les ouvriers* is a key oeuvre of Quebec documentary photography from the sixties. In this personal project, executed over a period of two years, Gaudard examined the world of workers in detail: he shared their daily lives, picturing them at the factory, at home, at union meetings. For him, photography was a vital tool for social understanding: "I try as much as possible to deal simply and respectfully with people. I try, and this isn't always easy, to understand the people I photograph and do them justice. The important thing is to spend time with them and see how they live and what their concerns are."[151] Gaudard's account is direct, even harsh: his grainy, contrasted images do nothing to embellish the factories and workshops they describe or to lighten their gritty, sooty atmospheres.

Although Gaudard's documentary series came at a time when Quebec society was being swept by a wave of militancy and revolutionary feeling, his view remained a personal one. His objective was to communicate the results of his explorations and observations of the world

93   Orest Semchishen
Church near Redwater, Alberta 1968
cat. 67

94   Gabor Szilasi
Mrs. Alexis (Marie) Tremblay, île aux
Coudres, Quebec 1970
cat. 72

by fully exploiting photography's expressive power. This explains his choice of the medium close-up view used for *Pointe-Saint-Charles Factory, Montreal, Quebec* (1969, rep. 92), which focuses on the face and garb of a factory worker. Despite the dark goggles concealing his eyes, the man – pictured against the backdrop of a graffiti-covered wagon – is clearly looking straight at us. The mood of the scene is distinctly odd. Evidently, Gaudard's goal was to describe the world of Quebec's workers in a voice uniquely his own. His work reveals a constant interaction between factual truth and the felicity of the photographer's view. That this view is frontal, direct, clear and unaffected is a choice that is as inherently significant as the choice of subject itself. The transparency of the photographer's message never obscures his choices, but rather re-inforces them.

Clarity and precision characterize the practices of both Orest Semchishen, working in the Canadian West, and Gabor Szilasi, whose pictures depict various rural areas of Quebec. Semchishen, a radiologist by profession, turned to photography in the late sixties. From the outset he opted to work with a view camera, focusing his attention on the architecture and landscape of the Prairies. We are struck first by the purity of his vision – which gives pride of place to the subject – and his familiarity with the very particular space of the Prairies. His relationship with his subjects is a close one: "When you work on a topic not only are you working on technique but you're trying to get at and understand your subject. It's only by staying with it, by persevering, that you get to understand it better."[152]

Church near Redwater, Alberta (1968, rep. 93) was the image that triggered Semchishen's first major series. Byzantine churches had twofold significance for the photographer: they served as a reminder of his Ukrainian origins and as landmarks in a vast geographical space colonized by immigration. This duality is evident in his treatment of the relationship between the church's architecture and the infinite horizon of the plain. The feeling of horizontality is heightened by the image's framing, while the built structure stands like a beacon in the desolate space. Semchishen's goal was to produce a portrait at once detailed and accurate. It was between 1973 and 1975 that he executed his series devoted exclusively to the theme of the Byzantine church, photographing over two hundred and fifty – most of which no longer exist. During this period his approach became more flexible and his compositions freer, revealing the full complexity of the subject.

In the fall of 1970, Gabor Szilasi produced a personal document in the Charlevoix and île aux Coudres region of Quebec that would have as great an impact on documentary photography as Gaudard's. Szilasi was on familiar ground: employed by the Office du film du Québec since 1959, he had already visited virtually every corner of the province. His series of portraits and interiors, taken with a view camera, highlights the uniformity of values and rituals among his chosen subjects. His stylistically spare and systematically frontal technique records many of the signs that embody the identity of this cultural group. Moreover, the relationship between these signs structures the images by contrasting tradition and modernity. Szilasi focuses attention on this somewhat uneasy coexistence by showing it with maximum clarity. This particular conception of time is at the heart of his practice: "I am not interested in the past or the future: I am interested in the present. Through the photographic image, I can directly record the signs of the past and the future as they appear in this moment."[153]

As in the image of Madame Tremblay standing in front of her china cabinet (1970, rep. 94), Szilasi invariably pictures people in their everyday environment. While the static, almost ritualized pose underscores the distance between the photographer and his model, the detachment is only apparent: we sense rather a respectful and respected reserve that is actually undermined by the directness of Madame Tremblay's gaze and her appeal to the spectator as witness. Like a mirror, the portrait becomes a reflection of resemblance and familiarity, deriving its style from the encounter between subject and photographer.

The project devoted to île aux Coudres was the first in a series focusing on the increasing urbanization of rural Quebec that would occupy Szilasi for the following decade and take him to the Beauce, Abitibi-Témiscamingue, Saguenay-Lac-Saint-Jean and Lotbinière regions.

In sketching the portrait of their time, Gaudard, Semchishen and Szilasi highlighted the cultural specificity of different milieus by offering a detailed account of their vernacular features. In the social realm, the acknowledgement of particularity signalled a growing questioning of values taken hitherto to be shared and immutable. This celebration of difference can be seen in a sense as the antithesis of *The Family of Man*. According to this view, universality lies neither in reduction to a single type nor in a hypothetical nature common to all, but in the ubiquity of the differences that are the foundation of identity.

A Personal Vision of the Human Condition

For some practitioners, photography serves as a tool for the exploration and understanding not only of society, but also of their own inner world. In the productions of Michel Saint-Jean, Dave Heath and John Max, for example, vision is everything and expression takes precedence over subject.

95   **Michel Saint-Jean**
Sacred Heart, Blainville, Quebec 1970
cat. 61

What if this present were the worlds last night?
Marke in my heart, O Soule, where thou dost dwell,
The picture of Christ crucified...
                                                    John Donne

Quebec photographer Michel Saint-Jean categorically dismisses all notions of objectivity: "Photography should and does serve to express an idea, a conception of the world. It is a way of learning both about people and things, and about oneself. Basically, whether the subject is a tree, a woman or a factory, a good photographer never photographs anything but himself."[154]

The power of Saint-Jean's work lies in the dramatic intensity that emanates from the scenes he captures. *Sacred Heart, Blainville, Quebec* (1970, rep. 95) is part of the *Amérique québécoise* collection that occupied him for almost a decade. The huge statue of Christ that dominates the image bears a "for sale" sign. The irony of the situation is underscored by the low-angle shot, which causes the statue's two sections to occupy virtually the entire visual field. A relatively ordinary roadside scene becomes a quasi-surrealist image, whose mood of mystery is enhanced by sharp contrasts and a grainy finish. Viewpoint and execution have been combined here to create a caustic comment on the Church's stranglehold over Quebec society. It is an approach that reveals the bizarre lurking beneath the surface of the ordinary and transforms the street into a theatre where everyday dramas are played out. The photographic image becomes a source of aesthetic experience not through the subject it depicts but through its capacity to present that subject in its own unique visual language.

Dave Heath was born in Philadelphia in 1931. In 1947 he adopted photography as the chief vehicle for his personal reflections on existence. It was in Chicago, in the mid-1950s, that he began organizing his pictures into books and sequences. The single image was no longer sufficient, he felt, to render the complexity of a quest for authenticity that reached an initial culmination in 1965, with the publication of *A Dialogue with Solitude*. Subsequently, Heath

continued to work on the issue of sequence and to hone his capacity to "create poetic structure, a connective linkage, not chronological or narrative in development such as a photo-essay, but emotional in development."[155]

Meditation (in 5 Parts) (c. 1964, rep. 96) sketches a self-portrait of Heath through the people and situations he photographs. His capacity to identify with his subjects, who become almost like the embodiments of his own feelings, seems boundless. He shares with these people a sense of aloneness that he sees as the fate of all humanity. Each particular situation – we are all, as Montaigne wrote, "of the common sort" – is translated into a symbolic language that joins the universal. Each image freezes the emotional intensity of a moment at its peak, suspending the action in an eternal present. We move into an experiential temporality that leads towards the intense lyricism of an acknowledged subjectivity. This process unfolds according to a visual logic of lines, tonalities and forms, creating a network of echoes and resonances. As part of a chronology, the image acquires a poetic force that transcends its individual power of evocation.

In the mid-sixties, Heath gradually turned away from black and white photography and pursued his explorations in slide shows, to which he added narration and sound and time elements. In 1970 he moved to Toronto, where he taught at Ryerson Polytechnic Institute for more than twenty years.

John Max was born to parents of Ukrainian origin in Montreal in 1936. He studied painting and music before discovering photography in the late 1950s, in the work of Lutz Dille. This highly personal approach to the human condition had an immediate impact on him, and he set about to teach himself photography.

98   Charles Gagnon
Greenwich Village, New York City 1966
cat. 23

During the sixties Max undertook many projects, all of which he used – ignoring the imperatives of documentary description – to crystallize his own particular vision. For him, photography is a tool for introspection, something that allows him to create a journal of his life. He describes his mission thus: "What I am attempting to do is to get underneath the mask, the numerous masks that man wears, through to the spirit underneath. On the other hand, sometimes I emphasize the mask to show that this is the dominant thing that motivates a person, propels him and brings him to life."[156]

Max's images bear the stamp of his personality. Their technique is unusual: the grainy textures and striking contrasts magnify the tensions between areas of deep, impenetrable shadow and expanses of blinding white. His subjects are generally members of his family, close friends or fellow artists. Each image represents a sealed instant: in *Julian Beck and the Living Theatre* (1967, rep. 97), photographed in Paris, an extraordinary range of expressions and emotions ripples through the bodies of the actors. His close-up portraits present a huge variety of physiognomies on which can be read their owners' inner state. As the faces and gestures are those of all humanity, this voyage into individual emotion and ritual takes us inexorably towards the universal.

The Social Landscape

The expression "social landscape" was coined by the American photographer, critic and educator Nathan Lyons,[157] for whom landscape was essentially cultural – the realm of urban structures with which human beings interact.

Lyons's photographic approach is based on the medium's most ordinary form: the snapshot. It is an approach well suited to his study of social structures, since it allows that spontaneous, unstudied reaction that establishes a correspondence between the photographer's psyche and the physical world. This reaction is embodied in the action of the photographer, who, submerged in the flood of sensations triggered by the urban milieu, becomes one with the moment, seizes it as it materializes, and records it in his shot. His own movement becomes an integral part of the image: cut-off perspectives, chaotic compositions, fragile equilibriums and visual ruptures translate a teeming reality that spills continually out of the frame.

Lyons draws the line once and for all between reality and its representation: the image is a reality in its own right, with its own truth, whose existence is rooted in the tools of its production. It possesses no meaning outside itself and what it presents. Breaking sharply with the tradition that aimed to establish correspondences between the physical and imaginal realms, Lyons defines the latter as a self-sufficient whole, governed by its own laws, and employs the photographic act as both its foundation and its junction.

Charles Gagnon is one of the Canadian artists influenced by Lyons' ideas. Known for his multidisciplinary practice, which encompasses painting, photography, film and assemblage (see "Perception, Perception, Perception," p. 61), Gagnon studied at New York's Parsons School of Design from 1955 to 1960. It was there that he was introduced to Abstract Expressionism, the writers of the Beat Generation, jazz, and the films of Robert Frank.

Gagnon's first photographs, taken in 1959, follow in the vein of Lee Friedlander and Garry Winogrand. Like them, he cast an often ironic eye over the urban jungle. The street was for him a stage where the figures of the collective imagination performed. His shots of an ambiguous, fragmented urban space are filled with recurring visual motifs that create a mood of alienation. The photographic space becomes the meeting place for a collection of diverse signs forming a web of visual correspondences (see rep. 98). As the sixties progressed, Gagnon's increasingly purified formal vocabulary focused on the more symbolic, even meta-physical aspects of the North American cityscape. His pared-down images push the spectator towards a certain introversion. Gagnon has said: "I don't believe that art has anything to do with communication – art really deals with communion … Communion demands much greater participation on several levels, whereas in communication you're getting information thrown at you."[158]

All through the sixties, Gagnon engaged in photography and painting simultaneously. For him, the two disciplines represent the two faces of being: "As I see it, to take photographs is to perceive; to paint is to conceive. And this notion of perception is so vital that when I move through the world with a photographer's eye, reality becomes a performance (in the artistic sense) of infinite richness."[159] Freed of the conflicts that had divided them since the mid-nineteenth century, their particular strengths well defined, the two disciplines can be seen as two complementary and reciprocally illuminating ways of presenting the visible as an object of contemplation, entirely open to communion with the spectator.

Tom Gibson's background was also in painting. Born in Edinburgh, Scotland, in 1930, Gibson moved in 1952 to Toronto, where he studied painting and drawing at the Ontario College of Art. He then embarked on a career as a painter, achieving considerable success before turning to photography in the late sixties. After two years of study with Nathan Lyons at the Visual Studies Workshop, in Rochester, his future was confirmed.

Photography is similar to painting, Gibson believes, "if you view the world as a studio in which you take elements and you put them together to create a photograph. You go out with a camera and you create a kind of collage, putting together elements that make a coherent statement."[160] As a photographer, he juxtaposes the signs of the urban world in a highly par-ticular way. In *My Shadow at Comber, near Chatham, Ontario* (1970, rep. 99), for example, a row of gravestones appears connected to the photographer's own cast shadow. We are taken back to one of the basic motifs of the snapshot, where so many picture-takers' shadows inadver-tently become part of the image, an accidental non-presence. But Gibson exploits such accidents. The shadow serves as his double, underscoring his part in the photographic act and sealing his encounter with his surroundings. The transparency and evanescence of the shadow are materialized in and by the photograph, which becomes at the same time a screen on which the photographer projects his preoccupations and obsessions.

While Gagnon and Gibson were exploring the forms of urban life, the Vancouver-based Tim Porter was finding ways of transcribing it visually. Born in Washington in 1946, he studied philosophy and English literature at the University of Virginia from 1964 to 1966, before immi-grating to Canada in 1967 and taking up photography.

In *Lawn Party, Vancouver* (1970, rep. 100), Porter makes skilful use of photography's intrinsic properties to create an image of rigorously structured planes. The fence running along the bottom of the picture defines an entry point for the eye, which is guided by the chevrons of light that strike its points and firmly demarcate the foreground. The vast expanse of shade that stretches across the lawn from one fence to the other remains impenetrable. This dense mass nonetheless draws the eye, and renders all the more mysterious the presence of the empty chaise longue. This architecture of planes, defined by alternating areas of deep shadow and

99   Tom Gibson
My Shadow at Comber, near Chatham, Ontario 1970
cat. 30

100 Tim Porter
Lawn Party, Vancouver 1970
cat. 55

The Sixties in Canada: Photography in Question

cascades of vividly sharp light, creates a purely photographic space that is a combination of reality and its transcription via the medium. Garry Winogrand explained the social landscape approach in the following terms: "A still photograph is the illusion of a literal description of how a camera saw a piece of time and space ... I photograph to see what things look like photographed."[161]

Forms: Architecture and Landscape

Photography enjoys a special relationship with both architecture and landscape. From the medium's earliest days, it has been used to gather evidence of past realizations and to celebrate technological progress. Initially, photography documented constructions that expressed the modern spirit. Gradually, a poetics of the city emerged, which involved a systematic search for new perspectives on architectural forms: shots from above and below, angled views, close-ups and cubist-style fragmentation were all elements of a formal photographic vocabulary that was entirely in tune with the avant-garde movements of the twenties.

By the dawn of the sixties, the unwavering optimism of the early part of the century was showing signs of erosion: forms are not eternal, and the products of material civilization get old – even die. Numerous photographers therefore undertook the task of registering, cataloguing and studying examples of vernacular architecture, in order to sketch the anatomy of the social body as manifest in the evidence of its members' activities.

John Flanders, architect and professor of architecture at Ottawa's Carleton University, aims to rescue from oblivion the vernacular architecture of the towns and villages of eastern Ontario. He explains: "Industrialization and urban problems have made us overlook the rural dilemma – economic decline and urban growth. A whole way of life is rapidly disappearing and with it an important part of our heritage. There is no way that this can be stopped, even if stopping it were possible. But we must look and learn before it disappears completely."[162] Over a period of four years, he photographed old family homes, barns, business establishments, service stations, blacksmith's shops, posters, store windows and all sorts of other evidence of the popular tradition. He saw these anonymous vestiges as the expression of age-old skills and of an original material culture.

Flanders' description of structures and buildings from the past are meticulously detailed. The invariably frontal viewpoint and lack of aesthetic effects create a sense of neutrality that allows the subject to take centre stage. His shots clearly reveal both the structure of the buildings and their materials, while the bright, diffuse light picks up the relief of architectural details and the patinas of age. Each carefully framed image takes in a portion of the building's surroundings, establishing both its setting and its original function (see rep. 101).

Individually, Flanders' photographs capture the basic forms of a built environment; together, they constitute a veritable catalogue raisonné of these forms' multiple permutations as expressed across the spectrum of a culture. Through his images, we discover the lifestyles and values of that culture's anonymous creators who constructed it using local materials and the techniques of their time. While many studies of the past reek of nostalgia, Flanders surveys and records for the purposes of history. The architecture of the past, still part of our present, bears vital witness to the standards and mores of those who produced it.

101 John Flanders
Coke and Pepsi Signs Reflected
in a Barber Shop Window, Lyndhurst,
Ontario 1966-70
cat. 17

Jean-Paul Morisset's interest in the traditional arts of Quebec developed early. Born in Quebec City, he studied at Université Laval and later at the École nationale supérieure des beaux-arts and the Institut d'arts et d'archéologie, in Paris. In 1954 he began taking part in the huge project to inventory Quebec's works of art set up by his father, art historian Gérard Morisset. Throughout the sixties, Jean-Paul Morisset continued working on an individual basis towards the same objective.

Although the goal was to document every manifestation of his province's cultural heritage, Morisset was not content to slavishly record the external appearance of his subjects: his views possess an inventive flair that has the effect of enhancing the originality of the object on which his camera is focused. The buildings he photographs are transposed into a very particular pictorial world. It is an approach that coincides precisely with the ideas of André Malraux: "The world of photographs is, unquestionably, only the servant of the world of originals; and yet, appealing less directly to the emotions and far more to the intellect, it seems to reveal or to 'develop' – in the sense in which the world is used in photography – the creative act; to make of the history of art primarily a continuing succession of creations."[163]

Morisset's shots are often taken from an unusually low angle, which distorts and exaggerates the perspective. The views include the buildings' immediate surroundings, and their framing sets off some expressive detail of the facade or decorative elements. The generally powerful contrasts of light and dark serve to model the volumes and structure the image. In some cases, a use of filters or infrared film intensifies tonal values, lending the image a slightly unreal quality (see rep. 102). Morisset's exploitation of the properties and materials of the medium is never arbitrary, but contributes towards a visual approach whose goal is to offer an interpretation of the subject, to convey its meaning and to reveal its beauty.

102 Jean-Paul Morisset
House, Saint-François, île d'Orléans,
Quebec 1959–60
cat. 50

103 Jeremy Taylor
Montreal, Quebec 1963
cat. 81

Born in Montreal in 1938, Jeremy Taylor began taking photographs in 1959 while staying in San Miguel de Allende, Mexico, with his father, the painter Frederick B. Taylor. On his return home, Taylor began combing the streets of Montreal armed with his Hasselblad or a view camera. Anything and everything became a potential subject, for he was like Walter Benjamin's *flâneur*, whose intoxication "not only feeds on the sensory data taking shape before his eyes but often possesses itself of abstract knowledge – indeed, of dead facts – as something experienced and lived through."[164] Taylor sought out the hidden facets of his city, but his project remained a personal one: his objective was not to document – his aim was simply to discover and assemble a wealth of images as he wandered. Not everything was of equal interest to him: he ignored the slick surfaces of glass-and-concrete towers and the sharp angles of modern architecture in favour of structures worn by time, which in his hands become textured mosaics and black and white paintings that are practically abstract (see rep. 103).

From July 1968 to August 1969, Taylor travelled and photographed throughout the American Southwest and Canada's West Coast. During much of this trip, he made landscapes with an 11 x 14-inch view camera. In the introduction to an exhibition of his work held in Montreal on his return, Taylor wrote: "The photographer distills the gross to reveal the essence. He looks for something significant, often familiar, takes it out of context and presents it to the viewer, who may then really see it for the first time."[165]

Like the city, the countryside also offers Taylor an inexhaustible photographic source, and he captures its images using the same purely formal approach (see rep. 104). For Taylor, as for his model Edward Weston, the subjectivity of the photographer lies in his capacity to seize the essence of the visible and to transpose it in truly photographic terms. His contact prints display a range of subtle shades that enhance the simplicity of the forms. Tight framing

frees the subject from any superfluous detail, accentuating the spareness of the lines. Light sculpts the volumes and separates the planes. Through the intense presence of its subject, each of Taylor's landscapes is a blueprint of the visible world that transcribes the immutable essence of nature.

Robert Bourdeau also strives, in his landscapes, to capture the meaning and essence of the visible world. Born in Kingston, Ontario, in 1931, he studied architecture and interior design at the University of Toronto and at the New School of Design in Boston before becoming a self-taught photographer in the late 1950s. Bourdeau's meeting with the American photographer and educator Minor White in 1959 had a decisive impact on his approach to the medium. White saw photography as a spiritual exercise, both for the photographer, in close interaction with the world, and for the spectator, to whom the image reveals the hidden face of reality. The image, a metaphor for the photographer's experience, sheds its literality and assumes a symbolic meaning disclosed by the photographic act.

In the introduction to a monograph on Bourdeau's works from the sixties and seventies, Ronald Solomon describes this fusion of the photographer and his subject: "Beyond the photographer and the camera there is only the subject. Quietly, gently, the photographer releases himself to the subject, for he is the camera and there is no ego, no anger, no surrender, no victory; only total consciousness and presence. And there – full, luminous and free – is the subject."[166] It is this communion with the subject that gives Bourdeau's landscapes their serene power. Their symbolic significance arises from the close correspondence, in the photographer's vision, between the act of apprehending the physical world and the internalization of that apprehension (see rep. 105).

The taking of the shot is for the photographer, then, an experience of communion with the world; its reception, on the other hand, requires the spectator to be open-minded and reflective. Far from being passive, this type of reception obliges the viewer to *read* the image. For images, like texts, possess a logic and a vocabulary that bear meaning. The meaning of the image is the result of an inner process that mobilizes the sensitivity, affectivity and rationality of the person interpreting it.

Forms: The Photographic Medium

While subject and style were explored in depth by numerous photographers during the sixties, others made use of photography's fundamental properties to create a personal visual vocabulary and push the image into the realm of art. Going beyond conventional genres and techniques, these practitioners saw in formal invention the possibility of photographic truth. For them, an image's meaning lies in the reality of photographic forms, and its referents can be found in the nature of the medium itself – its materials, techniques and aesthetics. In John Szarkowski's famous words, "whatever else a photograph may be about, it is inevitably about photography."[167]

Born in Germany in 1931, Guenter Karkutt came to Canada in 1957, embarking immediately on a career as an industrial and commercial photographer. Through his personal practice and his work as an exhibition organizer, critic and teacher, he became one of the leading proponents of so-called "creative photography." In his view, a photograph is a pure image that achieves abstraction when freed from the burden of representation (see rep. 106). From the outset, he has situated photography in the realm of the visual arts: "Deliberate concentration on the elements common to photography and other related disciplines is the purpose of my work. Despite the apparent complexity of the technical aspects of photography it is imperative to me to fuse visual awareness and photographic technique."[168]

First, Karkutt copies the elements he wishes to combine onto orthochromatic film, retaining only the blacks and whites in order to bring out the main shapes and contours. He may make other interventions at this stage, such as drawing with ink on the transparent support or using solarization, which reverses the tones and gives the objects a ghostly look. He then composes these elements into an image where the forms, lines and tonalities interact with one another as in an abstract painting. No longer tied to figurative representation, the image – a pure product of the photographer's actions – creates a peculiarly photographic pictorial space.

Vancouver resident Fred Herzog could be described as an "enlightened amateur," since his personal practice was conducted as a sideline to his main work as a medical photographer at the University of British Columbia. In his wanderings through the streets of Vancouver, he produced over fifty thousand slides over the years, using a variety of visual vocabularies to interpret his urban subjects, from street photography to experimentation with photographic materials. Helga Pakasaar describes his work this way: "Herzog's approach was that of a subjective witness recording traces of earlier times and the social impact of Vancouver's rapid growth. His formalist eye was drawn to the prosaic – corroded surfaces, decrepit signs and dusty junk store windows. These lushly colored abstract images were indicative of modernist photography and sixties pop art."[169]

106 Guenter Karkutt
Crusader 1965
cat. 39

In certain shots, Herzog combines a highly personal form of realism with a manipulation of the photographic finish. His unusual approach to colour, especially, sets his images apart. Colour, still relatively unexploited at the start of the sixties, was generally used decoratively, to heighten realism or intensify picturesque effects. In *Rescue, Vancouver* (1960, rep. 107), Herzog has made it an essential element of the image, whose pointillist quality is due to extreme enlargement of the negative. The result is the transformation of the subject into a constellation of diffuse colours and vaguely defined forms. The points of colour constituting each of the layers reveal the structure of the image, whose surface and its treatment take precedence over the subject – ultimately less important than its photographic interpretation.

Marc-André Gagné became a full-time photographer on graduating from the École des beaux-arts de Montréal in 1962. Throughout the sixties, he served as chronicler of Montreal's art scene. In his personal photographic work he conjured a dreamlike world that was at once a foray into surrealism and an exploration of image construction. Like Karkutt, he employed a range of techniques to produce composite works that often resemble engravings. Solarization, masking, multiple exposures and the superimposition and juxtaposition of negatives, as well as different interventions on the surface of the prints, are used to emphasize the strangeness and incongruity of scenes that could only exist through photography (see rep. 108).

In contrast to the collages created by the Surrealists, who used clashes of idea and image to conjure multiple levels of reality, the components of Gagné's pictures were slowly developed and assembled in the darkroom, the joins obliterated by the effect of light on the photographic support. We are no longer in the realm of swiftly captured instants but have entered a photographic space-time, created slowly and painstakingly with multiple components and a variety of procedures and interventions.

Time also plays a significant role in the photography of Normand Grégoire, who was born in 1944 in Montreal, where he studied photography at the Institut des arts graphiques. In 1968, at the Bibliothèque nationale du Québec in Montreal, he exhibited *Polyptych One* – a series of short photographic sequences that used minimalist scenes to create symbolic schemas of human experience.

With *Polyptych Two* (1969, rep. 109), Grégoire moved closer to animation and film. In his presentation of this slideshow, Grégoire wrote: "Man and his camera seeking an adventure: photography / – trying to capture a moment of life as it flows by, breathe life into it, reveal its inner meaning. / Polyptych two – face to face with its own image, scanned in a new perspective, offering new dimensions. / There is no magic clue, Polyptych two is a looking glass."[170] The starting point is stylized reality: man, alone and naked, faces an invasion of images and advertisements that leave him uncertain of his own true desires. The theatricality of the scene is entirely deliberate. The actor improvises, moves around, makes use of several "props." The camera follows his performance, and we are constantly aware of the photographer's presence as he closely watches the subject's every action, moves with him, inhabits the same space as him. The images are of the simplest, instantly readable and instilled with the enhanced presence of beings and things.

The images succeed one another on the screen, forming an uninterrupted flow whose alternating scenes seem to hover between reality and illusion. A soundtrack of noises, voices and percussive sounds imposes its beat on the visual sequence. The acoustic rhythms empha-

107 **Fred Herzog**
Rescue, Vancouver 1960
cat. 36

108 **Marc-André Gagné**
Untitled 1969
cat. 22

109 **Normand Grégoire**
Polyptych Two (detail) 1969
cat. 34

size and reinforce the visual ones, and some images reappear regularly in the slideshow like a leitmotif, taking on fresh symbolic significance each time.

Born in 1928, Jack Dale left the Ontario College of Art in 1953 with a diploma in industrial design and went on to take a degree in architecture at the University of Toronto. He was drawn to photography for its multidisciplinary potential. *Cubed Woman No. 5* (1970, rep. 110) is one of a series of photo-sculptures he made in the early 1970s. Although the photographic materials he employed in making these works are entirely traditional – glass plates coated with a light sensitive emulsion on which images (some solarized) are reproduced – the constructed effect of their assemblage is most unusual. The flat surfaces of the fragments, stacked up in superimposed rows, create a transparent column that forms a cubist nude, shot through with reflections created by transparency effects and the layering of positive and negative images. The composition changes according to the viewpoint of the spectator, who is free to approach the work from any angle.

Two of Dale's photo-sculptures were included in the exhibition *Photography into Sculpture*, organized by MoMA in 1970.

A Tool for Artists

Although throughout the sixties photography continued to strive to establish itself as an autonomous art form – by seeking new subjects, adopting fresh narrative strategies, or exploring its expressive and formal potential – it was radically affected by the emergence of artists who saw it as a new tool for questioning the conventions and status of the work of art. As Walter Benjamin put it, questions now had to be asked not about "photography as an art" but about "art as photography."[171] By reversing the terms of the axiom that had guided much of the work produced during the decade, these artists redefined the art/photography debate and opened the way to a new formulation of artistic practice. Photography would enable them to break down the barriers between disciplines and to imbue art with a new logic.

Of all the artists working with photography during this period, Michael Snow's approach seems the most idiomatic. On the occasion of a recent survey exhibition of his photographic works and films, Snow wrote: "The actors in the events-that-become-objects that are my photographic works are the manipulable variables of photographic image-making. That cameras are mirrors with memories is the first important understanding. That 'subjects' are transformed to become photographs is the second."[172]

Authorization (1969, rep. 111), a landmark work of the sixties, consists of five Polaroid images showing the artist photographing himself in a mirror, onto which he tapes each new photograph. The pictures of the artist that make up the image are not self-portraits – they show the artist creating the work. Here, the work is embodied entirely in the process of its production and the evidence of its execution. This doubling and redoubling, this *mise en abyme* effect – not of reality but of its representation – could be repeated ad infinitum. The pictures-within-pictures represent a series of variations that, like the *Goldberg Variations* or the *Musical Offering* by Bach, exploit the possibilities of a theme that grows increasingly complex with each mutation. The spectator plays a vital role in this game of Russian dolls: the real mirror that serves as the construction's support captures his or her reflection and makes it part of the composition. Photography thus becomes neither a window, nor a mirror, but a production process that is constantly renewed and enlivened by the image of the spectator, whose every encounter with it constitutes a unique moment.

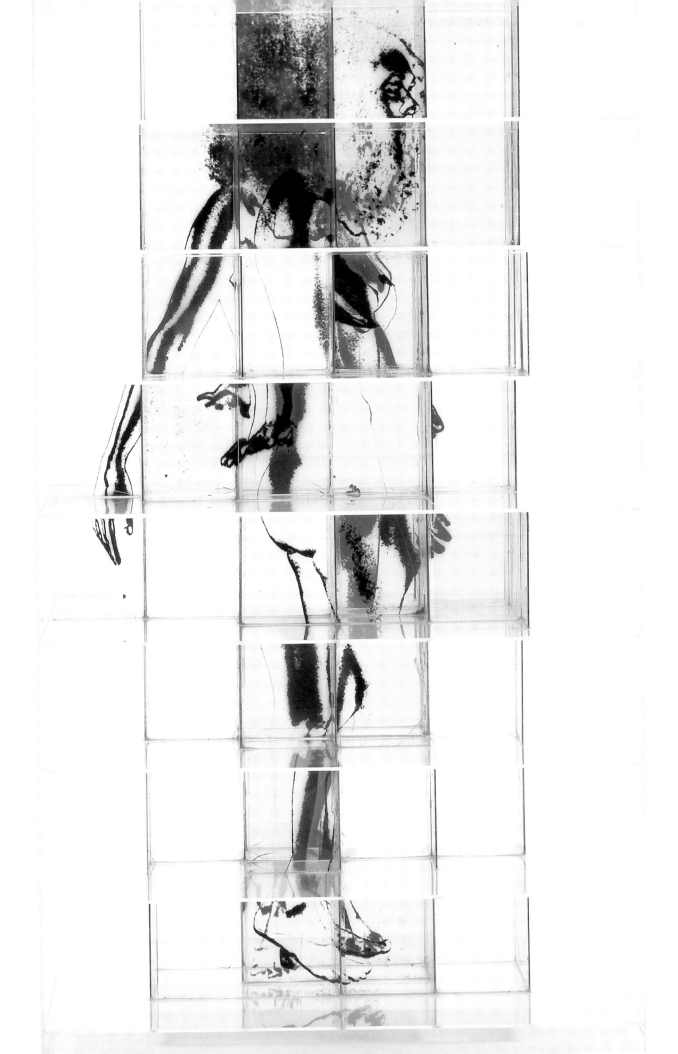

After signing the *Refus Global* manifesto in 1948, Françoise Sullivan continued working as a dancer and then, throughout the sixties, as a sculptor. Towards the end of the decade, she began re-examining her commitment to the art world and the idea of the art "product." A couple of years later, she declared: "Our world is saturated with art objects. So what are we to do? I don't believe that today's artists are happy, because of the gulf between what they do and what they would like to do. When one creates, one attempts to capture the spirit of something that would be relevant to art. It is perhaps the hope of finding a new possibility that makes us leave painting and sculpture and pushes us towards something other than the object."[173]

Sullivan would redefine her practice by turning back to performance and devoting the 1970s to an exploration of the relationship between a meaningful act and its transcription in a photographic, filmic or videographic image. *Promenade from the Musée d'art contemporain to the Montreal Museum of Fine Arts* (1970, rep. 112) was the first of four walks undertaken by the artist during the decade. The idea, for Sullivan, was to get back to basics and to a form of production that drew directly on her own experience as an artist and her way of living each moment. Her 1948 performance entitled *Dance in the Snow*, photographed by Maurice Perron, was a largely improvised choreography in which she responded with subtle spontaneity to the natural setting in which she found herself. *Promenade* abandons the vocabulary of automatism in favour of a conceptual approach.

While Sullivan does not actually appear in the images, her presence is clearly felt as the subject of a chronological action that we are able to trace on the map that is part of the installation. Her itinerary links two Montreal institutions devoted to the conservation of art –

111 Michael Snow
Authorization 1969
cat. 69

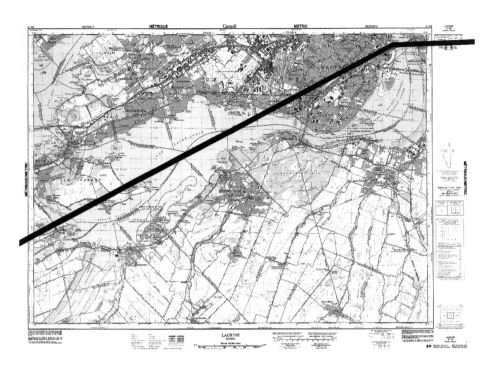

one of the past, the other of the present. Between these two worlds, the sign-infested streets and highways reflect a bustling urban culture. In this work, photography does more than record the artist's performance: it becomes an integral part of the project's process and conception. It provides a marker for each stage of the artist's expedition and allows Sullivan to transcribe her movements through the city in a series of pictures that provide evidence of her own view of the event.

Born in Toronto, in 1933, Bill Vazan studied first at the Ontario College of Art and subsequently at the École des beaux-arts in Paris. In 1968 he abandoned hard-edge painting and embarked on a conceptual and land art practice in which photography plays a vital role. Between 1969 and 1971 he executed several conceptual projects that explored the idea of a line linking a number of geographical points. One of these was *Cross Canada Line* (1969–70, rep. 113), for which Vazan enlisted the collaboration of eight museums and galleries across the country, who agreed to place a line of tape on the floor of one of their exhibition spaces in a position dictated by him. As in some giant game of "join the dots," each point of the carefully planned circuit was connected to the next. This ambitious communications project can be seen as the embodiment of the McLuhanesque dream of the world as a global village, united by media that transcend the frontiers of time and space. Vazan set up the system of coordinates that made the event possible, but it was actually executed by people on the spot at each location and given visible form through photography.

The photographs provided the raw material for the documentation produced by the artist. His goal was not to report the event as it unfolded, but rather to give tangible form to the idea behind it. For each location, Vazan produced two panels – one with a map showing

113   Bill Vazan
Cross Canada Line (details) 1969–70
(reconstructed in 1999)
cat. 88

114   N.E. Thing Co.
North American Time Zone Photo –
VSI Simultaneity Oct.18, 1970 (detail)
1970
cat. 54

the angle of the line at that location, and the second bearing a photographic record of the line's installation and a diagram showing its coordinates. Each pair of panels thus combined the abstract and the concrete, the concept and its realization, enabling spectators to intellectually reconstitute the path of the line, which existed, as a result, as a mental process and imagined place. "After all," said the artist at the time, "the essence of all art is the idea of the experience of it. The actual work that's left is just a shell."[174]

Founded in 1966 in Vancouver by Iain and Ingrid Baxter, the N.E. Thing Co. would act as a stimulus in the contemporary art world, both in Canada and internationally. In their multi-disciplinary practice, photography was used as a medium in the McLuhanesque sense of the word – as a relay between producer and public: "The camera is now being reintroduced as the artist's main working surface (paper, canvas). From altering perception to recording it. Wire-photos and telecopiers and telex and phone, and radio, and TV are all electric power tools for recording information – sensitizing it with ideas – and sending it on, or out into display patterns globally."[175]

North American Time Zone Photo – VSI Simultaneity Oct. 18, 1970 (see rep. 114) illustrates this idea of photography as a transmitter. The project required six artists distributed across Canada's time zones to take a photograph of a specific subject at the same moment. Every fifteen minutes, each participant took a photo on a predetermined theme: time, the nude, still life, urban landscape, earth, air, fire, water, the North, the South, the East, the West, shadow and self-portrait. All used a 35 mm camera and identical materials. Processed in exactly the same way, without alterations or cropping, each of the images was later assembled with the others in its category, creating a panel showing six views of the same subject.

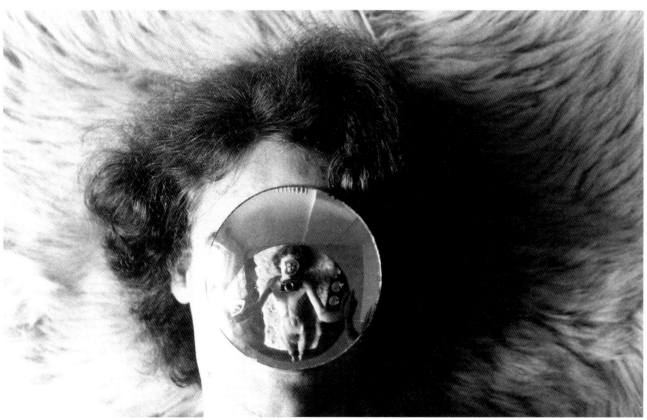

115 AA Bronson
Mirror Sequences (details) 1969-70
cat. 8

While the basic idea, the operational framework and the uniformity of materials would seem likely to reduce subjectivity and to undermine the notion of personal style, the diversity of the images produced indicates the opposite. Although the camera is a machine that methodically records and organizes what it is focused on, the intention of the person holding the instrument reveals itself in the interpretation of the subject and the way it is presented. With its juxtaposition of images, each panel becomes an exploration of simultaneity and an exercise in the organization and communication of visual information. From a single, linear space-time we move into a multifaceted register of a complex ensemble.

From 1969 to 1994, AA Bronson was part of General Idea, a collective whose favoured theme was the role of the artist as creator of mythologies and critic of popular culture (see also "The Expanding Field of Painting," p. 82). In the early days of the group, Bronson and his two fellow members pursued individual practices centered on photography, and the body was the focal point around which Bronson's work of the period revolved: "In 1968, when I began taking self-portraits, I was concerned with the body: more specifically, with my body, and with my body in relation to my friends' bodies. I had no other way to measure the world. Lacking an identity, or any way to judge my separation from others, I began with my physical self."[176]

Among the many works on the theme he produced between 1969 and 1971 is a series of images entitled *Mirror Sequences* (1969–70, rep. 115) that reflect the artist's body in a circular mirror. The goal was to explore the image of the body and the different ways in which the self is perceived by the other. Here, the mirror becomes a protagonist in the interplay between the artist and his image. His own naked form is shot from unusual angles and presented in a series of visual puzzles, where reflections interlock and perspectives and vanishing lines are

(next pages)
116 Roy Kiyooka
Van Gogh and the Bird of Paradise
1970-75
cat. 42

superimposed. The mirror cannot retain the constantly moving images that ripple across its surface: it is the camera that fixes their trace. This personal dimension of Bronson's work would blend into the collective identity of General Idea, which he and his two partners developed using a range of artistic personae.

Roy Kiyooka, already a well-known painter of geometric abstractions, took up photography in 1969 and devoted himself henceforth to a multifaceted conceptual oeuvre that encompassed photography, sculpture, printmaking, video, music and writing. One of his first works from this period was *The Eye in the Landscape Photo/graphs, of The Point, Hornsby Island*, commissioned by the Still Photography Division of the National Film Board of Canada as part of its *B C Almanac(h) C-B* project. In the spring of 1970 Lorraine Monk, executive producer of the Division, asked Jack Dale and Michael de Courcy to mount an exhibition featuring the emerging generation of Vancouver artists. The event assembled the work of fifteen creators, each of whom produced a booklet.[177]

Kiyooka's contribution as a member of this eclectic group was notable for its fusion of art and life. His booklet was a kind of diary of images, made throughout the month of August and consisting of a collage of impressions formed by clusters of pictures showing events from multiple viewpoints. The logic of the sequence was based on free association and visual connections.

Van Gogh and the Bird of Paradise (1970–75, rep. 116) is a fragment of the original project, reworked by Kiyooka in 1975 into its definitive, autonomous form. This grid of thirty images, with its highly personal, even intimate tone, reflects the autobiographical subtext characteristic of the artist's work from this period. It is clearly the artist himself who invites us to witness his reading of a book on Van Gogh, while at the same time recording the process of that reading.

The structuring of the images into a grid conjugates two parallel actions. On the one hand, the turned pages reveal the progress of the reading. The artist and his camera move around the book, shooting it from a succession of fluid viewpoints. This movement establishes the artist as the subject of the scene/image. On the other hand, the changing light creates a series of forms that vacillate between shadow and brilliance. The ensemble presents a sequence of appearances and disappearances that revolve around an interiorized event, which becomes a comprehensive experience for the subject. Kiyooka was among those artists who "wanted to radicalize our time sense, to draw a plenitude of experience out of empty time, to turn clock time into organic time. The allegory of their desire was an artistic method that turned banal photos into literature, into narrative epiphanies."[178]

Like Kiyooka, Michael Morris – born in England in 1942 – worked first as a painter. His contribution to *B C Almanac(h) C-B*, entitled *Alex & Rodger, Rodger & Alex* (1970, rep. 117), was one of his first forays into a form of photography that serves a living art, spontaneous and directly involved in the activities and experiences of its protagonists. Morris's approach reflects the spirit of Fluxus, the neo-Dada inspired European movement of the early sixties that prioritized action rather than the artwork as defined by the classical parameters of artistic production. His practice was especially influenced by the vision of Frenchman Robert Filliou, who defended an art based not on market value or the talent of an exceptional individual but on "innocence," "imagination" and "freedom." Morris's work celebrates the playful, collective nature of the act of recording an event and of the network of relations within which the artist acts as both mobilizer and catalyst.

The situation that is the focus of *Alex & Rodger, Rodger & Alex*, although directed and probably rehearsed, leaves considerable scope for improvisation, both in the actions of the participants and the interventions of the photographer. Two naked men face one another: the mirror being manipulated by one of them captures the sun's reflection and uses it to trace the outline of the body of the other, who is seated in shadow. From a fixed position, Morris records the action while altering and magnifying it. The camera's framing defines the space of the action and splits it in two – the shaded side and the lit side, which the reflection in the mirror brings together. Each snapshot captures an instant, dividing the action into a series of images that reconstruct in photographic form the path of the light moving over the skin of the actor.

Born in Montreal in 1943, Pierre Ayot studied at the city's École des beaux-arts from 1959 to 1963. Rejecting the rules of abstraction then in vogue, he turned for inspiration to Pop art (see also "The Pop Aesthetic," p. 38) and his work as a printmaker moved rapidly towards a figurative approach in which the photographic image occupied centre stage.

Ayot's serigraphs frequently feature the *trompe-l'œil* combination of an object and its image. *Do Not Flush the Toilet While Train Is in Station* (1967, rep. 118) is a case in point: the toilet roll dispenser is an image, but the paper itself is entirely real. From the image – a simple outline – the object represented can be instantly deciphered. The addition of "real" toilet paper heightens the illusion and introduces a note of humour. The somewhat cryptic title is itself a comment on what constitutes a suitable artistic subject: the answer is clearly absolutely anything, including details of everyday life and popular culture. The deliberate vulgarity of the piece makes it a critique of elitist art, to which artistic ability and good taste are all important. Moreover, Ayot's principal technique – serigraphy – is a populist form that entered the art world via printmaking, long considered one of the minor arts. It is a technique that permits the inexpensive, mass reproduction of images and the resulting introduction of artworks into an everyday world that is increasingly image-oriented.

Ayot and the artists of the Pop movement used various forms of printmaking to appropriate the images of popular culture; others, such as Jennifer Dickson, have used the plasticity and malleability of the medium to their own personal ends. Dickson, who was born in South Africa in 1936, studied painting and printmaking in London and in Paris, where between 1960 and 1965 she attended Stanely William Hayter's Atelier 17. In the 1966 series *Alchemic Images*, she developed a personal vocabulary in order to express "levels of reality: external realities as perceived through the senses, and internal reality, which is largely irrational and intuitive." The artist explained: "In my work I want to arrive at a fusion of the two realities. Symbols are the means I use to do this. These have specific personal meanings, apart from their obvious universal ones."[179]

For Dickson, the surface of the print acts as a meeting place for all sorts of different materials and images. The diptych entitled *The Great Apocalypse – Poem for Bel-Ami; The Great Apocalypse – Ritual Procession* (1966, rep. 119) is an assemblage whose diverse, even antagonistic elements are juxtaposed and fused on the support. The artist's first step is to deconstruct the individual images and signs in order to transform them and move them to another level. The eighteenth-century print that occupies the lower part of the composition, a photo transfer of the original, marks the beginning of Dickson's exploration into the relationship between photography and printmaking. The image's shifting from one technique to another transforms it by lending it qualities borrowed from another visual vocabulary. In reconstructing

do not flush the toilet while train is in station.

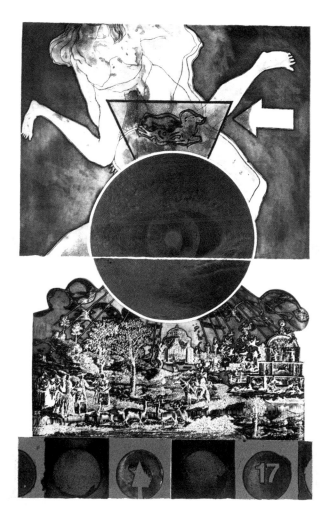

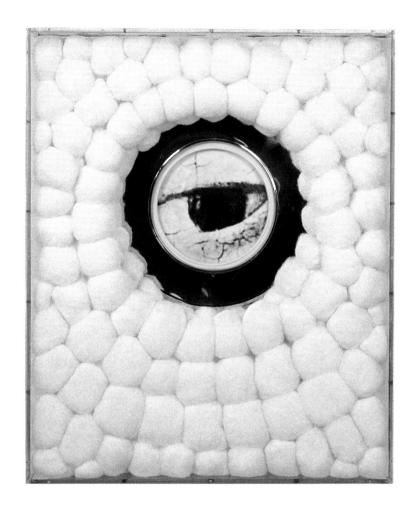

120 Irene F. Whittome
L'œil 1970
cat. 89

her images, Dickson builds a graphic world of unusual formal associations that open the door to a hitherto concealed reality.

From 1965 to 1968, Irene F. Whittome also attended Hayter's studio in Paris. Almost from the outset, her work as printmaker revealed a growing impulse to draw the printed image out of the two-dimensional realm by juxtaposing it with real objects or altering it with the addition of a diversity of manually applied materials. Between 1969 and 1972, a detail from *Portrait of a Young Girl*, painted in the fifteenth century by the Flemish artist Petrus Christus, became a recurring element of Whittome's work, and in *L'œil* (1970, rep. 120) a photomechanical reproduction of this detail – an eye – occupies the centre of the composition. The enlargement of the fragment has revealed the paint's craquelure, which appears as a network of tiny veins. The eye is also overlaid by the mass of small dots left by the serigraphy screen, which makes the reproductive nature of the image eminently clear. By means of such historical quotes and their alteration via the photographic medium, Whittome uses the image to link past and present.

A metal ring encircles the serigraph, repeating the shape of the eye and giving volume to the image. This central motif is surrounded by rows of cotton wool balls, and the whole is contained in a transparent plastic box. The downy texture of the cotton echoes the surface quality of the screenprint, while the balls themselves evoke the pores of the skin. The plastic box places boundaries on the various elements, while simultaneously providing them with a context in which to coexist. Through the resulting interplay of antithetical materials and images, Whittome weaves a tapestry of metaphors that exhaust the meaning of the components by constantly reinventing it and making it entirely open-ended.

All the work produced by Serge Tousignant during the decade following his graduation from the École des beaux-arts de Montréal in 1962 was part of a systematic attempt to deconstruct the art object by means of the image and its many aberrations. On leaving art school, he began producing prints that used a powerfully calligraphic style to explore the intrinsic beauty of matter and colour. Then, gradually, his visual language was refined into a type of formalist abstraction reminiscent of the Plasticiens. In a series of geometric paintings executed in Montreal and London, England, in 1966–67, Tousignant undertook a rigorous investigation into the capacity of colour to structure pictorial space and engender optical illusion. Following this formalist period, he produced a series of sculptures made of metal, glass and mirrors that heightened perceptual aberration.

This research into the strategies of illusion led to a series of five installations that included *Duo-reflex* (1969, rep. 121). In this piece, the setup is minimal: footprints traced on the gallery floor indicate to spectators where they are to stand in relation to the mirrors that are part of the installation. Arranged so as to offer the reflection of a section of their own body and their surroundings integrated into the real image of someone standing opposite them, these mirrors trigger a network of optical fragmentation, transfer and substitution that produces the illusion and constitutes the image. In the artist's skilful installation, the illusion is not some kind of perversion of reality or a formal anomaly designed to mystify the observer. Tousignant is not attempting to draw a clear division between the True and the False: his work is located in the reality of illusion, his art in the shifting world of images that change with each new participant.

In his optical installations, Tousignant is concerned with the "natural" objectivity of the camera and its capacity to introduce illusion in the guise of neutrality and truth. What interests him is photography's impersonality and its status as an optical device. The object is not to produce a true image that structures reality, but a real image that crystallizes a process. In 1972 Tousignant turned definitively to photography, making its mechanisms part of a process of recording ephemeral interventions.

Conclusion

Photography emerged considerably enriched from its self-examination of the sixties. The burst of experimentation that accompanied the challenging and collapsing of forms resulted in a salutary eclecticism. Its capacities have spread from the utilitarian fields of information and communication, which provide us with personal representations of the world and its events, into the realm of art, where it has become an instrument that stamps a new logic on the work of groundbreaking artists. Relying on its own unique vocabulary, photography has ushered in an era of multidisciplinarity.

In the wake of the sixties, we can no longer view and analyze photographs out of context, divorced from the situation that gave rise to them; we now see this medium as an integral part – indeed, the cornerstone – of the world of images for which it is the matrix out of which sprang film, television, video, virtual imaging and the other media. Images of the world and of society now serve as a substitute for the immediate grasp of reality: the systematic "mediaization" of human experience – in the West, at any rate – has begun.

What has fundamentally changed is our relationship to representations of the world and to the mechanisms of imagery. The French psychoanalyst Serge Tisseron describes this new relationship in these terms:

> The *visual* surrounds us without enveloping us and influences us without contributing towards the transformation of our mental processes because it does not contribute to our symbolic operations. It's a little like an article of clothing hanging on a coat rack, a piece of fabric with no body to inhabit and transform it. The garment only exists when worn – otherwise, it's just material. By contrast, the *visual* 'inhabited' by our attention becomes an image. As far as the symbolic process is concerned, it is the gaze that turns the image into a space to be inhabited and transformed – in other words, a space of freedom. But it is the gaze that causes the image's imaginative powers to come alive.[180]

Notes

intro

1 Some of the Structuralist theories that gradually go beyond closed linguistic circles also consider language and knowledge as patriarchal tools of bourgeois domination.

2 See Canadian economist John Kenneth Galbraith, *The Affluent Society*. (Boston, 1958).

3 The author has in mind the evocative title of a book by Roland Barthes, *Writing Degree Zero*. (London, Cape, 1967). First published in French in 1953.

4 The definition of counterculture proposed by Theodore Roszak, history professor at California State University, in "Youth and the Great Refusal," *The Nation* (March 25, 1968) has since then gained ground: "The counter culture is the embryonic cultural base of New Left politics, the effort to discover new types of community, new family patterns, new sexual mores, new kinds of livelihood, new aesthetic forms, new personal identities on the far side of power politics, the bourgeois politics, the bourgeois home, and the Protestant work ethic."

5 See Jean-François Lyotard, *The Postmodern Condition: A Report on Knowledge,* an influential study commissioned initially by the *Conseil des universités du Québec* (Minneapolis, 1984). First published in French in 1979.

6 Gilles Kepel, "La modernité comme différentiation des champs sociaux, politique, religieux, culturel, etc." (loosely translated as: "Modernity as a differentiation of the social, political, religious, cultural spheres, etc.") in *Jihad : expansion et déclin de l'islamisme* (Paris, 2000, coll. "Folio actuel") p. 57. (translated by Anthony F. Roberts in: *Jihad: The Trail of Political Islam*, Cambridge, Mass., 2003).

7 Fredric Jameson, *Postmodernism, or the Cultural Logic of Late Capitalism* (Durham, 1991).

8 Jürgen Habermas, "Modernity: An Unfinished Project," in Hal Foster, ed., *The Anti-Aesthetic: Essays on Postmodern Culture* (Port Townsend, Washington, 1983), pp. 3–15.

9 In 1966, Robert Venturi writes *Complexity and Contradiction in Architecture*, New York, a seminal book on post-modern architecture. The same year, Denise Scott Brown, teacher at UCLA, presents the Las Vegas project. The results of this project will be transcribed by Robert Venturi, Denise Scott Bown, and Steven Izenour in *Learning from Las Vegas: The Forgotten Symbolism of Architectural Form* (Cambridge, Mass., 1977).

10 Gene Youngblood, " Synaesthetic Cinema and Extra-Objective Reality," *Expanded Cinema*, New York, 1970, p. 127: "We have been taught by modern science that the so-called objective world is a relationship between the observer and the observed."

11 Hal Foster, *The Return of the Real: Art and Theory at the End of the Century* (Cambridge, Mass., and London, 1996).

12 Aldous Huxley, *The Doors of Perception* (London, 1954), p. 25.

13 Marshall McLuhan, *Counterblast* (Toronto/Montreal, 1969), p. 120.

14 The concept of 'catching up' (*rattrapage*) was first voiced by the sociologist Marcel Rioux in "Sur l'évolution des idéologies au Québec," *Revue de l'Institut de sociologie*, vol. 41, no. 1 (1968), pp. 95–124.

15 Michael Morris states: "The Canada Council helped us to travel, if we wanted to, and later, also if we wanted to, to remain and work here." Quote from an interview by Peter Selz with Alvin Balkind, "Vancouver Scene and Unscene: A Conceit in Eight Scenes and an Epilogue," *Art in America* (January–February 1970), p. 125.

16 Henry Geldhazer as quoted in Charlotte Townsend, " New York Expert Praises Art Show," *Vancouver Sun*, 22 January 1969.

17 Exhibitions on the effervescence of London, "The Heart of London (Ontario)" in 1968–69, and also on the N.E. Thing Co. from Vancouver in the summer of 1969.

18 The role played by some members of the Regina Five in the revitalization of the Emma Lake Artists' Workshops as well as the group's contribution to the advancement of Canadien art at the turn of the sixties are more closely examined in an other catalogue by the same author, *The Crisis of Abstraction in Canada: The 1950s*, exhib. cat., Ottawa, National Gallery of Canada, 1992. See also John O'Brian, ed., *The Flat Side of the Landscape: The Emma Lake Artists' Workshops*, exhib. cat., Saskatoon, Mendel Art Gallery, 1989.

19 Jack Chambers in Diana Nemiroff, *A History of Artist-Run Spaces in Canada, With Particular Reference to Vehicule, A Space and the Western Front.* MA thesis, Concordia University, Montreal, 1985, p. 6.

20 McLuhan, *Counterblast* (Toronto, 1969), p. 65.

21 Michael Snow in "Michael Snow. A Filmography," *Afterimage*, no. 11 (winter 1982–83), p. 4.

1

22 Marcel Duchamp in an interview with Herbert Crehan broadcast on WBJA FM radio, New York, and published in *Evidence*, no. 3 (fall 1961), Toronto, p. 37.

23 Sarah Milroy, "Greg Curnoe: Time Machines," in Dennis Reid and Matthew Teitelbaum (eds.), *Greg Curnoe: Life and Stuff* (Toronto/Vancouver, 2001), p. 21.

24 Judith Rodger, "Chronology," in Reid and Teitelbaum, *Greg Curnoe*, p. 145.

25 Michel Sanouillet, "The Sign of Dada," *Canadian Art*, vol. 19, no. 2 (March–April 1962), p. 111.

26 "There has appeared in New York recently a new, and still esoteric, genre of spectacle. At first sight apparently a cross between art exhibit and theatrical performance, these events have been given the modest and somewhat teasing name of 'Happenings.' They have taken place in lofts, small art galleries, backyards, and small theatres before audiences averaging between thirty and one hundred persons. To describe a Happening for those who have not seen one means dwelling on what Happenings are not. They don't take place on a stage conventionally understood, but in a dense object-clogged setting which may be made, assembled, or found, or all three. In this setting a number of participants, not actors, perform movements and handle objects antiphonally and in concert to the accompaniment (sometimes) of words, wordless sounds, music, flashing lights, and odors. The Happening has no plot, though it is an action, or rather a series of actions and events. It also shuns continuous rational discourse…" Susan Sontag, "Happenings: An Art of Radical Juxtaposition" (1962), in *Against Interpretation, and Other Essays* (New York, 1979), pp. 263–264.

27 "It was at Black Mountain College that I made what is sometimes said to be the first happening. The audience was seated in four isometric triangular sections, the apexes of which touched a small square performance area that they faced and that led through the aisles between them to the large performance area that surrounded them. Disparate activities, dancing by Merce Cunningham, the exhibitions of paintings and the playing of a Victrola by Robert Rauschenberg, the reading of his poetry by Charles Olson or hers by M. C. Richards from the top of a ladder outside the audience, the piano playing of David Tudor, my own reading of a lecture that includes silences from the top of another ladder outside the audience, all took place within chance-determined periods of time within the over-all time of my lecture." John Cage, "An Autobiographical Statement," delivered in November 1989 at the Inamori Foundation, Kyoto. The full text of this statement is reproduced on the Internet at: http://www.newalbion.com/artists/cagej/autobiog.html (accessed 10.12.04).

28 Josef Albers, quoted in RoseLee Goldberg, *Performance: Live Art 1909 to the Present* (New York, 1979), p. 79.

29 He defined a happening as "the assemblage of events performed or perceived in more than one time and place. Its material environments may be constructed, taken over directly from what is available, or altered slightly; just as its activities may be invented or commonplace. A Happening, unlike a stage play, may occur at a supermarket, driving along a highway, under a pile of rags, and in a friend's kitchen, either at once or sequentially. If sequentially, time may extend to more than a year. The Happening is performed according to plan but without rehearsal, audience, or repetition. It is art but seems closer to life." Allan Kaprow, quoted in *Vancouver: Art and Artists, 1931–1983*, exhib. cat. (Vancouver: Vancouver Art Gallery, 1983), p. 190.

30 In 1965, for example, on the advice of Charles Comfort, then Director of the National Gallery of Canada, Canadian customs authorities ruled that Warhol's silkscreened Brillo boxes were not art, but "merchandise" and therefore subject to import taxes if they were to enter the country.

31 Andy Warhol, quoted in an unreferenced photocopy of a 1966 magazine article, Archives of the Morris and Helen Belkin Art Gallery, University of British Columbia, Vancouver, Alvin Balkind Fonds, Festival of the Contemporary Arts file.

32 "Rayner was involved in a performance piece of a three-person abstract expressionist, over large, action painting at Burton's studio … The nine by twelve foot white photo cartridge paper was stapled over an entire wall." Joan Murray, "Gordon Rayner: Charting the Course," in *Gordon Rayner Retrospective*, exhib. cat. (Oshawa: The Robert McLaughlin Gallery, 1978), p. 9. A detailed account of the creation-happening appears on p. 10.

33 The original group consisted of Dennis Burton, Graham Coughtry, Richard Gorman, Nobuo Kubota, Robert Markle, Gordon Rayner and, on occasion, Michael Snow.

34 Hugo McPherson, "The Isaacs Gallery," *Evidence*, no. 3 (fall 1961), p. 22.

35 The original concept was described thus: "Les Levine discussed his proposed environment … It will consist of 8 large galvanized boxes to which have been attached enormous silver vinyl bags, vacuum cleaner motors will constantly inflate and deflate what can only be described as a large breathing environment." Letter from Brydon Smith (Toronto) to Alvin Balkind (Vancouver), 20 June 1966, Archives of the Morris and Helen Belkin Art Gallery, University of British Columbia, Vancouver, Alvin Balkind Fonds, Festival of the Contemporary Arts file.

36 "A 'happening' – as the Dada-inspired mixed-media performances of the day were called – was being planned for London, Ontario … it was hoped Duchamp could be brought up for the occasion. *The Celebration*, as the London event was called, turned out to be a momentous affair in the artistic life of that city." Dennis Reid, "Marcel Duchamp in Canada," *Canadian Art*, vol. 4, no. 4 (winter 1987), p. 54.

37 For a description of the concept and events of the happening, see Judith Rodger, "Chronology," in Reid and Teitelbaum, *Greg Curnoe*, pp. 145 and 147.

38 On 1 March 1962, Greg Curnoe wrote: "I imagine myself cut in the crotch – corduroy crawling with blood, cut with a stencil knife – by myself … painting in the chair holding my split genitals …" Handwritten document, Archives of the Art Gallery of Ontario, Greg Curnoe Fonds, box no. 2, writings 1956–1984.

39 The original group consisted of John Boyle, John Clement, Greg Curnoe, Bill Exley, Murray Favro, Hugh McIntyre and Art Pratten.

40 Normand Thériault spoke of the "…'medicine cabinets' he exhibited in 1962 at the Museum of Fine Arts." "Le tableau est aussi le monde," *La Presse* (Montreal), 8 March 1969. Around 1968 Iain Baxter of Vancouver would make use of metal bathroom cabinets, transforming them into light boxes.

41 Claude Gosselin, *5 attitudes/1963–1980*, exhib. cat. (Montreal: Musée d'art contemporain, 1981), p. 73.

42 Serge Lemoyne, quoted in Lysiane Gagnon and Normand Cloutier, "Le mot d'ordre des jeunes artistes : après le refus global, l'art total," *Culture vivante*, no. 5 (1967), p. 85.

43 Christian Allègre, "Serge Lemoyne: ne plus regarder la peinture," *Le Devoir* (Montreal), 18 July 1970, p. 11.

44 Serge Lemoyne, pamphlet/manifesto, written and distributed in May 1964 during La Semaine "A," held at the Centre social de l'Université de Montréal.

45 This group included percussionist Jean Sauvageau, poets Baron Filip Gingras and Claude Péloquin, pianist Dominic Macchiagodena, painters Serge Lemoyne and Pierre Cornellier, and dancer Suzanne Verdal.

46 Serge Lemoyne, quoted in Yves Robillard, "Serge Lemoyne et Gilles Boisvert face au Happening," *La Presse* (Montreal), 3 September 1966.

47 See Marc Vachon, *L'arpenteur de la ville : L'utopie urbaine situationniste et Patrick Straram* (Montreal, 2003), p. 97.

2

48 Richard Hamilton, quoted in Mark Francis (ed.), *Les années pop, 1956–1968*, exhib. cat. (Paris: Centre Pompidou, 2001), n.p.

49 Nicole Dubreuil-Blondin, *La Fonction critique dans le Pop Art américain* (Montreal, 1980), p. 9.

50 "Notre perspective," *Parti Pris*, no. 1 (October 1963), p. 2.

51 Quoted in Yves Robillard (ed.), *Québec Underground 1962–1972*, vol. 1 (Montreal, 1973), p. 357.

52 During the occupation of the École des beaux-arts de Montréal, the students developed the concept of a "free university of everyday art" and published a magazine article based on documents from the *Internationale Situationniste* dealing with the question of self-management. This issue is also mentioned in the summaries of the various discussions. See Archives de l'Université du Québec à Montréal, Yves Robillard Fonds, file 146P (201/001).

53 Michèle Grandbois, *L'art québécois de l'estampe 1945–1990. Une aventure, une époque, une collection*, exhib. cat. (Quebec City: Musée du Québec, 1996), p. 51: "Industrial serigraphy was now being used for all manner of things, including logos, wallpaper, food cans, blinds, blow-up toys, electronic billboards, mirrors, stickers and fabric."

54 Interest in Che Guevara and the Cuban cause was revived in left-wing Montreal circles following the Tri-Continental Conference of revolutionary movements held in Cuba on 3 January 1966.

55 As the artist put it so neatly, he painted "Greenbergian abstractions based on skin book photos." Dennis Burton and Joan Murray, *Dennis Burton Retrospective*, exhib. cat. (Oshawa: The Robert McLaughlin Gallery, 1977), p. 22.

56 Ibid.

57 Pierre Elliott Trudeau, "Transcript of Remarks of the Honorable Pierre E. Trudeau at the Liberal Leadership Convention, Apr 5/68," file " Speeches 5 April, 1968 – Remarks at the Liberal Leadership Convention, 1968," National Archives of Canada, Ottawa, box MG 26,013, vol. 40, p. 2. I am grateful to Brian Worobey for his tenacity in tracking down this quotation.

58 Joyce Wieland in an interview with Susan M. Crean, "Notes from the Language of Emotion: A Conversation with Joyce Wieland," *Canadian Art*, vol. 4, no. 1 (spring–March 1987), p. 65.

59 Margaret Trudeau, *Margaret Trudeau: Beyond Reason* (New York, 1979).

60 Greg Curnoe, in *Greg Curnoe: Some Lettered Works 1961–1969*, exhib. cat. (London, Ont.: London Art Gallery, 1975), p. 4.

61 John [Jack] Chambers, "Perceptual Realism," *artscanada*, vol. 24, no. 5 (October 1969), p. 7. Chambers had put the finishing touches to this text on 21 August 1969, while in hospital awaiting the results of diagnostic tests.

62 John B. Boyle, "Continental Refusal/Refus Continental," *20 Cents Magazine* (April 1970), London, Ontario.

63 Greg Curnoe, in Frank Davey (ed.), *Deeds/Abstracts: The History of a London Lot* (London, Ont., 1995), p. 27.

3

64 Marshall McLuhan (Toronto), in a letter to Alvin Balkind (Vancouver), 23 February 1963, Archives of the Morris and Helen Belkin Art Gallery, University of British Columbia, Vancouver, Alvin Balkind Fonds, Festival of the Contemporary Arts file.

65 Aldous Huxley, *The Doors of Perception and Heaven and Hell*, foreword by J. G. Ballard (London, 1994)

66 The Blake quote is taken from "The Marriage of Heaven and Hell," 1790.

67 The term was first used publicly by British psychiatrist Dr. Humphry Osmond during a 1957 meeting of the New York Academy of Sciences. According to Osmond's definition, the word means "mind manifesting." In the late fifties, Osmond conducted his research and clinical trials into the effects of LSD and mescalin in Weyburn, Saskatchewan. See Douglas Martin, "Humphry Osmond, 86, Who Sought Medicinal Value in Psychedelic Drugs, Dies," *The New York Times*, February 22, 2004. Osmond apparently first employed the term in a 1956 letter to Aldous Huxley ("To fathom hell or soar angelic/Just take a pinch of Psychedelic"). See Anne Collins, *In the Sleep Room: The Story of the C.I.A. Brainwashing Experiments in Canada* (Toronto, 1997), p. 129.

68 Huxley, *The Doors of Perception*, p. 14.

69 When interviewed by the author around 1990, both artists said that the study had not seemed to them conclusive.

70 Carolle Gagnon and Ninon Gauthier, *Marcel Barbeau : Le regard en fugue* (Montreal, 1990), p. 142.

71 Strictly speaking, synesthesia means the production of a mental sense impression relating to one sense by the stimulation of another sense, or another part of the body (as in the association of certain sounds with colours). In the late nineteenth century, musicians, poets and painters began using the phenomenon as a source of artistic inspiration. Interest was revived during the sixties, partly owing to the synesthetic effects observed and reported by those who had experimented

with drugs like LSD. Marshall McLuhan employed the concept to describe the impact of the electronic environment on our senses. Gene Youngblood also used the adjective "synesthetic" in his analysis of many of the experimental films produced in New York in the mid-sixties, including Michael Snow's *Wavelength*. See Gene Youngblood, "Synaesthetic Cinema and Extra-Objective Reality," in *Expanded Cinema* (New York, 1970), p. 122.

72 Claude Tousignant, quoted in James D. Campbell, *After Geometry: The Abstract Art of Claude Tousignant* (Toronto, 1995), p. 85.

73 Claude Tousignant, quoted in Pierre Théberge, *Canada art d'aujourd'hui*, exhib. cat. (Brussels: Palais des beaux-arts, 1968), n.p.

74 This apt description comes from Dore Ashton, "Yves Gaucher at the New York Cultural Center," *artscanada*, vol. 32, no. 2 (June 1975), p. 81.

75 Michel Martin, *Yves Gaucher. Récurrences*, exhib. cat. (Quebec City: Musée du Québec, 2000), p. 15.

76 Yves Gaucher, quoted in "Yves Gaucher: Galerie Godard Lefort," *artscanada*, vol. 25, no. 1 (February 1969), p. 45.

77 Les Levine, quoted in Douglas Pringle, "Les Levine: Body Control Systems and John and Mimi's Book of Love, The Isaacs Gallery, Toronto April 1970," *artscanada*, vol. 27, no. 3 (June 1970), p. 60.

78 Les Levine, quoted in Geoffrey James, *Transparent Things/Transparences*, exhib. cat. (Ottawa: The Canada Council, 1977), n.p.

4

79 Rudi Fuchs (ed.), *Royden Rabinowitch: Sculpture 1962/1992*, exhib. cat. (The Hague: Gemeentemuseum, 1992). This catalogue includes an inventory of the artist's work.

80 Kenneth Baker, "Identity and Praxis – The work of David Rabinowitch," in Jochen Poetter (ed.), *David Rabinowitch: Werke 1967–1976* (Stuttgart-Bad Cannstatt, 1992), pp. 62–64.

81 Walter Redinger in an interview with Joan Murray, "A Conversation with Joan Murray and Walter Redinger," *artmagazine*, vol. 9, no. 38/39 (June 1978), p. 63.

82 Serge Tousignant, quoted in Normand Thériault, "Dialoguer avec le spectateur," *La Presse* (Montreal), 23 November 1968.

83 Jean-Pierre Latour, *Serge Tousignant. Signalements : œuvres formelles et géométriques*, exhib. cat. (Montreal: Galerie Graff, 2000), p. 10.

5

84 Constance Naubert Riser, *Jean McEwen: Colour in Depth. Paintings and Works on Paper 1951–1987*, exhib. cat. (Montreal: The Montreal Museum of Fine Arts, 1987), p. 157.

85 This is the expression used by McEwen in a conversation with the author at the artist's home in Montreal, on 6 March 1991.

86 Guido Molinari, "L'expérience plastique," text of a lecture given on 14 March 1974 at the Université du Québec à Montréal, Archives of the National Gallery of Canada, Ottawa, artist's file.

87 Guido Molinari, quoted in Sandra Grant Marchand, *Guido Molinari, une rétrospective*, exhib. cat. (Montreal: Musée d'art contemporain, 1995), p. 17.

88 The arrow metaphor is particularly apposite in light of the artist's Aboriginal origins. Resolutely abstract in her approach, she has nonetheless instilled her art with traces of age-old memories.

89 Rita Letendre, quoted in Anne-Marie Ninacs, *Rita Letendre. Aux couleurs du jour*, exhib. cat. (Quebec City: Musée national des beaux-arts du Québec, 2003), p. 99. Original interview in Gary Michael Dault, "Prolific Artist Works on a Majestic Scale," *Toronto Sun*, 18 October 1977.

90 Bodo Pfeifer, quoted in Eileen Johnson, "Bodo the Bold," *Vancouver Life* (September 1967).

91 Michael Morris, in conversation with the author, Vancouver, 12 September 2000.

92 Ibid.

93 Michael Kimmelman writes: "Early in his career, he invented what came to be called mail art, a modest byway, which consisted mostly of his photocopied drawings and assemblages of found images stuffed into envelopes, sometimes customized for particular people, often conceived to be chain letters and passed on. He sent out thousands of these." See "A Collage in Which Life = Death = Art," *The New York Times*, 6 October 2002.

94 Diana Nemiroff, justification, 30 November 1992, National Gallery of Canada, Ottawa, curatorial file.

95 Although General Idea adopted its group identity and began its joint artistic practice in 1969, it appropriated certain individual works from 1968 in the name of the collective. For more on the precise chronology, see Fern Bayer, *The Search for the Spirit: General Idea 1968–1975*, exhib. cat. (Toronto: Art Gallery of Ontario, 1998), p. 10.

96 AA Bronson, in an e-mail to the author, 1 June 2004.

6

97 Letter from Marshall McLuhan (Toronto) to Alvin Balkind (Vancouver), 25 September 1963, Archives of the Morris and Helen Belkin Art Gallery, University of British Columbia, Vancouver, Alvin Balkind Fonds.

98 Marshall McLuhan, *Counterblast* (Toronto/Montreal, 1969), p. 116.

99 Yves Robillard (ed.), *Québec Underground 1962–1972*, vol. 1 (Montreal, 1973), p. 204.

100 Tony Tascona, quoted in James Patten, "Tony Tascona and the Modern Imagination," in Patricia E. Bovey, Robert Enright and James Patten, *Tony Tascona: Resonance*, exhib. cat. (Winnipeg: Winnipeg Art Gallery, 2001), p. 22.

101 See Jill Johnston, "Liking Things for What They Are," *Canadian Art*, vol. 23, no. 3 (July 1966), p. 15.

102 See Nan R. Piene, "Sculpture and Light: Toronto and Montreal," *artscanada*, vol. 25, no. 5 (December 1968), p. 46–47.

103 Michael Snow, in an interview with Jonas Mekas, "Movie Journal," *The Village Voice* (New York), 27 January 1972, p. 65.

104 Michael Snow, "Landscape," typescript, Archives of the Art Gallery of Ontario, Toronto, Michael Snow Papers, box 14 (6, p. 2).

105 Pierre Boutin, *Le Monde*, press cutting, 5 October 1973, Archives of the Art Gallery of Ontario, Toronto, Michael Snow Papers, box 14 (6).

106 Michael Snow, in Mekas, "Movie Journal," *The Village Voice*, p. 65.

7

107 For more on the evolution of exhibition concepts for the Indian pavilion, see Richard Gordon Kicksee, "'Scaled Down to Size': Contested Liberal Commonsense and the Negotiation of 'Indian Participation' in the Canadian Centennial Celebrations and Expo '67, 1963–1967," 1995. Master's thesis, Queen's University, Kingston.

108 Ross Montour, "Delisle Named to Receive Aboriginal Achievement Award" (online), *The Eastern Door*, vol. 13, no. 1, 23 January 2004, at: http://www.easterndoor.com/VOL.13/13-1.htm (accessed 10.12.04).

109 Doris Shadbolt, in "Harry Malcomson," *The Telegram* (Toronto), 9 September 1967.

110 Norval Morrisseau, *Legends of My People: The Great Ojibway*, ed. Selwyn Dewdney (Toronto, 1965), n.p.

111 I would like to thank Christine Lalonde, Associate Curator of Inuit Art at the National Gallery of Canada, for her help in selecting the Inuit prints included in the exhibition.

112 Pitseolak Ashoona, from recorded interviews by Dorothy Eber, *Pitseolak: Pictures Out of My Life* (Montreal/Toronto, 1972), n.p.

113 Sakiassie Ragee, quoted in Jean Blodgett and Susan Gustavison, *Strange Scenes: Early Cape Dorset Drawings*, exhib. cat. (Kleinburg: McMichael Canadian Art Collection, 1993), p. 98.

114 Terence Heath, *Ronald L. Bloore. Not Without Design*, exhib. cat. (Regina: Mackenzie Art Gallery, 1993), p. 29.

115 Ronald Bloore, "R.L. Bloore on Permanence," *artscanada*, vol. 25, no. 1 (April 1968), p. 31.

116 Clement Greenberg, "Clement Greenberg's View of Art on the Prairies," *Canadian Art*, vol. 20, no. 2 (March–April 1963), p. 92.

117 Art McKay, quoted in *Arthur McKay: Recent Paintings*, exhib. cat. (Vancouver: Vancouver Art Gallery, 1964), n.p.

118 For more on this group, see Ross Fox, *The Canadian Painters Eleven (1953–1960) from The Robert McLaughlin Gallery*, exhib. cat. (Amherst, Mass., Mead Art Museum, Amherst College, 1994).

119 Excerpt from a poem by John Meredith, "The John Meredith Poems Untitled. Unsigned," *Exile*, vol. 1, no. 3 (1972), p. 85.

120 Scott Watson, *Jack Shadbolt*, Vancouver/Toronto, 1990, p. 121.

121 A poem by Jack Shadbolt. I am grateful to the owners of the manuscript for having provided me with a photocopy. A longer version of the poem appears in Scott Watson, *Jack Shadbolt* (Vancouver/Toronto, 1990), p. 123.

8

122 This expression was used by Lucy Lippard in a lecture entitled "Toward a Dematerialized or Non Object Art," given at the Nova Scotia College of Art and Design on 29 November 1969, photocopy of a typescript, Archives of the National Gallery of Canada, Ottawa.

123 Letter from Alvin Balkind (Vancouver) to Mr. and Mrs. Ragley Wright (Seattle), 7 February 1964, Archives of the Morris and Helen Belkin Art Gallery, University of British Columbia, Vancouver, Alvin Balkind Fonds, Festival of the Contemporary Arts file.

124 Letter from Av Isaacs (Toronto) to Douglas Christmas (Vancouver), 26/27 August 1967(?), Archives of York University, Toronto, Av Isaacs Fonds, *Vancouver 5* file (1996–036/014).

125 Nancy Shaw, "Expanded Consciousness and Company Types: Collaboration Since Intermedia and the N.E. Thing Company," in Stan Douglas (ed.), *Vancouver Anthology: The Institutional Politics of Art* (Vancouver, 1991), p. 86.

126 Michael de Courcy, in conversation with the author in New Westminster, B.C., in the spring of 2002. I would like to take this opportunity of thanking him for having shown me his photographs of various Intermedia activities.

127 Iain Baxter made this point in a phone conversation with the author in August 2004.

128 Roy Kiyooka, quoted in Charlotte Townsend, "Kiyooka," *The Vancouver Sun*, 23 January 1970.

129 Roy Kiyooka, quoted in "Roy Kiyooka. 'aumône pour douces paumes,'" exhibition brochure (Paris: Canadian Cultural Centre, 1972), n.p.

130 Roy Kiyooka (Vancouver) in a letter to Pierre Théberge (Ottawa), 15 February 1970, Archives of the National Gallery of Canada, Ottawa, exhibition file of *StoneDGloves: Alms for Soft Palms* [photographs and poems by Roy Kiyooka], circulated from 15 August 1970 to 31 January 1972.

131 Robin Laurence, "Remembering an Artistic Guru," *The Georgia Straight* (Vancouver), 28 May 1998.

132 Roy Kiyooka, *StoneDGloves* (Toronto, 1970), n.p.

133 See Les Levine, "The Best Art School in North America?" *Art in America*, vol. 61, no. 4 (July–August 1973), p. 15.

134 Garry Neill Kennedy, quoted in Robert Stacey and Liz Wylie, *Eighty/Twenty: 100 Years of the Nova Scotia College of Art and Design*, exhib. cat. (Halifax: Art Gallery of Nova Scotia, 1988), p. 76.

135 Garry Neill Kennedy, "The Nova Scotia College of Art and Design and the Sixties: A Memoir," *Canadian Literature*, no. 152/153 (spring–summer 1997), p. 196.

136 Bill Vazan in an interview with John Grande, "A Conversation with Bill Vazan: Cosmological Shadows," *Sculpture*, vol. 21, no. 10 (December 2002), p. 2. This interview is accessible on the Internet at: http://www.sculpture.org/documents/scmag02/dec02/Vazan/Vazan.htm (accessed 10.12.04).

137 Ibid., p. 3.

9

138 Marshall McLuhan, *Understanding Media: The Extensions of Man* (New York, Toronto, London, 1964), p. 189.

139 Ibid., p. 18.

140 Edward Steichen, Introduction to *The Family of Man*, exhib. cat. (New York: Museum of Modern Art, 1955), n.p.

141 Lutz Dille, *Confessions of a Streetwalker*, unpublished manuscript, c. 1980–85, Archives of the Canadian Museum of Contemporary Photography, artist's file.

142 Roloff Beny, in an extract from his autobiographical writings quoted by Mitchell Crites in *Visual Journeys: Roloff Beny* (Vancouver, 1994), p. 61.

143 Rose Macaulay, *Pleasure of Ruins* (London, 1965), p. 26.

144 Henri Cartier-Bresson, *Images à la sauvette* (Paris: Éditions Verve, 1952), n.p. This translation taken from *Photographers on Photography; A Critical Anthology*, Nathan Lyons (ed.) (Englewood Cliffs, N.J., 1966), p. 43.

145 "One Man Show: Sam Tata," *Photo Age*, vol. 9, no. 2 (April 1962), p. 20.

146 Interview with Tess Taconis conducted by Pierre Dessureault in Toronto in November 1982 preparatory to the exhibition *On Assignment*, organized by the Still Photography Division of the National Film Board of Canada, Ottawa.

147 See "A Boy in the Dark," *Star Weekly*, October 7, 1961, and "The Gentle Troublemakers," *Star Weekly*, May 18, 1967.

148 Michel Lambeth, "Statement on Photography," in *Michel Lambeth, Photographer*, exhib. cat. (Ottawa: Public Archives Canada, 1986), p. 60.

149 Nina Raginsky, "Statements," in a brochure published by the Art Gallery of Ontario to accompany the exhibition *Nina Raginsky: Photographs*, August 25 to September 30, 1979, n.p.

150 Michael Semak, "Statement," *Photo Age*, vol. 14, no. 1 (January 1967), p. 17.

151 Pierre Gaudard, introduction to his exhibition *Prisons*, Still Photography Division of the National Film Board of Canada, Ottawa, April 1977, n.p.

152 Orest Semchishen, quoted by par Kate Davis in "Profile: Orest Semchishen," *Photo Communiqué* (winter 1986–1987), p. 9.

153 Gabor Szilasi, introduction to his exhibition *Images of Quebec*, Still Photography Division of the National Film Board of Canada, Ottawa, April 1977, n.p.

154 Michel Saint-Jean, quoted by Jean-Claude Germain in "Le monde de Michel Saint-Jean : à mi chemin entre la tristesse et la colère," *Dimension*, vol. 6, no. 3 (1969), p. 52.

155 Dave Heath in an interview with Michael Torosian in *Extempore – David Heath: Reflections & Ruminations on Art & Personal History* (Toronto, 1988), p. 7.

156 John Max in an interview with Sam Tata in "On Assignment: John Max," *Foto Canada* vol. I, no 3, p. 33.

157 Lyons employed the expression for the exhibition *Toward a Social Landscape*, presented at the George Eastman House in Rochester, New York in 1966, and at the National Gallery of Canada in 1968. This exhibition brought together the work of Bruce Davidson, Lee Friedlander, Garry Winogrand, Danny Lyon and Duane Michaels.

158 Charles Gagnon, speaking of his film *The Sound of Space* (1967–1968), quoted in Philip Fry, *Charles Gagnon*, exhib. cat. (Montreal: The Montreal Museum of Fine Arts, 1978), p. 91.

159 Charles Gagnon, quoted by Jean Dumont in "Charles Gagnon: La photo comme discipline métaphysique," *Le Devoir* (Montreal), 4 April 1992.

160 Tom Gibson in an interview with Martha Langford in *Tom Gibson: False Evidence, Appearing Real* (Ottawa: Canadian Museum of Contemporary Photography, 1993), p. 95.

161 Garry Winogrand, "Understanding Still Photographs," in Brooks Johnson (ed.), *Photography Speaks* (New York, 1989), p. 96.

162 John Flanders, "Ontario Vernacular," *Habitat*, vol. XIII, no. 3 (1970), p. 33.

163 André Malraux, *Le Musée Imaginaire* (Paris, 1965), p. 148. This translation taken from *Museum Without Walls*, trans. Stuart Gilbert and Francis Price (Garden City, New York, 1967), p. 148.

164 Walter Benjamin, "The Flâneur," *The Arcades Project*, trans. Howard Eiland and Kevin McLaughlin (Cambridge, Mass, 1999), p. 417.

165 Jeremy Taylor, *Statement*, brochure accompanying the exhibition *Photography in the Landscape*, Studio 23, Montreal, 4 December 1969, n.p.

166 Ronald Solomon, *Robert Bourdeau* (Ottawa and Toronto, National Film Board of Canada, Still Photography Division in collaboration with Mintmark Press, 1979), n.p.

167 John Szarkowski, *William Eggleston's Guide* (New York: Museum of Modern Art, 1976), p. 6.

168 Guenter Karkutt, *Statement*, unpublished manuscript, Ottawa, National Film Board of Canada, Still Photography Division, September 1970, n.p.

169 Helga Pakasaar, "Memory Images from a City of Tomorrow," *The Just Past of Photography in Vancouver*, exhib. cat. (Vancouver: Presentation House Gallery, 1997), p. 17.

170 Normand Grégoire, "Polyptych two," *Image 7* (Ottawa: National Film Board of Canada, Still Photography Division, 1970), n.p.

171 Benjamin developed this famous idea in "A Short History of Photography" and "The Work of Art in the Age of Mechanical Reproduction." An English translation of the former appears in *Artforum*, vol. 15 (February 1977), and of the latter in *Illuminations* (New York, 1968).

172 Michael Snow, "Notes on the Whys and Hows of My Photographic Works," *Michael Snow Panoramique: Photographic Works & Films 1962–1999*, rep. (Brussels: Société des Expositions du Palais des Beaux-Arts de Bruxelles/Paris: Centre national de la photographie/ Geneva: Centre pour l'image contemporaine Saint-Gervais/ Cinémathèque royale de Belgique, 1999), p. 99.

173 Françoise Sullivan, quoted by Gilles Toupin in "La nostalgie de l'art," *La Presse*, Montreal, January 13, 1973. p. D–14.

174 Bill Vazan, "Artist Draws a Line Across Canada – Why?," *The Sun* (Vancouver), January 10, 1970.

175 N.E. Thing Co., "Some Thoughts re: Communications and Concepts," *You Are Now in the Middle of a N.E. Thing Landscape: Works by Iain and Ingrid Baxter 1965–1971*, exhib. cat. (Vancouver: UBC Fine Arts Gallery, 1993), p. 42.

176 Excerpt from a web project by AA Bronson for the Vienna Secession (October, 2000) entitled *Looking Glass*; accessible on the artist's Web site at http://www.aabronson.com/art/LookingGlass/Wien15.htm (accessed 10.12.04).

177 The fifteen artists were Jack Dale, Michael de Courcy, Christos Dikeakos, Judith Eglington, Gerry Gilbert, Roy Kiyooka, Glen Lewis, Taras Masciuch, Michael Morris, N.E. Thing Co. Ltd., Jone Pane, Timothy Porter, Peter Thomas, Vincent Trasov and Robertson Wood. The fifteen booklets were published in a boxed set by the Still Photography Division of the National Film Board of Canada, Ottawa, in 1970.

178 Robert Linsley, "Roy Kiyooka's Yonville," *art/text*, no. 64 (February–April 1999), Rose Bay (Australia), p. 73.

179 Jennifer Dickson, from a brochure accompanying an exhibition of her paintings and prints, *Through A Glass Darkly*, held at the Arts Centre of the University of Sussex from 8 November to 6 December 1967, Archives of the Canadian Museum of Contemporary Photography, artist's file.

180 Serge Tisseron, *Le bonheur dans l'image* (Paris, 2003), p. 153.

List of Works

National Gallery of Canada
Canadian Museum of Contemporary Photography, see p. 176

National Gallery of Canada (NGC)

cat. 1   Pitseolak Ashoona
Woman Hiding from Spirit 1968 [rep. 64]
colour stonecut on laid japan paper
68.7 x 62.6 cm
National Gallery of Canada, Ottawa
Gift of the Department of Indian and
Northern Affairs, 1989

cat. 2   Pierre Ayot
Untitled 1966 [rep. 16]
Acrylic on masonite
183 x 122 cm
National Gallery of Canada, Ottawa
Purchased 1999

cat. 3   Pierre Ayot
You Let My Toast Burn Again 1969
[rep. 17]
Serigraphy, bread slices and resin on
plexiglas
77 x 50.2 x 5.8 cm
Musée d'art contemporain de Montréal
Gift of Mrs. Madeleine Forcier

cat. 4   Marcel Barbeau
Retina 999 1966 [rep. 34]
Acrylic on canvas
168.3 x 168 cm
Winnipeg Art Gallery
Anonymous Donor

cat. 5   Iain Baxter
Red Still Life 1965 [rep. 33]
Vacuumed-formed plastic relief
67.6 x 84.7 x 5 cm
Art Gallery of Windsor
Gift of the artist, 2001

cat. 6   Ronald Bloore
Painting No. 11 1965 [rep. 66]
Oil on masonite
121.5 x 243.7 cm
National Gallery of Canada, Ottawa
Purchased 1965

cat. 7   John Boyle
Rebel Series: Totem 1967 [rep. 30]
Oil on plywood, painted on both sides
214.2 x 61.6 x 1.2 cm (irregular)
National Gallery of Canada, Ottawa
Purchased 1969

Rebel Series: Big Bear and Brendan
1967 [rep. 30]
Oil on plywood, painted on both sides
161.4 x 60.7 x 1.2 cm (irregular)
National Gallery of Canada, Ottawa
Gift of Janet Perlman Boyle, Victoria,
2000

Rebel Series: Louis and Gregory 1967
[rep. 30]
Oil on plywood, painted on both sides
110.2 x 60.7 x 1.2 cm (irregular)
National Gallery of Canada, Ottawa
Gift of the artist, Allenford, 2000

cat. 8   Claude Breeze
Sunday Afternoon: From an Old
American Photograph c.1964–65
[rep. 32]
Acrylic on canvas
258.6 x 167.1 cm
National Gallery of Canada, Ottawa
Acquired 1999

cat. 9   Dennis Burton
Mother, Earth, Love 1965 [rep. 21]
Oil and acrylic copolymer on canvas
152.4 x 203.2 cm
Art Gallery of Ontario, Toronto
Gift from the Junior Women's
Committee Fund, 1965

cat. 10   Dennis Burton
Mothers and Daughters 1966 [rep. 22]
Oil, acrylic copolymer and graphite on
linen canvas
152.2 x 152.6 cm
The Robert McLaughlin Gallery,
Oshawa
Purchase 1976

cat. 11   Jack Bush
English Visit 1967 [rep. 51]
Acrylic on canvas
208.2 x 281.9 cm
Anne Lazare-Mirvish, Toronto

cat. 12   Eric Cameron
Reds and Yellows on Green (type 111q,
½" tape) 1968 [rep. 55]
Oil on canvas, mounted on fibreboard
183 x 183 x 6.8 cm
National Gallery of Canada, Ottawa
Gift of the artist, Calgary, 1992

cat. 13   Jack Chambers
Victoria Hospital 1969–70 [rep. 29]
Oil on wood
121.9 x 243.8 cm
Private collection

cat. 14   Greg Curnoe
Hurdle for Art Lovers 1962 [rep. 7]
Assemblage of wood, cast iron, plastic
belt, oil-based paint, ink, silver knives,
stainless steel knives with wooden and
plastic handles, aluminum knitting needles, bamboo stick, silver spoons, steel
screw-driver blade, and mastic knife
99 x 158.5 x 26.5 cm
National Gallery of Canada, Ottawa
Purchased 1994

cat. 15   Greg Curnoe
The True North Strong and Free
[rep. 27]
No. 1–Canada Feeds the Brain! G.C.
No. 2–Close the 49th Parallel, Etc.
No. 3–Can. CostsLess than Drugs
No. 4–Canada Always Loses!
No. 5–Did Chartier Die in Vain??
19 April 1968 [rep. 27]
No. 1: Stamp pad ink and polyurethane
on paper on plywood; nos. 2–5: Stamp
pad ink and polyurethane on plywood
59.7 x 63.5 cm each, 59.7 x 317.5 cm
assembled
Museum London, Ontario

cat. 16   Greg Curnoe
View of Victoria Hospital, Second Series
(February 10, 1969-March 10, 1971)
1969–71 [rep. 28]
Oil, rubber stamp and ink, graphite,
and wallpaper on plywood, in plexiglas
strip frame, with audiotape, tapeplayer,
loudspeakers, and eight-page text
(photocopied from a rubber-stamped
notebook)
243.8 x 487 cm assembled
National Gallery of Canada, Ottawa
Purchased 1971

cat. 17   François Dallegret
US Paper Dollar 1968 [rep. 18]
serigraphy on Kromekote paper
36 x 105 cm
Artist, Montreal

cat. 18   François Dallegret
US Silver Dollar 1968 [rep. 19]
Serigraphy on acetate mirror finish
36 x 105 cm
Collection of the artist, Montreal

cat. 19   Jean-Marie Delavalle
Roller 1968 [rep. 48]
Steel with enamel paint
15.5 x 129 x 129 cm
Musée national des beaux-arts du
Québec, Quebec City
Gift of Mr. René Crépeau

cat. 20   Murray Favro
Guitar #1 1966 [rep. 8]
Wood, masonite, enamel and guitar
hardware
108 x 32 x 7 cm
David Rabinowitch, New York

cat. 21   Brian Fisher
Indirections No. 1 1968 [rep. 35]
Acrylic on canvas
172.6 x 172.6 cm
Vancouver Art Gallery
Gift of J.R. Longstaffe

cat. 22   Charles Gagnon
No Vacancy 1962 [rep. 11]
Collage of papers and objects with
enamel paint in a glazed wooden box
65.2 x 80.9 x 14.2 cm
National Gallery of Canada, Ottawa.
Gift from the Estate of Charles
Gagnon, Montreal, 2004

cat. 23   Charles Gagnon
November Steps 1967–68 [rep. 38]
Oil on canvas
183 x 365.6 cm
National Gallery of Canada, Ottawa
Purchased 1968

cat. 24   Yves Gaucher
Triptych: Signals, Another Summer;
Signals, Very Softly; Silences/Silence
1966 [rep. 37]
Acrylic on canvas
203.2 x 152.7 cm (each)
203.2 x 483.6 cm (overall)
Art Gallery of Ontario, Toronto
Purchased with assistance of the
Canada Council Special Purchase
Assistance Program and Wintario,
1977

cat. 25   General Idea
Pascal 1968–69 [rep. 56]
Acrylic and latex on canvas
201.3 x 300 cm
AA Bronson, New York

cat. 26   Michael Hayden
Head Machine 1967 [rep. 61]
Anodized aluminum, Plexiglas, acrylic,
fluorescent and phosphorescent paint,
fluorescent lights, stroboscope and
sound
244 x 244 x 244 cm
National Gallery of Canada, Ottawa
Purchased 1969

cat. 27   Jacques Hurtubise
Eloise 1969 [rep. 59]
Neon tubes, light bulbs, and aluminum
198 x 121.5 x 29 cm
Canada Council Art Bank, Ottawa

cat. 28   Garry Neill Kennedy
Bisected 1969 [rep. 78]
41 gelatin silver prints
7.6 x 610 cm (installed)
Art Gallery of Windsor, Ontario
Purchased with financial support from
the Canada Council for the Arts, Acqui-
sitions Assistance Program, and with
funds from the Walter and Duncan
Gordon Foundation and the Art Gallery
of Windsor Volunteer Committee, 2000

cat. 29   Roy Kiyooka
StoneDGloves 1970 [rep. 75]
Gelatin silver print, mounted on
cardboard
100.4 x 67,9 cm
National Gallery of Canada, Ottawa
Purchased 1998

cat. 30   Roy Kiyooka
StoneDGloves 1970 [rep. 76]
Gelatin silver print, mounted on
cardboard
67.9 x 100.4 cm
National Gallery of Canada, Ottawa
Purchased 1998

cat. 31   Roy Kiyooka
StoneDGloves 1970 [rep. 77]
Gelatin silver print, mounted on card-
board
67.9 x 100.4 cm
National Gallery of Canada, Ottawa
Purchased 1998

cat. 32   Gary Lee-Nova
Menthol Filter Kings 1967 [rep. 31]
Acrylic on canvas
152.7 x 121.9 cm
Vancouver Art Gallery
Murrin Estate Funds

cat. 33   Serge Lemoyne
Ironing Board (Cape Canaveral) 1963
[rep. 12]
Oil and retail enamel paint on wooden
ironing board with cotton
batting and fabric
143.7 x 48.5 x 8 cm
National Gallery of Canada, Ottawa
Purchased 1998

cat. 34   Serge Lemoyne
Quebec Prisoner of Confederation
1969 [rep. 13]
Acrylic on glass
79 x 59 cm
Musée national des beaux-arts du
Québec, Quebec City

cat. 35   Rita Letendre
Lodestar 1970 [rep. 52]
Acrylic on canvas
366 x 274 cm
Canada Council Art Bank, Ottawa

cat. 36   Les Levine
Untitled 1965 [rep. 5]
silkscreen on acetate transparency in
a lightbox
80 x 65.1 x 15 cm
Art Gallery of Ontario, Toronto
Gift of Ann and Harry Malcolmson, 1990

cat. 37   Les Levine
Slipcover 1966 [rep. 6]
Environment of mixed media
56 m^2
Reconstructed and adapted in 2004
by The National Gallery of Canada in
collaboration with the artist

cat. 38   Les Levine
Topesthesia 1968 1968 [rep. 41]
Six photographs on mat board
63 x 72 cm
Canada Council Art Bank, Ottawa

cat. 39   Les Levine
Plug Assist II 1966 [rep. 60]
Vacuum formed uvex plastic
128 x 55 x 88 cm
Art Gallery of Hamilton
Gift of Nancy Hushion, 1981

cat. 40   Jean McEwen
Jubilant Red 1963 [rep. 49]
Oil on canvas
269 x 450 cm
Power Corporation of Canada,
Montreal

cat. 41   Art McKay
Blue Image 1966 [rep. 67]
Oil on masonite
122 x 182.5 cm
Canada Council Art Bank, Ottawa

cat. 42   John Meredith
Prophecy 1967   [rep. 68]
Oil on canvas
198.7 x 162.2 cm
National Gallery of Canada, Ottawa
Purchased 1967

cat. 43   Guido Molinari
Orange and Green Bi-serial 1967
[rep. 50]
Acrylic on canvas
203 x 363 cm
National Gallery of Canada, Ottawa
Purchased 1968

cat. 44   Guy Montpetit
Series E – Sex Machine No. 8 1969
[rep. 20]
Acrylic on canvas
204 x 163 cm
Canada Council Art Bank, Ottawa

cat. 45   Michael Morris
Peking Letter 1968   [rep. 54]
Acrylic on canvas with mirrors and
plexiglas
184 x 323 cm
Canada Council Art Bank, Ottawa

cat. 46   Norval Morrisseau (Copper
Thunderbird)
Merman Ruler of Water 1969   [rep. 63]
Acrylic on paper
101.6 x 162.5 cm
McMichael Canadian Art Collection,
Kleinburg, Ontario
Gift of Mr. and Mrs. James J. Casey

cat. 47   Jean-Paul Mousseau
Untitled (Dolmen Series) 1961
[rep. 58]
Fibreglass, metal mesh, coloured
resin,
metal base and electrical equipment
with neons
185.5 x 46 x 40.2 cm
Katerine Mousseau, Montreal

cat. 48   N.E. Thing Co.
ACT No. 19: Marcel Duchamp's Total
Art Production Except His Total Ready-
Made Production (1968)/ ART No. 19:
Marcel Duchamp's Total Ready-Made
Production Except His Total Art Produc-
tion (1968) 1969   [rep. 70]
Felt pen and collage on black & white
photograph
70.6 x 100.2 cm
National Gallery of Canada, Ottawa
Purchased 1970

cat. 49   N.E. Thing Co.
ART No. 16: Robert Smithson's "Non-
Sites" (1968) 1969   [rep. 71]
Felt pen and collage on black & white
photograph
70.4 x 100.3 cm
National Gallery of Canada, Ottawa
Purchased 1970

cat. 50   N.E. Thing Co.
Telexed Triangle 1969   [rep. 72]
telex, b/w offset lithograph (map),
felt pen, foil seal, offset lithography
on paper
45.6 x 60.9 cm
Morris and Helen Belkin Art Gallery,
Vancouver

cat. 51   N.E. Thing Co.
Lucy Lippard Walking Towards True
North 1969   [rep. 73]
silver print, felt pen, foil seal, b/w offset
lithograph on paper
45.6 x 60.9 cm
Morris and Helen Belkin Art Gallery,
Vancouver

cat. 52   N.E. Thing Co.
Circular Walk Inside Arctic Circle
Around Inuvik, N.W.T. 1969   [rep. 74]
18 silver prints, felt pen, ink stamp, foil
seal, offset lithograph on paper
44 x 44 cm
Morris and Helen Belkin Art Gallery,
Vancouver

cat. 53   Bodo Pfeifer
Untitled 1967   [rep. 53]
Acrylic on canvas
185.7 x 299 cm
Vancouver Art Gallery
McLean Foundation Grant

cat. 54   David Rabinowitch
The Phantom: Conic (Elliptical) Plane
with 2 Double Breaks I (Convergent)
1967   [rep. 45]
hot-rolled steel
10 x 305 x 95.3 cm
National Gallery of Canada, Ottawa
Purchased 1978

cat. 55   Royden Rabinowitch
Barrel Construction: Double Curvature
at Right Angles 1966 ?   [rep. 42]
oak barrel staves and bottoms
19 x 87 x 89 cm
National Gallery of Canada, Ottawa
Gift of an anonymous donor, 2000

cat. 56   Royden Rabinowitch
Barrel Construction: Double Curvature
at Right Angles 1966 ?   [rep. 43]
oak barrel staves
21.5 x 88 x 93 cm
National Gallery of Canada, Ottawa
Gift of an anonymous donor, 2000

cat. 57   Royden Rabinowitch
Barrel Construction: Double Curvature
at Right Angles 1966 ?   [rep. 44]
oak barrel staves
18 x 87 x 92 cm
National Gallery of Canada, Ottawa
Gift of an anonymous donor, 2000

cat. 58   Sakiassie Ragee
Sea Goddess Feeding Young 1961
[rep. 65]
stonecut on laid japan paper
30.7 x 41.3 cm
National Gallery of Canada, Ottawa
Gift of the Department of Indian and
Northern Affairs, 1989

cat. 59   Gordon Rayner
Homage to the French Revolution 1963
[rep. 1]
assemblage of wood, metal, cardboard
with paint
179.5 x 114.3 x 19 cm
Art Gallery of Ontario, Toronto
Purchase, 1964

cat. 60   Walter Redinger
Spermatogenesis #1 1968   [rep. 46]
fibreglass
91.5 x 125.5 x 297 cm
Canada Council Art Bank, Ottawa

cat. 61   Henry Saxe
Collage No. 2 1961   [rep. 10]
Acrylic and mixed media on panel
92.5 x 70.7 cm
The Montreal Museum of Fine Arts
Gift of Esperanza and Mark Schwartz

cat. 62   Jack Shadbolt
The Bride 1969–74   [rep. 69]
pen and ink, latex, acrylic, crayon and
conté on watercolour board
151.3 x 304.8 cm (a triptych)
Private collection

cat. 63   Michael Snow
Window 1960   [rep. 2]
wood, acrylic, polyethylene, glass,
paper, cotton, wire, sheet metal,
chrome-plated sheet metal
86.4 x 67.3 x 10.2 cm
National Gallery of Canada, Ottawa
Purchased 1970

cat. 64   Michael Snow
Atlantic 1967 (reconstructed in 1980)
[rep. 39]
metal, photographs, wood, arborite
171.1 x 245.1 x 39.9 cm
Art Gallery of Ontario, Toronto
Purchase 1980

cat. 65   Michael Snow
Five Girl-Panels 1964   [rep. 40]
acrylic on five canvases
15.2 x 101.6 cm, 63.5 x 83.8 cm, 134.6 x
50.8 cm, 177.7 x 24.5 cm, 35.5 x 199.3 cm
Department of Foreign Affairs and
International Trade Canada
Courtesy of Canada's Consulate
General in Los Angeles

cat. 66   Michael Snow
De La 1969–72   [rep. 62]
aluminum and steel mechanical
sculpture with surveillance camera,
electronic controls, and four monitors
189.2 x 142.2 cm without base
base: 45.7 x 243.8 cm diameter
National Gallery of Canada, Ottawa
Purchased 1972

cat. 67   Tony Tascona
Yellow Transmission 1969   [rep. 57]
Lacquer on masonite
110.5 x 111.6 cm
Faculty of Law, University of Manitoba,
Winnipeg

cat. 68   Claude Tousignant
Chromatic Accelerator 96–10–68
October 1968   [rep. 36]
acrylic on canvas
243.8 cm diameter
Artist, Montreal

cat. 69   Serge Tousignant
Exit 1966   [rep. 47]
painted steel
41.5 x 206 x 40.5 cm
Canada Council Art Bank, Ottawa

cat. 70   Tony Urquhart
Pillar Landscape 1969   [rep. 9]
papier mâché, wire, nails, paint, on
wood base
102.5 x 39.6 cm (including base)
Art Gallery of Windsor, Ontario
Purchase 1969

cat. 71   Bill Vazan
Land Filling (Water Depletion – Silting –
Land Reclamation [Political]) 1966–69
[rep. 14]
Collage of map components
51 x 66 cm
Collection of the artist, Montreal

cat. 72   Bill Vazan
North Reclaim (Lakes Dry Up –
Sediment Pile Up – Rebound Up-French
Reclaim) 1966–69 [rep. 15]
Collage of map components
51 x 66 cm (appr.)
Artist, Montreal

cat. 73   Bill Vazan
14 Time Lines Readied 1969 (printed
2004)
Square of Ripples 1967–69 (printed 2004)
[rep. 79]
Chromogenic print (Lambra-Flex
process)
66.2 x 99 cm (image)
152.4 x 127 cm (print)
Artist, Montreal

cat. 74   Bill Vazan
Two Angles Readied 1969 (printed 2004)
Square with Tangents 1967–69 (printed
2004) [rep. 80]
Chromogenic print
66.2 x 99 cm (image)
152.4 x 127 cm (print)
Artist, Montreal

cat. 75   Bill Vazan
Low Tide Sand Form – Level – Side to
Side 1967–69 (reprinted 2004)
Low Tide Sand Form – Pyramid After
High Tide 1967–69 (reprinted 2004)
[rep. 81]
Chromogenic print
66.2 x 99 cm (image)
152.4 x 127 cm (print)
Artist, Montreal

cat. 76   Bill Vazan
Low Tide Sand Form – Impact Crater
1969 (reprinted 2004)
2" High Tide Level 1969 (reprinted
2004) [rep. 82]
Chromogenic print (Lambra-Flex
process)
66.2 x 99 cm (image)
152.4 x 127 cm (print)
Artist, Montreal

cat. 77   Bill Vazan
Low Tide Sand Form 1969 (reprinted
2004)
After One High Tide 1969 (reprinted
2004) [rep. 83]
Chromogenic print
66.2 x 99 cm (image)
152.4 x 127 cm (print)
Artist, Montreal

cat. 78   Joyce Wieland
Young Woman's Blues 1964 [rep. 3]
Mixed media construction
44.5 x 33 x 22.9 cm
The University of Lethbridge Art
Collection
Purchased 1986 with funds provided
by the Province of Alberta Endowment
Fund.

cat. 79   Joyce Wieland
Home Movie 1966 [rep. 4]
Mixed media
104.6 x 20 cm
Geraldine Sherman and Robert
Fulford, Toronto

cat. 80   Joyce Wieland
Balling 1961 [rep. 23]
oil on canvas
193.2 x 233.6 cm
National Gallery of Canada, Ottawa
Purchase 1968

cat. 81   Joyce Wieland
Reason over Passion 1968 [rep. 24]
quilted cotton
256.5 x 302.3 x 8 cm
National Gallery of Canada, Ottawa
Purchase 1970

cat. 82   Joyce Wieland
La raison avant la passion 1968–69
[rep. 25]
quilted cotton, commercial and
domestic dyes
244.7 x 305.5 x 8 cm
Estate of Pierre Elliott Trudeau,
Montreal

cat. 83   Joyce Wieland
O Canada 1969 [rep. 26]
Lithograph in red on wove paper
57.4 x 76.4 cm
National Gallery of Canada, Ottawa
Purchased 1971

cat. 1   Pierre Ayot
Do Not Flush the Toilet While Train Is
in Station 1967 [rep. 118]
Silkscreen print and bathroom tissue
66 x 51 cm
Musée national des beaux-arts du
Québec, Quebec

cat. 2   Roloff Beny
Ancient Cathedral in Antigua,
Guatemala 1968 [rep. 85]
Gelatin silver print
50.2 x 38 cm
Canadian Museum of Contemporary
Photography, Ottawa

cat. 3   Roloff Beny
Polonnāruwa, Ceylon 1962
Gelatin silver print
20.3 x 25.8 cm
Canadian Museum of Contemporary
Photography, Ottawa

cat. 4   Robert Bourdeau
Ireland 1967 [rep. 105]
Gelatin silver print
19.2 x 24 cm
Canadian Museum of Contemporary
Photography, Ottawa

cat. 5   Robert Bourdeau
Ontario 1970
Gelatin silver print
11.7 x 16.8 cm
Canadian Museum of Contemporary
Photography, Ottawa

cat. 6   Robert Bourdeau
Untitled 1969
Gelatin silver print
19.3 x 24.5 cm
Canadian Museum of Contemporary
Photography, Ottawa

cat. 7   Robert Bourdeau
Nova Scotia 1968
Gelatin silver print
24.3 x 19.3 cm
Canadian Museum of Contemporary
Photography, Ottawa

cat. 8   AA Bronson
Mirror Sequences 1969–70 [rep. 115]
7 Gelatin silver prints
6 elements 11.7 x 19 cm
1 element 25.4 x 20.3 cm
Collection of the artist

cat. 9   Walter Curtin
Stripper Ann Howe with Reporter
Robert Thomas Allen, Toronto 1960
[rep. 86]
Gelatin silver print
33.6 x 26.4 cm
Canadian Museum of Contemporary
Photography, Ottawa

cat. 10   Walter Curtin
Carnaby Street, London England 1967
Gelatin silver print
33.7 x 23.5 cm
Canadian Museum of Contemporary
Photography, Ottawa

cat. 11   Walter Curtin
Tokyo-born Kazuyoshi Akiyama,
rehearses the Toronto Symphony,
Massey Hall, Toronto 1968–69
Gelatin silver print
23.1 x 34.3 cm
Canadian Museum of Contemporary
Photography, Ottawa

cat. 12   Jack Dale
Cubed Woman No. 5 1970 [rep. 110]
Photosentized glass, Plexiglas
89 x 51 x 51 cm
Canadian Museum of Contemporary
Photography, Ottawa

cat. 13   Jennifer Dickson
The Great Apocalypse – Poem for Bel-
Ami; The Great Apocalypse – Ritual
Procession 1966 [rep. 119]
Etching and photo transfer
57.3 x 157.5 cm
Musée national des beaux-arts du
Québec, Quebec

cat. 14   Lutz Dille
New York, U.S.A. 1962 [rep. 84]
Gelatin silver print
22.6 x 29.3 cm or 22. 9 x 30.5 cm
With the kind permission of the
Stephen Bulger Gallery, Toronto

cat. 15   Lutz Dille
Speaker's Corner, London, England
1961
Gelatin silver print
38.3 x 48.5 cm
Canadian Museum of Contemporary
Photography, Ottawa

cat. 16   Lutz Dille
Naples, Italy 1962
Gelatin silver print
38.2 x 48.9 cm
Canadian Museum of Contemporary
Photography, Ottawa

cat. 17   John Flanders
Coke and Pepsi Signs Reflected in a
Barber Shop Window, Lyndhurst,
Ontario 1966–70 [rep.101]
Gelatin silver print
33.8 x 22.7 cm
Canadian Museum of Contemporary
Photography, Ottawa

cat. 18   John Flanders
Lisson's Cold Storage and The Red
and White Stores, Merrickville, Ontario
1966–70
Gelatin silver print
22.7 x 34.5 cm
Canadian Museum of Contemporary
Photography, Ottawa

cat. 19   John Flanders
Photographs in a Window Showing Five
Generations, Pakenham, Ontario 1967
Gelatin silver print
22.9 x 34 cm
Canadian Museum of Contemporary
Photography, Ottawa

cat. 20   Marc-André Gagné
Untitled 1969 [rep. 108]
Gelatin silver print
32.5 x 21.6 cm
Canadian Museum of Contemporary
Photography, Ottawa

cat. 21   Marc-André Gagné
Untitled 1967
Gelatin silver print
29.4 x 25.2 cm
Canadian Museum of Contemporary
Photography, Ottawa

cat. 22   Marc-André Gagné
Untitled 1967
Gelatin silver print
32.4 x 24.4 cm
Canadian Museum of Contemporary
Photography, Ottawa

cat. 23   Charles Gagnon
Greenwich Village, New York City 1966
[rep. 98]
Gelatin silver print
23.7 x 34.8 cm
Canadian Museum of Contemporary
Photography, Ottawa

cat. 24   Charles Gagnon
New York State, near Albany 1966
Gelatin silver print
23.1 x 34.4 cm
Canadian Museum of Contemporary
Photography, Ottawa

cat. 25   Charles Gagnon
Untitled, Maine 1965
Gelatin silver print
23.6 x 34.8 cm
Canadian Museum of Contemporary
Photography, Ottawa

cat. 26   Charles Gagnon
Men's Room, Union Station, Toronto
1969
Gelatin silver print
16.5 x 25.2 cm
Canadian Museum of Contemporary
Photography, Ottawa

cat. 27   Pierre Gaudard
Pointe-Saint-Charles Factory,
Montreal, Quebec 1969 **[rep. 92]**
Gelatin silver print
20.5 x 30.4 cm
Canadian Museum of Contemporary
Photography, Ottawa

cat. 28   Pierre Gaudard
Demonstration of the unemployed in
East Montreal 1969
Gelatin silver print
20.4 x 30.5 cm
Canadian Museum of Contemporary
Photography, Ottawa

cat. 29   Pierre Gaudard
Roy Display Co., Montreal 1970
Gelatin silver print
21.4 x 30.4 cm
Canadian Museum of Contemporary
Photography, Ottawa

cat. 30   Tom Gibson
My Shadow at Comber, near Chatham,
Ontario 1970 **[rep. 99]**
Gelatin silver print
21.7 x 32.6 cm
Canadian Museum of Contemporary
Photography, Ottawa

cat. 31   Tom Gibson
Riding Boots, Toronto 1969
Gelatin silver print
18.3 x 37.7 cm
Canadian Museum of Contemporary
Photography, Ottawa

cat. 32   Tom Gibson
Funeral Parlour, Toronto 1970
Gelatin silver print
21.7 x 32.7 cm
Canadian Museum of Contemporary
Photography, Ottawa

cat. 33   Tom Gibson
Toronto 1970
Gelatin silver print
12.9 x 19.6 cm
Canadian Museum of Contemporary
Photography, Ottawa

cat. 34   Normand Grégoire
Polyptych Two 1969 **[rep. 109]**
125 slides with a soundtrack by
Robert Blondin
24 minutes 33 seconds
Canadian Museum of Contemporary
Photography, Ottawa

cat. 35   Dave Heath
Meditation (in 5 parts) c. 1964 **[rep. 96]**
Portfolio of six plates with gelatin silver
prints, illustration and texts mounted
on board
35.8 x 43.4 each
Canadian Museum of Contemporary
Photography, Ottawa

cat. 36   Fred Herzog
Rescue, Vancouver 1960 **[rep. 107]**
Chromogenic print
27.8 x 35.4 cm
Canadian Museum of Contemporary
Photography, Ottawa

cat. 37   Fred Herzog
Chinese Store, Vancouver 1960
Gelatin silver print
25.6 x 34.3 cm
Canadian Museum of Contemporary
Photography, Ottawa

cat. 38   Fred Herzog
"U. R. Next," Vancouver 1960
Chromogenic print
37 x 34.7 cm
Canadian Museum of Contemporary
Photography, Ottawa

cat. 39   Guenter Karkutt
Crusader 1965 **[rep. 106]**
Gelatin silver print
34.2 x 27.2 cm
Canadian Museum of Contemporary
Photography, Ottawa

cat. 40   Guenter Karkutt
Symbol 1965
Gelatin silver print
27 x 34.8 cm
Canadian Museum of Contemporary
Photography, Ottawa

cat. 41   Guenter Karkutt
GEFAEHRLICH IST'S DURCH'S MOOR
ZU GEH'N (It is Dangerous to Go
Through the Bog) 1965
Gelatin silver print
19.1 x 23.8 cm
Canadian Museum of Contemporary
Photography, Ottawa

cat. 42   Roy Kiyooka
Van Gogh and the Bird of Paradise
1970–75 **[rep. 116]**
30 gelatin silver print mounted and
framed
112.5 x 163.6 cm
Canadian Museum of Contemporary
Photography, Ottawa

cat. 43   Michel Lambeth
St. Joseph's Convent School, Toronto,
Ontario 1960 **[rep. 89]**
Gelatin silver print
29.1 x 35.5 cm
Canadian Museum of Contemporary
Photography, Ottawa

cat. 44   Michel Lambeth
Orange Parade, Toronto, Ontario 1960
Gelatin silver print
35.5 x 26.7 cm
Canadian Museum of Contemporary
Photography, Ottawa

cat. 45   Michel Lambeth
Allen Gardens, Toronto, Ontario 1965
Gelatin silver print
25.4 x 17.3 cm
Canadian Museum of Contemporary
Photography, Ottawa

cat. 46   John Max
Julian Beck and the Living Theatre,
Paris, France 1967 **[rep. 97]**
Gelatin silver print
33.8 x 50 cm
Canadian Museum of Contemporary
Photography, Ottawa

cat. 47   John Max
Untitled 1965–70
Gelatin silver print
48 x 32.5 cm
Canadian Museum of Contemporary
Photography, Ottawa

cat. 48   John Max
Untitled 1965–70
Gelatin silver print
48 x 32.5 cm
Canadian Museum of Contemporary
Photography, Ottawa

cat. 49   John Max
Untitled 1963
Gelatin silver print
50.2 x 40.9cm
National Gallery of Canada, Ottawa

cat. 50   Jean-Paul Morisset
House, Saint-François, île d'Orléans,
Quebec 1959–60 **[rep. 102]**
Gelatin silver print
26.8 x 34 cm
Canadian Museum of Contemporary
Photography, Ottawa

cat. 51   Jean-Paul Morisset
House at the Corner of Couillard and
Christie, Quebec City 1959–60
Gelatin silver print
35.3 x 28 cm
Canadian Museum of Contemporary
Photography, Ottawa

cat. 52   Jean-Paul Morisset
Church Facade, Sainte-Famille, île
d'Orléans, Quebec 1959–60
Gelatin silver print
34 x 26.8 cm
Canadian Museum of Contemporary
Photography, Ottawa

cat. 53   Michael Morris
Alex & Rodger, Rodger & Alex 1970
(printed in 2004) **[rep. 117]**
Gelatin silver prints mounted on 20
panels
40.5 x 51 cm each
Collection of the artist

cat. 54   N.E. Thing Co.
North American Time Zone Photo –
VSI Simultaneity Oct. 18, 1970 1970
[rep. 114]
18 photo-offset lithographies
44.5 x 44.5 cm each
Morris and Helen Belkin Gallery
Vancouver

cat. 55   Tim Porter
Lawn Party, Vancouver 1970 **[rep. 100]**
Gelatin silver print
11.4 x 16.4 cm
Canadian Museum of Contemporary
Photography, Ottawa

cat. 56   Tim Porter
Lower Granville, Vancouver 1970
Gelatin silver print
16.4 x 11.3 cm
Canadian Museum of Contemporary
Photography, Ottawa

cat. 57   Tim Porter
Untitled, Vancouver 1970
Épreuve argentique
16.4 x 11.4 cm
Canadian Museum of Contemporary
Photography, Ottawa

cat. 58   Nina Raginsky
Colonel Langley with his Dog Toga,
England 1967 **[rep. 90]**
Gelatin silver print
23.4 x 34.3 cm
Canadian Museum of Contemporary
Photography, Ottawa

cat. 59   Nina Raginsky
Mrs. Smith, Montreal, Quebec 1965
Gelatin silver print
18.4 x 23.8 cm
Canadian Museum of Contemporary
Photography, Ottawa

cat. 60   Nina Raginsky
Reverend Harold Noakes and his 1927
Bentley, London, England 1967
Gelatin silver print
23.5 x 35 cm
Canadian Museum of Contemporary
Photography, Ottawa

cat. 61   Michel Saint-Jean
Sacred Heart, Blainville, Quebec 1970
[rep. 95]
Gelatin silver print
23.5 x 33.7 cm
National Gallery of Canada, Ottawa

cat. 62   Michel Saint-Jean
Garden of Stars, La Ronde, Montreal
1967
Gelatin silver print
29.4 x 26.4 cm
Canadian Museum of Contemporary
Photography, Ottawa

cat. 63   Michel Saint-Jean
Untitled 1963
Gelatin silver print
46 x 32.8 cm
Canadian Museum of Contemporary
Photography, Ottawa

cat. 64   Michael Semak
Italian Community, Toronto 1963
[rep. 91]
Gelatin silver print
22.6 x 34 cm
Canadian Museum of Contemporary
Photography, Ottawa

cat. 65   Michael Semak
Ukrainian Parishioners Pray in the
Church in Pine River, Manitoba 1964
Gelatin silver print
26 x 33 cm
Canadian Museum of Contemporary
Photography, Ottawa

cat. 66   Michael Semak
Lady Reading, Montorio Nei Frentani,
Italy 1961
Gelatin silver print
26.2 x 33.8 cm
Canadian Museum of Contemporary
Photography, Ottawa

cat. 67   Orest Semchishen
Church near Redwater, Alberta 1968
[rep. 93]
Gelatin silver print
18.8 x 38 cm
Canadian Museum of Contemporary
Photography, Ottawa

cat. 68   Orest Semchishen
Furrows and House, near Edmonton,
Alberta 1968
Gelatin silver print
27.3 x 37.2 cm
Canadian Museum of Contemporary
Photography, Ottawa

cat. 69   Michael Snow
Authorization 1969   [rep. 111]
Instant silver prints and adhesive tape
on mirror in metal frame
54.6 x 44.4 x 1.4 cm
National Gallery of Canada, Ottawa

cat. 70   Michael Snow
Slidelength 1969–71
Eighty 35 mm colour slides
Dimensions variable
National Gallery of Canada, Ottawa

cat. 71   Françoise Sullivan
Promenade from the Musée d'art
contemporain to the Montreal Museum
of Fine Arts 1970   [rep. 112]
32 gelatin silver print and 1 map
26.5 x 26.5 each
Montreal Museum of Fine Arts
Gift of Françoise Sullivan

cat. 72   Gabor Szilasi
Mrs. Alexis (Marie) Tremblay, île aux
Coudres, Quebec 1970   [rep. 94]
Gelatin silver print
24 x 18.6 cm
Canadian Museum of Contemporary
Photography, Ottawa

cat. 73   Gabor Szilasi
Television, île aux Coudres, Quebec
1970
Gelatin silver print
34.9 x 27.7 cm
Canadian Museum of Contemporary
Photography, Ottawa

cat. 74   Gabor Szilasi
Pascal Dufour, île aux Coudres, Quebec
1970
Gelatin silver print
18.9 x 24 cm
Canadian Museum of Contemporary
Photography, Ottawa

cat. 75   Kryn Taconis
A Hutterite Guides his Geese, Ewelme
Colony, Fort McLeod, Alberta 1962
[rep. 88]
Gelatin silver print
23.1 x 34.5 cm
Canadian Museum of Contemporary
Photography, Ottawa

cat. 76   Kryn Taconis
Blind Boy Barry Scheur at Camp
Arowhon, Algonquin Park, Ontario 1961
Gelatin silver print
30.7 x 20.3 cm
Canadian Museum of Contemporary
Photography, Ottawa

cat. 77   Kryn Taconis
Children, School for the Deaf, Milton,
Ontario 1964
Gelatin silver print
23.5 x 33.2 cm
Canadian Museum of Contemporary
Photography, Ottawa

cat. 78   Sam Tata
Saint-Jean-Baptiste Day Parade,
Montreal 1963   [rep. 87]
Gelatin silver print
25.5 x 16.5 cm
Canadian Museum of Contemporary
Photography, Ottawa

cat. 79   Sam Tata
Pat Pearce, T. V. Columnist, Montreal
1962
Gelatin silver print
15.7 x 23.9 cm
Canadian Museum of Contemporary
Photography, Ottawa

cat. 80   Sam Tata
Navjote, the Ceremony of Initiation
into the Zoroastrian Faith of the Parsis,
Montreal 1969
Gelatin silver print
22.4 x 33.5 cm
Canadian Museum of Contemporary
Photography, Ottawa

cat. 81   Jeremy Taylor
Montreal, Quebec 1963   [rep. 103]
Gelatin silver print
19.1 x 24.2 cm
Canadian Museum of Contemporary
Photography, Ottawa

cat. 82   Jeremy Taylor
Point Lobos, California 1968   [rep. 104]
Gelatin silver print
24.5 x 19.4 cm
Canadian Museum of Contemporary
Photography, Ottawa

cat. 83   Jeremy Taylor
Parc Viger, Montreal 1963
Gelatin silver print
19 x 20.3 cm
Canadian Museum of Contemporary
Photography, Ottawa

cat. 84   Jeremy Taylor
Montreal 1963
Gelatin silver print
17.4 x 16.5 cm
Canadian Museum of Contemporary
Photography, Ottawa

cat. 85   Jeremy Taylor
Saint-Hilarion, Quebec 1964
Gelatin silver print
19.4 x 24.4 cm
Canadian Museum of Contemporary
Photography, Ottawa

cat. 86   Jeremy Taylor
Hoo-Doos, Drumheller, Alberta 1969
Gelatin silver print
26.4 x 34.4 cm
Canadian Museum of Contemporary
Photography, Ottawa

cat. 87   Serge Tousignant
Duo-reflex 1969   [rep. 121]
Mirrors, metal and tape
Dimensions variable
Collection of the artist

cat. 88   Bill Vazan
Cross Canada Line 1969–70 (reconstructed in 1999)   [rep. 113]
Maps, gelatin silver prints and drawing
on board
120 x 762 cm (overall dimension)
Collection of the artist

cat. 89   Irene F. Whittome
L'œil 1970   [rep. 120]
Wood, Plexiglas, metal, cotton balls,
silkscreen print
63.5 x 55.3 x 10.1 cm
Musée national des beaux-arts du
Québec, Quebec

Bibliography

Intro and chapters 1 to 8

For Chapter 9 references on photography, see p. 184

General references

Arbour, Rose Marie, et al. *Déclics, art et société : le Québec des années 1960 et 1970*. Exhibition Catalogue. Saint-Laurent, Quebec: Fides, 1999.

Aquin, Stéphane, ed. *Global Village: The 1960s*. Exhibition catalogue. Montreal: Montreal Museum of Fine Arts in collaboration with Snoek Publishers, 2003.

Bronson, AA, ed. *From Sea to Shining Sea*, Toronto: Power Plant, 1987.

Calas, Nicolas and Elena Calas. *Icons and Images of the Sixties*, New York: E.P. Dutton & Co., 1971.

Couture, Francine, ed. *Les arts visuels au Québec dans les années soixante. Vol. II : L'éclatement du modernisme.* Montreal: VLB éditeur, 1997.

Crow, Thomas. *The Rise of the Sixties: American and European Art in the Era of Dissent*. New York: Harry N. Abrams Inc., 1996.

Douglas, Stan, ed. *Vancouver Anthology: The Institutional Politics of Art.* Vancouver: Talon Books, 1991.

Foster, Hal. *The Return of the Real: Art and Theory at the End of the Century.* Cambridge Mass./London: MIT Press, 1996.

Galbraith, John Kenneth. *The Affluent Society.* Boston: Houghton Mifflin, 1958.

Habermas, Jürgen. "Modernity: An Unfinished Project," in Hal Foster, ed., *The Anti-Aesthetic: Essays on Postmodern Culture.* Port Townsend, Washington: Bay Press, 1983.

Huxley, Aldous. *The Doors of Perception.* London: Flamingo, 1994.

Jameson, Fredric. *Postmodernism, or, The Cultural Logic of Late Capitalism,* Durham: Duke University Press, 1991.

Lippard, Lucy R. *Six Years: The Dematerialization of the Art Object from 1966 to 1972.* New York: Praeger, 1973.

Lyotard, Jean-François. *The Postmodern Condition: A Report on Knowledge.* Translated by Geoff Bennington and Brian Massumi. Minneapolis: University of Minnesota Press, 1984

Marwick, Arthur. *The Sixties: Cultural Revolution in Britain, France, Italy, and the United States, c. 1958–c. 1974.* Oxford/New York: Oxford University Press, 1998.

Mastin, Catharine M. *Changing Spirits: Canadian Art of the 60s and 70s.* Exhibition catalogue. Kamloops, B.C.: Kamloops Art Gallery, 1998.

McKaskel, Robert, and Marco Y. Topalian. *Making it New!: (The Big Sixties Show).* Exhibition catalogue. Windsor: Art Gallery of Windsor, 2000.

McLuhan, Marshall. *Counterblast.* Toronto/Montreal: McClelland and Stewart, 1969.

"Michael Snow. A Filmography," *Afterimage*, no. 11 (winter 1982–1983).

Phillips, Lisa. *The American Century: Art and Culture, 1950–2000.* Exhibition catalogue. New York: Whitney Museum of American Art in association with W.W. Norton & Company, 1999.

Reid, Dennis. *Toronto Painting: 1953–1965.* Introduction by Barrie Hale. Exhibition catalogue (bilingual).Ottawa: National Gallery of Canada, 1972.

Rioux, Marcel. "Sur l'évolution des idéologies au Québec," *Revue de l'Institut de sociologie*, vol. 41, no. 1 (1968).

Robillard, Yves, ed. *Québec Underground 1962–1972.* 3 Volumes. Montreal: Les Éditions Médiart, 1973.

Rorimer, Anne. *New Art in the 60s and 70s: Redefining Reality.* London: Thames & Hudson, 2001.

Roszak, Theodore. "Youth and the Great Refusal," *The Nation* (25 March 1968).

Round Table with Denis Hollier, Annette Michelson, Hal Foster, Silvia Kolbowski, Martha Buskirk, and Benjamin H.D. Buchloh, "The Reception of the Sixties," *October*, no. 69 (summer 1994).

Stephens, Chris and Katharine Stout, eds. *Art & the 60s: This Was Tomorrow.* Exhibition catalogue. London: Tate Publishing, 2004.

Townsend, Charlotte. "New York Expert Praises Art Show," *Vancouver Sun*, 22 January 1969.

Venturi, Robert, Denise Scott Brown, and Steven Izenour. *Learning from Las Vegas: The Forgotten Symbolism of Architectural Form.* Cambridge, Mass: MIT Press, 1977.

Youngblood, Gene. "Synaesthetic Cinema and Extra-Objective Reality," in: *Expanded Cinema*. New York: E.P. Dutton & Co., 1971.

1

Allègre, Christian. "Serge Lemoyne : ne plus regarder la peinture," *Le Devoir* (18 July 1970).

Av Isaacs Fonds. Toronto: York University Archives.

Cage, John. "An Autobiographical Statement," 1989. Web site (accessed 10–12–04) on the Internet at: www.newalbion.com/artists/cagej/autobiog.html.

Campbell, James D. *Murray Favro: The Guitars 1966–1989*. Exhibition catalogue. Regina: Mackenzie Art Gallery, 1991.

Crehan, Herbert. Interview with Marcel Duchamp. *Evidence*, no. 3 (autumn 1961).

Curnoe, Greg and Frank Davey, eds. *Deeds/Abstracts: The History of a London Lot*. London, Ont.: Brick Books, 1995.

Fleming, Marie, Lucy Lippard, and Lauren Rabinovitz. *Joyce Wieland*. Exhibition catalogue. Toronto: Art Gallery of Ontario and Key Porter Books, 1987.

Gagnon, Lysiane and Normand Cloutier. "Le mot d'ordre des jeunes artistes : après le refus global, l'art total," *Culture vivante*, no. 5, 1967.

Goldberg, RoseLee. *Performance. Live Art 1909 to the Present*. New York: Harry N. Abrams, 1979.

Gosselin, Claude. *5 attitudes 1963–1980 : Ayot, Boisvert, Cozic, Lemoyne, Serge Tousignant*. Exhibition catalogue. Montréal: Musée d'art contemporain, 1981.

Greg Curnoe Fonds. Toronto: Art Gallery of Ontario.

Hapgood, Susan. *Neo-Dada Redefining Art 1958–1962*. Exhibition catalogue. New York: American Federation of the Arts/Universe Publishing, 1994.

Holubizky, Ihor. "Small Villages: The Isaacs Gallery in Toronto: 1956–1991. Making the Frame," Toronto, 1992. At: www.ccca.ca/history/isaacs/english/sv-ihor/hol005t.html on the Web site for the Centre for Contemporary Canadian Art (accessed 12–20–04).

Holubizky, Ihor. "The Wunderkammer," Toronto, 1989. At: www.ccca.ca/history/isaacs/english/sv-ihor/hol003t.html on the Web site for the Centre for Contemporary Canadian Art (accessed 12–20–04).

Lind, Jane. *Joyce Wieland: Artist on Fire*. Toronto: J. Lorimer, 2001.

Lussier, Réal. *Henry Saxe, œuvres de 1960 à 1993*. Exhibition catalogue. Montreal: Musée d'art contemporain de Montréal, 1994.

Nowell, Iris. *Joyce Wieland: A Life in Art*. Toronto: ECW Press, 2001.

McPherson, Hugo. "The Isaacs Gallery," *Evidence*, no. 3 (autumn 1961).

McPherson, Hugo. "Toronto's New Art Scene," *Canadian Art*, vol. XXII, no. 1 (Jan.–Feb. 1965).

Motherwell, Robert. *The Dada Painters and Poets: An Anthology*. New York: Wittenborn, Schulz, 1951.

Murray, John. "Gordon Rayner: Charting the Course" in *Gordon Rayner Retrospective*. Exhibition catalogue. Oshawa: The Robert McLaughlin Gallery, 1978.

Reid, Dennis. "Marcel Duchamp in Canada," *Canadian Art*, vol. 4, no. 4 (winter 1987).

Reid, Dennis and Matthew Teitelbaum, eds. *Greg Curnoe: Life and Stuff*. Toronto/Vancouver: Art Gallery of Ontario/Douglas & McIntyre, 2001.

Robillard, Yves. "Serge Lemoyne et Gilles Boisvert face au Happening," *La Presse* (3 September 1966).

Saint-Pierre, Marcel. *Serge Lemoyne*. Exhibition catalogue. Quebec: Musée du Québec, 1988.

Sanouillet, Michel. "The Sign of Dada," *Canadian Art*, vol. XIX, no. 2 (March–April 1962).

Sontag, Susan. "Happenings: An Art of Radical Juxtaposition," 1962. Reprinted in *Against Interpretation, and Other Essays*. New York: Delta, 1979.

Thériault, Normand. "Le tableau est aussi le monde," *La Presse* (8 March 1969).

Vachon, Marc. *L'arpenteur de la ville : L'utopie urbaine situationniste et Patrick Straram*. Montreal: Tryptique, 2003.

Vancouver Art Gallery. *Vancouver, Art and Artists, 1931–1983*. Vancouver: Vancouver Art Gallery, 1983.

Vastokas, Joan M. *Worlds Apart: The Symbolic Landscapes of Tony Urquhart*. Exhibition catalogue. Windsor: Art Gallery of Windsor, 1988.

2

Archives of the Université du Québec à Montréal. Yves Robillard Fonds. Service des archives et gestion des documents.

Boyle, John B. "Continental Refusal/Refus Continental," *20 Cents Magazine* (April 1970).

Boyle, John B. and Barry Lord, eds. *John Boyle, A Retrospective*. Exhibition catalogue. London, Ont: London Regional Art and Historical Museums, 1991.

Burton, Dennis and Joan Murray. *Dennis Burton Retrospective*. Exhibition catalogue. Oshawa: The Robert McLaughlin Gallery, 1977.

Chambers, John [Jack]. "Perceptual Realism," *artscanada*, vol. 26, no. 5 (October 1969).

Crean, Susan M. "Notes from the Language of Emotion: A Conversation with Joyce Wieland," *Canadian Art*, vol. 4, no. 1 (Spring–March 1987).

Curnoe, Greg. *Greg Curnoe. Some Lettered Works 1961–1969*. Exhibition catalogue. London, Ont.: London Art Gallery, 1975

Dubreuil-Blondin, Nicole. *La Fonction critique dans le Pop Art américain*. Montreal: Les Presses de l'Université de Montréal, 1980.

Elder, Kathryn, ed. *The Films of Jack Chambers*. Toronto/Bloomington/Indianapolis, Cinématheque Ontario and Indiana University Press, 2002.

Francis, Mark, ed. *Les années pop, 1956–1968*. Exhibition Catalogue. Paris: Éditions du Centre Pompidou, 2001.

"François Dallegret's Art Fiction," *Art in America*, vol. 54, no. 2 (March–April 1966).

Gagnon, Serge. *François Dallegret. Réminiscences fluorescentes*. Exhibition catalogue. Quebec: Musée du Québec, 1999.

Grandbois, Michèle. *L'art québécois de l'estampe 1945–1990 : Une aventure, une époque, une collection*. Exhibition catalogue. Quebec: Musée du Québec, 1996.

Greenwood, Michael. *American Art of the Sixties in Toronto Private Collection*. Exhibition catalogue. Toronto: York University, 1969.

Johnson, Carl. *Greg Curnoe, Serge Lemoyne: Two Nationalisms?*. Exhibition catalogue (bilingual). Rimouski: Musée régional de Rimouski, 2001.

Krauss, Rosalind. "Theories of Art after Minimalism and Pop" in Hal Foster, ed. *Discussions in Contemporary Culture no. 1*. Dia Art Foundation. Seattle: Bay Press, 1987.

Lamy, Laurent. *Triptyques de Guy Montpetit*. Exhibition brochure. Montreal: Musée d'art contemporain de Montréal, 1972.

Lumsden, Ian, ed. *Close the 49th Parallel: The Americanization of Canada*. Toronto: University of Toronto Press, 1970.

"Notre perspective," *Parti Pris*, no. 1 (October 1963).

O'Brien, Paddy, ed. *Jack Chambers. The Last Decade*. Exhibition catalogue. London, Ont.: London Regional Art Gallery, 1981.

Scott, Jay. "Full Circle: True, Patriot Womanhood: The 30-year Passage of Joyce Wieland," *Canadian Art*, vol. 4, no. 1 (spring 1987).

Théberge, Pierre. *Greg Curnoe: Retrospective*. Exhibition catalogue (bilingual). Ottawa: National Gallery of Canada, 1982.

Théberge, Pierre. "London Recaptured," *Canadian Literature*, no. 152/153 (spring/summer 1997).

3

Archives of the Morris and Helen Belkin Art Gallery. Alvin Balkind Fonds. University of British Columbia, Vancouver, B.C.

Archives of the Morris and Helen Belkin Art Gallery. Morris/Trasov Fonds. University of British Columbia, Vancouver, B.C.

Ashton, Dore. "Yves Gaucher at the New York Cultural Center," *artscanada*, vol. 32, no. 2, (June 1975).

Campbell, James D. *After Geometry: The Abstract Art of Claude Tousignant.* Toronto: ECW Press, 1995.

Campbell, James D. *Claude Tousignant: Charged Spaces, 1955–1998.* Exhibition catalogue (bilingual). Montreal: Galerie de Bellefeuille, 1999.

Collins, Anne. *In the Sleep Room: The Story of the C.I.A. Brainwashing Experiments in Canada.* Toronto: Key Porter Books, 1997.

Corbeil, Danielle. *Claude Tousignant.* Exhibition catalogue (bilingual). Ottawa: National Gallery of Canada, 1973.

Dompierre, Louise. *Walking Woman Works: Michael Snow 1961–67.* Exhibition catalogue. Kingston, Ont.: Agnes Etherington Art Centre, 1983.

Fry, Philip. *Charles Gagnon.* Exhibition catalogue. Montreal: Montreal Museum of Fine Arts, 1978.

Gagnon, Carolle and Ninon Gauthier. *Marcel Barbeau : Fugato.* Montreal: Éditions du Centre d'étude et de communication sur l'art (CECA) Inc., 1990.

Godmer, Gilles, ed., with the collaboration of Olivier Asselin and Louis Goyette. *Charles Gagnon.* Exhibition catalogue. Montreal: Musée d'art contemporain de Montréal, 2001.

James, Geoffrey. *Transparences/ Transparent Things.* Exhibition catalogue (bilingual) Ottawa: Canada Council for the Arts, 1977.

Martin, Michel, *Yves Gaucher. Récurrences*, Exhibition catalogue. Québec, Musée du Québec, 2000.

Nasgaard, Roald. *Yves Gaucher: A Fifteen-Year Perspective, 1963–1978.* Exhibition catalogue (bilingual) Toronto: Art Gallery of Ontario, 1979.

Pringle, Douglas. "Les Levine: Body Control Systems and John and Mimi's Book of Love, The Isaacs Gallery, Toronto April 1970," *artscanada*, vol. 27, no. 3 (June 1970).

Théberge, Pierre. *Canada art d'aujourd'hui*, Exhibition catalogue. Brussels: Palais des beaux-arts, 1968.

"Yves Gaucher. Galerie Godard Lefort," *artscanada*, vol. 26, no. 1, (February 1969).

4

Bélisle, Josée. *David Rabinowitch.* Exhibition catalogue. Montreal/Ottawa: Musée d'art contemporain de Montréal and the National Gallery of Canada, 2003.

Burnett, David. *Serge Tousignant. Géométrisations.* Exhibition catalogue (bilingual) Montreal: Serge Tousignant, 1981.

Campbell, James D. *The Mirror, Method and Meaning in Monochrome: Jean-Marie Delavalle.* Exhibition catalogue. Toronto, Christopher Cutts Gallery, 1993.

Dessureault, Pierre. *Serge Tousignant: Phases in Photography.* Exhibition catalogue (bilingual). Ottawa: Canadian Museum of Contemporary Photography, 1992.

Fuchs, Rudi, ed. *Royden Rabinowitch: Sculpture 1962/1992.* Exhibition catalogue. The Hague: Gemeentemuseum, 1992.

Latour, Jean-Pierre. *Serge Tousignant. Signalements : œuvres formelles et géométriques.* Exhibition catalogue. Montreal: Galerie Graff, 2000.

Murray, Joan. "A Conversation with Joan Murray and Walter Redinger," *artmagazine*, vol. 9, no. 38/39 (June 1978).

Neiman, Catrina. *David Rabinowitch. Sculptures 1963–1970 with Selected Drawings, Plans and Notes.* Bielefeld: Karl Kerber Verlag, 1987.

Poetter, Jochen, ed. *David Rabinowitch: Werke 1967–1976.* Stuttgart-Bad Cannstatt: Edition Cantz, 1992.

Smith, Brydon and Pierre Théberge, eds. *Boucherville, Montreal, Toronto, London, 1973: Jean-Marie Delavalle, Henry Saxe, Robin Collyer, James B. Spencer, Murray Favro, Ron Martin.* Exhibition catalogue (bilingual). Ottawa: National Gallery of Canada, 1973.

Thériault, Normand. "Dialoguer avec le spectateur," *La Presse* (23 November 1968).

5

Bayer, Fern, ed. *The Search for the Spirit: General Idea 1968–1975.* Exhibition catalogue. Toronto: Art Gallery of Ontario, 1998.

Campbell, James D. *Molinari Studies.* New York: 49th Parallel, 1987.

Dault, Gary Michael. "Prolific Artist Works on a Majestic Scale," *Toronto Star* (18 October 1977).

Dault, Gary Michael. "Roll of the Dice: Guido Molinari in Conversation with Gary Michael Dault," *Canadian Art*, vol. 20, no. 4 (winter 2003).

Fenton, Terry. *Jack Bush: A Retrospective.* Exhibition catalogue. Toronto: Art Gallery of Ontario, 1976.

Fischer, Barbara, ed. *General Idea Editions: 1967–1995.* Exhibition catalogue. Toronto: Blackwood Gallery, 2003.

Grant Marchand, Sandra, et al. *Guido Molinari, une rétrospective.* Exhibition catalogue. Montreal: Musée d'art contemporain de Montréal, 1995.

Johnson, Eileen. "Bodo the Bold," *Vancouver Life* (September 1967).

Kimmelman, Michael. "A Collage in Which Life = Death = Art," *The New York Times* (5 October 2002).

National Gallery of Canada Archives, Ottawa.

Naubert-Riser, Constance. *Jean McEwen: Colour in Depth. Paintings and Works on Paper 1951–1987.* Exhibition catalogue. Montreal: Montreal Museum of Fine Arts, 1987.

Ninacs, Anne-Marie. *Rita Letendre. Aux couleurs du jour.* Exhibition catalogue. Quebec: Musée national des beaux-arts du Québec, 2003.

Théberge, Pierre. *Guido Molinari.* Exhibition catalogue (bilingual). Ottawa: National Gallery of Canada, 1976.

Wilkin, Karen, ed. *Jack Bush.* Toronto: McClelland and Stewart/Merritt Editions Ltd., 1984.

6

Aarons, Anita. "Plastic Paradise?" *Architecture Canada*, vol. 45, no. 2 (February 1968).

Art Gallery of Ontario Archives. Michael Snow Fonds. Toronto, Ont.

Bissonnette, Denise L., Mayo Graham, and François-Marc Gagnon. *Jacques Hurtubise: Four Decades, Image After Image.* Exhibition catalogue. Montreal: Montreal Museum of Fine Arts. 1998.

Bovey, Patricia E., Robert Enright, and James Patten. *Tony Tascona: Resonance.* Exhibition catalogue. Winnipeg: Winnipeg Art Gallery, 2001.
Dompierre, Louise (foreword). *The Michael Snow Project: The Collected Writings of Michael Snow.* Waterloo: Wilfrid Laurier University Press, 1994.

Johnston, Jill. "Liking Things for What They Are." *Canadian Art*, vol. XXIII, no. 3 (July 1966).

Klüver, Billy. "Experiments in Art and Technology (E.A.T.). Archives of Published Documents," 2000. Daniel Langlois Web site (accessed 21–12–04) at: www.fondation-langlois.org/flash/e/ stage.php?NumPage=306.

Landry, Pierre, ed. *Mousseau.* Exhibition catalogue. Montreal: Musée d'art contemporain de Montréal/Éditions du Méridien, 1996.

Lewis, Glenn. *New Media: Artwork from the 60s and 70s in Vancouver.* Burnaby, B.C.: Visual Arts Burnaby/Gallery at Ceperley House, 2002.

McPherson, Hugo. *Architecture and Sculpture in Canada. Canadian Government Pavilion, Expo 67, Montreal.* Ottawa: Queen's Printer, 1967.

Mekas, Jonas. "Movie Journal," *The Village Voice* (27 January 1972).

Piene, Nan R. "Sculpture and Light: Toronto and Montreal," *artscanada*, vol. 25, no. 5 (December 1968).

Roberts, Catsou and Lucy Steeds, eds. *Michael Snow: Almost Cover to Cover.* London/Bristol: Black Dog/Arnolfini, 2001.

7

Ainslie, Patricia. *Correspondences: Jack Shadbolt.* Exhibition catalogue. Calgary: Glenbow Museum, 1991.

Blodgett, Jean and Susan Gustavison. *Strange Scenes: Early Cape Dorset Drawings.* Exhibition catalogue. Kleinburg, Ont.: McMichael Canadian Art Collection, 1993.

Bloore, Ronald. "R. L. Bloore on Permanence," *artscanada* vol. 25, no. 1 (April 1968).

Brydon, Sherry. *The Indians of Canada Pavilion at Expo'67.* 1991. Honours B. A. Thesis. Ottawa: Carleton University.

Cardinal, Harold. *The Unjust Society: The Tragedy of Canada's Indians.* Edmonton: M.G. Hurtig, 1969.

Collins, Curtis J. *Janvier and Morrisseau: Transcending a Canadian Discourse.* 1994. M. A. Thesis. Montreal: Concordia University.

Enright, Robert. "Winnipeg's Benevolent Godfather. An Interview with Tony Tascona," *Arts Manitoba* (summer 1984).

Eric Cameron Process Paintings. Exhibition brochure. Halifax: The Art Gallery and Museum, Mount Saint Vincent University, 1972.

Fox, Ross. *The Canadian Painters Eleven (1953–1960) from The Robert McLaughlin Gallery.* Exhibition catalogue. Amherst, Mass.: Amherst College, 1994.

Greenberg, Clement. "Clement Greenberg's View of Art on the Prairies," *Canadian Art*, vol. xx, no. 2 (March–April 1963).

Heath, Terence. *Ronald L. Bloore. Not Without Design.* Exhibition catalogue. Regina: Mackenzie Art Gallery, 1993.

Howard, David. *Arthur F. McKay. A Critical Retrospective.* Exhibition catalogue. Regina: Mackenzie Art Gallery, 1997.

Kicksee, Richard Gordon. *'Scaled Down to Size': Contested Liberal Commonsense and the Negotiation of 'Indian Participation' in the Canadian Centennial Celebrations and Expo '67, 1963–1967*, 1995. M. A. Thesis. Kingston: Queen's University.

McLuhan, Elizabeth and Tom Hill. *Norval Morrisseau and the Emergence of the Image Makers*, Exhibition catalogue. Toronto: Art Gallery of Ontario and Mothuon Publications, 1984.

Montour, Ross. "Delisle Named to Receive Aboriginal Achievement Award," *The Eastern Door*, vol. 13, no. 1, 23 January 2004. Also published on the Internet at: www.easterndoor.com/VOL.13/13-1. htm#story7. (accessed 10–12–04).

Morrisseau, Norval. *Legends of My People: The Great Ojibway.* Selwyn Dewdney, ed. Toronto: Ryerson Press, 1965.

Morrisseau, Norval, Robert Houle et al. *Norval Morrisseau: Travels to the House of Invention.* Toronto: Key Porter Books, 1997.

Pitseolak: Pictures Out of My Life. Based on interviews recorded by Dorothy Eber. Montreal: Design Collaborative Books in association with Oxford University Press, 1971.

Shadbolt, Doris. "Harry Malcolmson," *The Telegram* (9 September 1967).

Tamplin, Illi-Maria. *R.L. Bloore: Drawings.* Exhibition catalogue. Peterborough, Ont.: The Art Gallery of Peterborough, 1988.

Vancouver Art Gallery. *Arthur McKay: Recent Paintings.* Exhibition catalogue. Vancouver: Vancouver Art Gallery, 1964.

Watson, Scott. *Jack Shadbolt.* Vancouver/Toronto: Douglas & McIntyre, 1990.

Watson, Scott. *Jack Shadbolt: Act of Painting.* Exhibition catalogue. Vancouver: Vancouver Art Gallery, 1985.

8

Balkind, Alvin. "Body Snatching: Performance Art in Vancouver A View of Its History," in *Living Art.* Vancouver: Western Front/Pumps/Video Inn, 1979.

Burnett, David and Pierre Landry. *Bill Vazan: Ghostings: Early Projects and Drawings* (bilingual). Montreal: Artexte Information Centre, 1985.

Domino, Christophe. "Iain Baxter: Art Is All Over," *Art Press*, no. 234 (April 1998).

Fleming, Marie L. *Baxter²: Any Choice Works 1965–1970.* Exhibition catalogue. Toronto: Art Gallery of Ontario, 1982.

Grande, John. "A Conversation with Bill Vazan. Cosmological Shadows," *Sculpture*, vol. 21, no. 10 (December 2002).

Kennedy, Garry Neill et al. *NSCAD: The Nova Scotia College of Art & Design: Prints and Books.* Exhibition catalogue. Halifax: The Press of the Nova Scotia College of Art & Design, 1982.

Kennedy, Garry Neill. "The Nova Scotia College of Art and Design and the Sixties: A Memoir," *Canadian Literature*, no. 152/153 (spring/summer 1997).

Kiyooka, Roy. *StoneDGloves*, Toronto: The Coach House, 1970.

Roy Kiyooka. Aumône pour douces paumes. Exhibition brochuro. Paris: Centre culturel canadien, 1972.

Knight, Derek. *N.E. Thing Co.: The Ubiquitous Concept.* Exhibition catalogue. Oakville, Ont.: Oakville Galleries, 1995.

Lawrence, Robin. "Remembering an Artistic Guru," *The Georgia Strait* (28 May 1998).

Levine, Les. "The Best Art School in North America?" *Art in America*, vol. 61, no. 4 (July–August 1973).

Lippard, Lucy R. "Iain Baxter: New Spaces," *artscanada*, vol. 26, no. 3 (June 1969).

Lippard, Lucy R. *Toward a Dematerialized or Non Object Art.* Transcript from a conference at the Nova Scotia College of Art and Design on 29 November 1969. Ottawa: Archives of the National Gallery of Canada.

Mewburn, Charity. *N.E. Thing Co.: Sixteen Hundred Miles North of Denver.* Exhibition catalogue. Vancouver: Morris and Helen Belkin Art Gallery, 1999.

Murchie, John et al. *Garry Neill Kennedy: Work of Four Decades.* (bilingual). Exhibition catalogue. Halifax/Ottawa: Art Gallery on Nova Scotia/National Gallery of Canada, 2000.

Nemiroff, Diana. *A History of Artist-Run Spaces in Canada With Particular Reference to Vehicule, A Space and the Western Front*, 1985. M. A. Thesis. Montreal: Concordia University.

Selz, Peter with Alvin Balkind. "Vancouver Scene and Unscene: A Conceit in Eight Scenes and An Epilogue," *Art in America* vol. 58, no. 1 (January–February 1970).

Shaw, Nancy and William Wood. *You Are Now in the Middle of a N.E. Thing Co. Landscape: Works by Iain and Ingrid Baxter 1965–1971.* Exhibition catalogue. Vancouver: UBC Fine Arts Gallery, 1993.

Sherrin, Robert, Ann Rosenberg et al. *Michael de Courcy: Surveying a Territory: Urban Wilderness Revisited A 25 Year Retrospective/Michael de Courcy.* Exhibition catalogue. Richmond, B.C.: Richmond Art Gallery, 1994.

Stacey, Robert and Liz Wylie. *Eighty/Twenty: 100 Years of the Nova Scotia College of Art and Design*, Exhibition catalogue. Halifax: Art Gallery of Nova Scotia, 1988.

Townsend, Charlotte. "Kiyooka," *The Vancouver Sun* (23 January 1970).

Varney, Ed and Gregg Simpson. *Intermedia: An Illustrated Chronology.* Web site at: www.greggsimpson.com/Imedia65_67.htm (accessed 21–12–04).

9

General references

Arbour, Rose Marie, et al. *Déclics, art et société : le Québec des années 1960 et 1970*, Saint-Laurent, Quebec: Fides, 1999.

Barthes, Roland. *Mythologies.* Translated by Annette Lavers. New York: Hill and Wang, 1972.

Barthes, Roland. *The Responsibility of Forms: Critical Essays on Music.* Translated by Richard Howard. New York: Hill and Wang, 1985.

Barthes, Roland. *The Rustle of Language.* Translated by Richard Howard. New York: Hill and Wang, 1986.

Roland Barthes. Le texte et l'image. Exhibition Catalogue. Paris: Pavillon des arts, 1986.

Roland Barthes, une aventure avec la photographie. Proceedings of a conference in Paris on 16 and 17 November 1990, *La Recherche photographique*, Maison européenne de la photographie, no. 12 (June 1992).

Couture, Francine, ed. *Les arts visuels au Québec dans les années soixante.* Montreal: VLB, 1993–1997.

Couture, Francine, *Les arts et les années 60 : architecture, arts visuels, chanson, cinéma, danse, littérature, musique, théâtre.* Montreal: Tryptique, 1991.

Dessureault, Pierre. *Exchanging Views: Quebec, 1939–1980.* Exhibition catalogue (bilingual) Ottawa: Canadian Museum of Contemporary Photography, 1999.

Expo 67. *International Exhibition of Photography: The Camera as Witness.* Exhibition catalogue (bilingual). Montreal: Expo 67, 1967.

Frank, Robert. *The Americans.* New York: Grossman, 1969.

Goldberg, Vicki, ed. *Photography in Print: Writing from 1816 to the Present.* Albuquerque: University of New Mexico Press, 1988.

Grandbois, Michèle. *L'art québécois de l'estampe, 1945–1990 : une aventure, une époque, une collection.* Exhibition catalogue. Quebec: Musée du Québec, 1996.

"La photographie au Québec," *Culture vivante.* Ministère des Affaires culturelles du Québec, no. 6 (1967).

Lyons, Nathan, ed. *Photographers on Photography; a Critical Anthology.* Englewood Cliffs, N.J.: Prentice Hall, 1966.

McKaskel, Robert and Marco Y. Topalian. *Making it New!: (The Big Sixties Show).* Exhibition catalogue. Windsor: Art Gallery of Windsor. 2000.

McLuhan, Marshall. *Understanding Media: The Extensions of Man.* New York: McGraw-Hill Book Company, 1964.

McLuhan, Marshall. *The Gutenberg Galaxy: The Making of Typographic Man.* Toronto: University of Toronto Press, 1962.

Musée d'art contemporain de Montréal. *Graff, 1966–1986,* Exhibition catalogue. Montreal, 1988.

Payne, Carol. *A Canadian Document.* Exhibition catalogue (bilingual). Ottawa: Canadian Museum of Contemporary Photography, 1999.

Pocock, Philip. "Photography and the Image of Canada," *Canadian Art* no. 76. (November–December, 1961).

Steichen, Edward. *The Family of Man.* Exhibition catalogue. New York: Museum of Modern Art, 1955.

Tisseron, Serge. *Le bonheur dans l'image.* Paris: Les Empêcheurs de penser en rond. 2003.

Vancouver Art Gallery. *Vancouver, Art and Artists, 1931–1983.* Vancouver: Vancouver Art Gallery, 1983.

Humanist Photography
Carey, Brian et al. *Kryn Taconis, Photojournalist.* Exhibition catalogue. (bilingual) Ottawa: Public Archives of Canada, 1989.

Cartier-Bresson, Henri. *Images à la sauvette.* Paris: Éditions Verve, 1952.

Crites, Mitchell. *Visual Journeys: Roloff Beny.* Vancouver: Douglas and McIntyre, 1994.

Curtin, Walter. *Curtin Call: A Photographer's Candid View of 25 Years of Music in Canada.* Toronto. Exile Editions, 1994.

Delius, Peggy. "The World of Roloff Beny," *The British Journal of Photography* (19 November, 1965).

Dessureault, Pierre. *The Tata Era.* Exhibition catalogue (bilingual). Ottawa: Canadian Museum of Contemporary Photography, 1988.

Dille, Lutz. *The Many Worlds of Lutz Dille.* Exhibition catalogue (bilingual). Ottawa: National Film Board of Canada, 1967.

Dille, Lutz. "The People of Naples," *Canadian Photographer* vol. 9, no. 10 (November 1962).

Edelson, Michael. "Michael Semak: A Photographer Involved with Life's Human Drama," *Popular Photography* (November 1970).

Hanna, Martha. *Walter Curtin: A Retrospective.* Exhibition catalogue (bilingual). Ottawa: Canadian Museum of Contemporary Photography, 1985.

Lambeth, Michel. *The Confessions of a Tree Taster.* Toronto: Lumiere Press, 1987.

Lambeth, Michel. "Lutz Dille, The Berthold Brecht of the Camera," *artscanada* (November 1967).

Lambeth, Michel. "The Americans," *The Canadian Forum* no. 40 (August 1960).

Lyons, Nathan, ed. *Vision and Expression.* New York: Horizon Press, 1969

Macaulay, Rose et al. *Pleasure of Ruins.* London: Thames and Hudson, 1965.

"One Man Show: Sam Tata," *Photo Age* vol. 9, no. 2 (April 1962).

Porteus, Hugh Gordon. "Pleasure of Ruins," *The British Journal of Photography* (19 November 1965).

Public Archives of Canada. *Michel Lambeth, Photographer.* Exhibition catalogue (bilingual). Ottawa: Public Archives of Canada, 1986.

Raginsky, Nina. *Statements.* Exhibition brochure. Toronto: Art Gallery of Ontario. 25 August–30 September 1979.

Reeves, John. "The Image Finders," *Toronto Life* (May 1979).

Semak, Michael. *Monograph.* Toronto: Impressions, 1974

Semak, Michael. "Statement," *Photo Age* vol. 14, no. 1 (January 1967).

Semak, Michael. *If This is the Time* (bilingual). Montreal: McGill-Queen's University Press for the National Film Board of Canada, 1969.

Sutnik, Maia-Mari. *Michel Lambeth: Photographer.* Exhibition catalogue. Toronto: Art Gallery of Ontario, 1998.

Tata, Sam. *Montreal.* Toronto: McClelland and Stewart, 1963.

Tata, Sam. *A Certain Identity: 50 Portraits.* Ottawa: Deneau, 1983.

Documentary Photography
Davis, Kate. "Profile: Orest Semchishen," *Photo Communiqué* (Winter 1986–1987).

Evans, Walker. *Walker Evans at Work: 745 Photographs Together with Documents Selected from Letters, Memoranda, Interviews, Notes/With an Essay by Jerry L. Thompson.* New York: Harper & Row, 1982.

Gaudard, Pierre. *Les ouvriers.* Exhibition catalogue (bilingual). Ottawa, National Film Board of Canada, 1971.

Hanna, Martha. *Orest Semchishen: In Plain View.* Exhibition catalogue (bilingual). Ottawa: Canadian Museum of Contemporary Photography, 1994.

Hohn, Hugh. *Byzantine Churches of Alberta: Photographs by Orest Semchishen.* Exhibition catalogue. Edmonton: Edmonton Art Gallery, 1976.

Kidd, Elizabeth. *Presence of the Prairie: Photographs by Orest Semchishen.* Exhibition catalogue. Edmonton: Edmonton Art Gallery, 1992.

Lambeth, Michel. "Les ouvriers – The workers," *Camera Canada* no. 11 (December 1971).

Madill, Shirley. *Orest Semchishen – Byzantine Churches: Selections from the Photography Collection of the Winnipeg Art Gallery.* Exhibition catalogue. Winnipeg: Winnipeg Art Gallery, 1997.

Sander, August. *Citizens of the Twentieth Century: Portrait Photographs, 1892–1952.* Translated by Linda Keller. Cambridge Mass.: MIT Press. 1986.

Semchishen, Orest. "In Plain View: Ukrainian Churches of Canada" *Queen's Quarterly: A Canadian Review* vol. 101, no. 1 (Spring 1994).

Steinman, Barbara. "In Looking, We Find Ourselves and the Places We've Been – Barbara Steinman interviews Gabor Szilasi." Canadian Art (Autumn 1997).

Szilasi, Gabor. Gabor Szilasi: Photographs 1954–1996. (bilingual). Montreal: McGill-Queen's University Press, 1997.

Szilasi, Gabor. "Intervention et appartenance," Actes du colloque Marques et contrastes. Éditions Sagamie, Quebec, 1987.

A Personal Vision of the Human Condition
Public Archives Canada, National Photography Collection. L'Amérique québécoise: Photographs by Michel Saint-Jean. Exhibition catalogue. Ottawa: National Archives of Canada, 1987.

Bibliothèque nationale du Québec. Montréal insolite – vu par Marc-André Gagné, Pierre Gaudard, Ronald Labelle, John Max, Michel Saint-Jean, Gabor Szilasi. Exhibition catalogue. Montreal: Ministère des Affaires culturelles du Québec, 1967.

Borcoman, James. David Heath: A Dialogue with Solitude. Exhibition catalogue (bilingual). Ottawa: National Gallery of Canada, 1979.

Germain, Jean-Claude. "Le monde de Michel Saint-Jean : à mi-chemin entre la tristesse et la colère," Dimension vol. 6, no. 3 (1969).

Heath, Dave. A Dialogue with Solitude. Culpeper, Virginia: Community Press, 1965.

Heath, Dave. Extempore – David Heath: Reflections & Ruminations on Art & Personal History. Elicited and edited by Michael Torosian. Toronto: Lumiere Press, 1988.

Lafortune, François. Où la lumière chante. Text by Gilles Vigneault. Quebec: Les Presses de l'Université Laval, 1966.

"Michel Saint-Jean/Photographe." Magazine OVO. vol. 16, no. 62 (1987).

Max, John. "Open Passport," Impressions (Toronto, 1973).

National Gallery of Canada. Four Montreal Photographers: Marc-André Gagné, Ronald Labelle, John Max, Michel Saint-Jean. Exhibition catalogue (bilingual). Ottawa: National Gallery of Canada, 1969

Tata, Sam. "On Assignment: John Max," Foto Canada vol. I, no. 3 (1967).

The Social Landscape
Ashton, Dore. "Charles Gagnon's Point of View," artscanada (August–September 1979).

"Charles Gagnon: Portfolio" Magazine OVO (June 1974)

Dumont, Jean. "Charles Gagnon. La photo comme discipline métaphysique," Le Devoir (4 April 1992).

Fry, Philip. Charles Gagnon. Exhibition catalogue (bilingual). Montreal: Montreal Museum of Fine Arts, 1978.

Gagnon, Charles. Observations. Exhibition catalogue (bilingual). Quebec: Musée du Québec, 1998.

Gibson, Tom. Signature I. Exhibition catalogue (bilingual). Ottawa: National Film Board of Canada, Still Photography Division, 1975.

Godmer, Gilles. Charles Gagnon. Exhibition catalogue. Montreal: Musée d'art contemporain de Montréal, 2001.

Lambeth, Michel. "Tom Gibson at the Merton Gallery," Proof Only vol. I, no. 3 (15 January 1974).

Langford, Martha. Tom Gibson: False Evidence Appearing Real. Exhibition catalogue (bilingual). Ottawa: Canadian Museum of Contemporary Photography, 1993.

Lyons, Nathan, ed. Toward a Social Landscape. Exhibition catalogue. New York: Horizon Press, 1966.

Lyons, Nathan, Photography in the Twentieth Century. Exhibition catalogue (bilingual). New York: Horizon Press, 1967.

Lyons, Nathan. Notations in Passing. Exhibition catalogue (bilingual). Ottawa: National Gallery of Canada, 1970.

"Tom Gibson/Interview." Magazine OVO (June 1974).

Winogrand, Garry. "Understanding Still Photographs," Photography Speaks. Brooks Johnson, ed. New York: Aperture/ The Chrysler Museum, 1989.

Forms: Architecture and Landscape
Benjamin, Walter. "The Flâneur," The Arcades Project. Translated by Howard Eiland and Kevin McLaughlin. Cambridge, Mass: Belknap Press, 1999.

Bourdeau, Robert. Robert Bourdeau: Landforms. Exhibition catalogue. Kingston: Agnes Etherington Art Centre, 1979.

Bourdeau, Robert. "The Meditated Image," Photo Age vol. 12, no. 3 (March 1965).

Burnett, David. Robert Bourdeau & Philip Pocock: Recent Photographs. Exhibition catalogue. Toronto: Art Gallery of Ontario, 1981.

Flanders, John. The Craftsman's Way: Canadian Expressions. Toronto: University of Toronto Press, 1981.

Flanders, John. "Ontario Vernacular," Habitat vol. XIII, no. 3 (1970).

Madill, Shirley. Breaking the Mirror: The Art of Robert Bourdeau. (bilingual). Exhibition catalogue. Winnipeg: Winnipeg Art Gallery, 1988.

Malraux, André, Museum Without Walls. Translated by Stuart Gilbert and Francis Price. London: Secker & Warburg. 1967.

Solomon, Ronald. Robert Bourdeau. (bilingual). Ottawa: National Film Board of Canada in collaboration with Toronto: Mintmark Press, 1979.

Thomas, Ann. "Robert Bourdeau's Landforms: In Praise of the Lucid," artscanada no. 214–215, (May–June 1977).

Weston, Edward. The Daybooks of Edward Weston. Rochester, N.Y.: George Eastman House, 1973.

White, Minor. Mirrors, Messages, Manifestations. New York: Aperture, 1969.

Forms: The Photographic Medium
Broadfoot, Barry. The City of Vancouver. Vancouver: J.J. Douglas, 1976.

Bunnell, Peter C. "Photography into Sculpture," artscanada vol. 27, no. 3 (June 1970).

Coleman, A.D. "Sheer Anarchy, or a Step Forward?" The New York Times (12 April 1970).

Grégoire, Normand. Normand Grégoire: Polyptych Two (bilingual), Lorraine Monk, ed. Ottawa: National Film Board of Canada, Still Photography Division, 1970.

Grégoire, Normand. Series 4 (bilingual). Ottawa: National Film Board of Canada, Still Photography Division 1972.

Hesse, Jurgen. "Art through the lens…" The Vancouver Sun (12 June 1970).

Hawkins, David. "Images by Marc-André Gagné," Camera Canada no. 18 (October 1973).

"Interview: Normand Grégoire," Magazine OVO no. 7 (May 1972).

Karkutt, Guenter. Photo-graphics. Halifax: Iris Books, 1974.

"L'homme et le photographe… Guenter Karkutt," Photo-Âge (September 1962).

Mendes, Ross. "Extensions: Revolutionary Directions in Photography," artscanada no. 138–139 (December 1969).

"Montreal Photographers," Image Nation no. 14, (Toronto: The Coach House Press, 1970).

Pakasaar, Helga. In Transition – Postwar Photography in Vancouver. Exhibition catalogue. Vancouver: Presentation House Gallery, 1986.

Pakasaar, Helga. The Just Past of Photography in Vancouver: Photographs by Bill Cunningham, Denes Devenyi, Fred Herzog, Dick Oulton, Foncie Pulice. Exhibition catalogue. Vancouver: Presentation House Gallery, 1997.

"Portfolio : Marc-André Gagné." Magazine OVO no. 8 (July 1972).

Simmins, Richard. "Photo Exhibition Simple, Strong," The Province (Vancouver, 20 November 1970).

Szarkowski, John. William Eggleston's Guide. New York: Museum of Modern Art, 1976.

Thornton, Gene. "Different – But is it Better?" The New York Times (27 December 1970).

Troster, Cyrel. "Photography as Process," *Art Magazine* (Autumn 1974).

University of British Columbia, *Extensions: Evolutions by Bob Flick, Environments by Fred Herzog, Erections by Jack Dale.* Exhibition catalogue. Vancouver: Fine Arts Gallery, 1969.

A Tool for Artists

Aquin, Stéphane. *Françoise Sullivan.* Exhibition catalogue. Montreal: Montreal Museum of Fine Arts/Éditions Parachute, 2003.

Ayot, Pierre. *Pierre Ayot Unlimited.* Exhibition catalogue. Montreal: Montreal Museum of Fine Arts, 2001.

Ayot, Pierre. *Le Monde selon Graff 1966–1986.* Montreal: Éditions Graff, 1987.

Baxter, Iain. *Reflections, Lethbridge.* Exhibition catalogue. Lethbridge: Southern Alberta Art Gallery, 1979.

Benjamin, Walter. "The Work of Art in the Age of Mechanical Reproductions," *Illuminations.* New York: Shocken Books, 1968.

Benjamin, Walter. "A Short History of Photography," *Artforum,* vol. 15 (February 1977).

Bronson, AA. *AA Bronson, 1969–2000.* Exhibition catalogue. Vienna: Vienna Secession, 2000.

Bronson, AA. *Mirror Mirror.* Exhibition catalogue. Cambridge, Mass., MIT, 2002.

Bronson, AA. *Negative Thoughts.* Exhibition catalogue. Chicago: Chicago Museum of Contemporary Art, 2001.

Dessureault, Pierre. *Serge Tousignant: Phases in Photography.* Exhibition catalogue (bilingual). Ottawa: Canadian Museum of Contemporary Photography, 1992.

Dickson, Jennifer. *A Retrospective – Selected Works 1963 to 1993.* Exhibition catalogue. Ottawa: Wallack Galleries, 1993.

Farr, Dorothy. *Jennifer Dickson,* Exhibition catalogue. Kingston, Ontario: Agnes Etherington Art Centre, 1986.

Fleming, Marie L. *Baxter: Any Choice Works 1965–1970.* Exhibition catalogue. Toronto: Ontario Art Gallery, 1982.

Fry, Jacqueline. *Irene Whittome, 1975–1980.* Exhibition catalogue (bilingual). Montreal: Montreal Museum of Fine Arts, 1980.

Galerie Dresdnere. *Jennifer Dickson: Paintings, Drawings and Graphics.* Exhibition catalogue. Toronto: Galerie Dresdnere, 1971.

Grande, John K. *Jumpgates: An Overview of Photoworks by Bill Vazan, 1981–1995.* Peterborough, Ont.: Art Gallery of Peterborough, 1996.

Gosselin, Claude. *5 attitudes 1963–1980 : Ayot, Boisvert, Cozic, Lemoyne, Serge Tousignant.* Exhibition catalogue. Montréal: Musée d'art contemporain, 1981.

Kiyooka, Roy. *Transcanada Letters.* Vancouver: Talon Books, 1975.

Kiyooka, Roy. *All Amazed for Roy Kiyooka.* Vancouver: Arsenal Pulp Press/Morris and Helen Belkin Gallery, Collapse, 2002.

Knight, Derek. *N.E. Thing Co.: The Ubiquitous Concept.* Exhibition catalogue. Oakville, Ont.: Oakville Galleries, 1995.

Lamoureux, Johanne. *Irene F. Wittome: Bio-fictions.* Exhibition catalogue (bilingual). Quebec: Musée du Québec, 2000.

Linsley, Robert. "Roy Kiyooka's Yonville," *art/text,* no. 64 (February–April 1999).

MacWilliam, Michael. *Michael Morris: Early Works 1965–1972.* Exhibition catalogue. Victoria, B.C.: Art Gallery of Greater Victoria, 1985.

Musée d'art contemporain de Montréal. *Périphéries.* Exhibition catalogue. Montreal: Musée d'art contemporain, 1974.

Musée d'art contemporain de Montréal. *Françoise Sullivan : Rétrospective.* Exhibition catalogue. Quebec: Ministère des Affaires culturelles, 1981.

Musée d'art contemporain de Montréal. *Michael Morris: Photographies.* Exhibition catalogue. Montreal: Musée d'art contemporain, 1980.

Musée d'art contemporain de Montréal. *Bill Vazan: Recent Land and Photoworks.* Exhibition catalogue (bilingual). Montreal: Musée d'art contemporain, 1980.

Musée d'art contemporain de Montréal. *Serge Tousignant : dessins, photos, 1970–74.* Exhibition catalogue. Montreal: Musée d'art contemporain, 1975.

Musée du Québec. *Bill Vazan.* Exhibition catalogue. Quebec: Musée du Québec, 1974.

National Film Board of Canada. *B.C. Almanac(h) C-B* (bilingual). Ottawa: National Film Board of Canada, 1970.

Ontario Art Gallery. *Michael Snow: A Survey.* Exhibition catalogue. Toronto: Ontario Art Gallery, 1970.

Palais de beaux-arts de Bruxelles. *Michael Snow: Panoramique: Photographic Works & Films 1962–1999.* Exhibition catalogue (bilingual). Société des expositions du Palais des beaux-arts de Bruxelles, Centre national de la photographie. Paris: Centre pour l'image contemporaine, Saint-Gervais, Geneva: Cinémathèque royale de Belgique, 1999.

Sayag, Alain. *Michael Snow.* Paris: Centre Georges Pompidou, 1978

Shaw, Nancy and William Wood. *You Are Now in the Middle of a N.E. Thing Co. Landscape: Works by Iain and Ingrid Baxter 1965–1971.* Exhibition catalogue. Vancouver: UBC Fine Arts Gallery, 1993.

Swain, Robert. *The Unknown Jennifer Dickson: A 25 Year Retrospective, 1959–1984.* Exhibition catalogue. Toronto: Galerie Dresdnere, 1985.

Visual Art 1951–1993 – The Michael Snow Project. Exhibition catalogue. Toronto: Knopf Canada, 1994. (Ontario Art Gallery and The Power Plant).

Terada, Ron. *N.E. Thing Co.: Selected Works 1967–1970.* Exhibition catalogue. Vancouver: Catriona Jeffries Galley, 1999.

Thériault, Normand. "L'art conceptuel : la mort de l'objet," *La Presse* (10 January 1970).

Toupin, Gilles. "La géographie de Bill Vazan," *Vie des arts* no. 69 (Winter 1972–1973).

Toupin, Gilles. "La nostalgie de l'art," *La Presse* (13 January 1973).

United Press International. "Artist Draws A Line Across Canada – Why?" *The Sun* (Vancouver, 10 January 1970).

Vazan, Bill. *Contacts 1971–1973.* Montreal: Véhicule Press, 1973.

Vazan, Bill. *Worldline 1969–71.* Montreal: William Vazan, 1971.

Véhicule Art. *Françoise Sullivan.* Exhibition catalogue (bilingual). Montreal: Véhicule Art, 1977.

Wood, William. *Roy Kiyooka.* Exhibition catalogue. Vancouver: Artspeak Gallery and the Or Gallery, 1991.